BREAKING INTO JAPANESE LITERATURE

BREAKING
INTO
JAPANESE
LITERATURE

Seven Modern Classics in Parallel Text

GILES MURRAY

KODANSHA INTERNATIONAL
Tokyo · New York · London

Go to **www.speaking-japanese.com** to get an overview
of *Breaking into Japanese Literature* and to download
free MP3 sound files of all seven stories in the book. The
site also profiles the author's other works, from the best-
selling *13 Secrets for Speaking Fluent Japanese* (with a
mini-movie theater feature) to his book and manga
translations, as well as *William Blake Interactive*, a lavish
audio-visual introduction to the famous English poet.

NOTE FROM THE PUBLISHER
All Japanese names appearing in this book are given in the Western order, sur-
name last. The exceptions are those of the authors of the original stories, Natsume
Sōseki and Akutagawa Ryūnosuke; Mori Ōgai and Tanizaki Jun'ichirō; and
those of the characters appearing in the English translations of the stories.

Distributed in the United States by Kodansha America, Inc., and in the United
Kingdom and continental Europe by Kodansha Europe Ltd.

Published by Kodansha International Ltd.,17–14 Otowa 1-chome, Bunkyo-ku,
Tokyo 112–8652, and Kodansha America Inc.

Text copyright © 2003 by Giles Murray.
Illustration copyright © 2003 by Tetsuji Kiwaki.
All rights reserved. Printed in Japan.
ISBN 978–4–7700–2899–0

First edition, 2003
15 14 13 12 11 10 09 08   15 14 13 12 11 10 9 8 7

www.kodansha-intl.com

CONTENTS

AIMS

This book is designed to propel you beyond the humdrum world of magazine and newspaper articles into the rewarding but relatively impenetrable world of Japanese literature. *Breaking into Japanese Literature* presents only complete and unedited short stories: extracts from longer works have been deliberately avoided. This guarantees that you can enjoy a full aesthetic experience and a sense of uncompromised achievement. The seven stories in this book are all recognized masterpieces: the two authors, Natsume Sōseki and Akutagawa Ryūnosuke, are both literary giants who form part of the Japanese national curriculum. The seven stories cover a variety of genres: "The Nose" is a comedy; "In a Grove" and "Rashōmon" are fast-paced thrillers set in ancient Japan; and the four tales from *Ten Nights of Dreams* are thrilling, hallucinatory accounts of love, death, suicide and murder.

THREE-LEVEL STRUCTURE

The book is divided into three increasingly challenging levels.

LEVEL ONE consists of four stories from Sōseki's *Ten Nights of Dreams* (1908). The *Dreams* are very short—only two or three pages each in the original Japanese—and are composed in short, simple sentences. The repetition which Sōseki uses to create a dreamlike atmosphere has the convenient side effect of providing automatic *kanji* review opportunities.

For all their gothic subject matter, the *Dreams* offer very practical study benefits: they contain a very high proportion of the 1,945 common-use *kanji* characters that all students of Japanese have to master.

LEVEL TWO consists of two Akutagawa stories, "In a Grove" (1922) and "The Nose" (1916). These two stories are about five times longer than their predecessors in Level One, while the sentences of which they are composed are also lengthier and more involved. "In a Grove" was selected not only for its exciting subject matter (robbery, rape and murder), but because its unusual structure—with seven different narrators retelling the same story with slight variations—again provides unconscious review opportunities. "The Nose," despite some difficult religious and historical vocabulary, is a humorous fable with a simple story line. Apart from its significance as Akutagawa's breakthrough work, "The Nose" also provides some comic relief in this slightly *noir* collection.

LEVEL THREE features a single Akutagawa story, "Rashōmon" (1916). "Rashōmon" is about the same length as "The Nose," but is more densely descriptive—and thus more difficult—than any of the other stories. This atmospheric story is historically significant both as the title story of Akutagawa's first collection and as one of the inspirations for Akira Kurosawa's celebrated 1951 film.

The illustrations and prefaces on the title pages should help you locate the story that is most to your taste. Most important though, is to choose a story of the appropriate ability level. Starting with one of the shorter *Dreams* is definitely a good idea.

CORE COMPONENTS

Reading Japanese literature unassisted can be frustrating. This book is designed to help you bypass all those feelings of bewilderment and irritation. With the story in Japanese on the left-hand page, the English translation on the right-hand page and the dictionary running along the bottom of both, each double-page spread is totally self-contained. There is no need for any dictionaries. *Since everything you need is right there in front of you, you can read the stories fast enough to enjoy them as works of literature.* On the one hand, the custom dictionary means you will not waste time deciphering words of little practical use, like proper names or official titles. On the other hand, it means that any useful *kanji* characters or expressions that occur are there ready to be memorized. It's no pain, all gain.'

ELEMENT 1: JAPANESE ORIGINAL

The Japanese text is based on the Iwanami bunko editions of Sōseki's *Ten Nights of Dreams* and Akutagawa's "In a Grove," and the Shincho bunko editions of the two other Akutagawa stories. These editions were selected because they reflect modern *kana* usage. Further modifications have been made: some words that are rarely seen in *kanji* anymore have been written in *hiragana*, and *hiragana* superscript has been added to difficult words that even some Japanese would find puzzling, as well as to a number of simple words that the reader might recognize if not for the *kanji*.

The Japanese text has been printed across the page (rather than from top to bottom) to allow for easy cross-referencing between the two languages. Large point-size makes the *kanji* physically bigger and thus easier to read. Generous line spacing also enhances readability while providing space for notes.

ELEMENT 2: LITERAL ENGLISH TRANSLATIONS

The translations follow the Japanese scrupulously. I have striven for direct semantic parity, omitting nothing and taking nothing away. Thus, if there is a noun in the Japanese, it is rendered—as much as possible—by a noun in the English. The old woman in "Rashōmon," for example, is referred to as "the old woman" if that is how she is described in the Japanese. I have tried not to substitute the pronoun "she," and I have tried not to make things more complicated by turning a simple "old woman" into a "crone," "hag," or "droopy-dugged trollop." With a few exceptions, sentence order and paragraphing in the English also follow the Japanese. The overriding aim is to help you figure out what in one language corresponds to what in the other.

The style of the seven translations is not completely uniform. Sōseki's four *Dreams*—which are short and relatively simple—have been translated literally (making them easy to follow), but with a hint of the literary (encouraging you to think about word choices and style). The English deliberately echoes the lushness of nineteenth-century authors like Oscar Wilde and Edgar Allan Poe who influenced Sōseki in the first place.

The three Akutagawa stories, which make up the two more-advanced levels of the book, are considerably longer and harder than the *Ten Nights of Dreams*. I have therefore translated them in a plain, austere manner, since too much polish would just be a distraction.

ELEMENT 3: THE ZERO-OMISSION DICTIONARY

The running dictionary at the bottom of the page provides a translation of words in the order that they appear in the text. The dictionary covers every *kanji*-based word in the book, as well as the more difficult *hiragana* words. Note that when a *kanji* word appears twice or more on the same page, it is listed only on its first appearance, but with a ☝ icon to warn you that it will recur. If a *kanji* character belongs to the 2,230 characters (including all the 1,945 common-use characters) featured in *The Kodansha Kanji Learner's Dictionary*, its entry number is provided in square brackets after the English definition. This means that you can track down the individual characters with ease and master their *on* and *kun* readings, meanings, compounds and so on in a time-efficient way.

The dictionary does not include basic particles, *ko-so-a-do* demonstratives, the auxiliary -*sō* (as in *nemu-sō* "looks sleepy"), or the copula *da* (including *desu* and *de aru*). It assumes knowledge of simple *hiragana* words (such as *anata*, *ikutsu*, *suru* or *naru*) that every student learns at beginner level. It also omits some phrasal conjunctions, such as *soko de* (at which point), *sore kara* (after that) and *suru to* (whereupon), which can be understood by their constituent parts. The definitions provided fit the usage in the Japanese story. Due to space constraints, no effort has been made to provide a comprehensive definition for the word in all possible contexts. Direct English equivalents, rather than academic explanations, are provided. On occasion multiple meanings are given. This is to highlight the fact that a single Japanese word can have a multiplicity of English equivalents. Frequently the definitions provided in the dictionary differ from the word used in my English translation. This is a deliberate ploy to encourge the reader to think about issues of style.

These stories are nearly a century old, so the language and orthography is archaic in places. Always use the *Kanji Learner's Dictionary* as your guide to correct contemporary *kanji* usage.

EXTRA FEATURES

To take reading Japanese out of the realm of mere code-breaking and into the realm of fun, *Breaking into Japanese Literature* includes various extras. The MINI-BIOGRAPHIES of the two authors provide insights into their private lives and their place in the Japanese literary pantheon. The seven MINI-PREFACES draw attention to links between the featured stories and other works of literature or film. The ILLUSTRATIONS make it easier for the reader to enter the world of the author's imagination. Finally, all the stories are available free of charge on the Internet as MP3 SOUND FILES read by professional Japanese actors. The four stories from Sōseki's *Ten Nights of Dreams* are available as single files, but the Akutagawa stories are broken up into sections to keep download times to a practical length. Details on the URL and number of files are provided in the mini-prefaces. I recommend that you download the relevant audio only after having worked your way through the story. Try to read along with the Japanese text as you listen. If you can follow the text at native reading speed, you can consider yourself to have mastered the *kanji*.

THANK YOU

Paul Hulbert, my former editor, first floated the idea of producing a reader book and suggested both *Ten Nights of Dreams* and "In a Grove." Lucy North kindly lent me several invaluable works of reference. Machiko Moriyasu painstakingly checked the draft translations and the blank-riddled dictionary in its earlier incarnations. Makiko Kamiya and Ikue Samuta nobly endured the grim task of checking all the *kanji* entry numbers. Thanks to Kazuhiko Miki for his excellent cover design and Tetsuji Kiwaki for his dark and dramatic illustrations. The stories were read for the Net by Ken Yoshizawa, Naoko Abe, Seishi Yamane, Mitsuyo Matsumoto and Zenji Hashimoto. Yukio Shimazu orchestrated the recordings with his usual mastery. The **www.speaking-japanese.com** website was expertly redesigned by Naoko Ito. Finally, a big thank you to Michael Staley, my editor at Kodansha International, who supervised the whole project.

ACKNOWLEDGEMENTS

In making *Breaking into Japanese Literature*, I have synthesized information from various scholarly sources. For the mini-biographies, I am greatly indebted to Jay Rubin, Van C. Gessel, Edwin McClellan, Howard Hibbett and G.H. Healey. Takashi Kojima's translations set me on course for my attempts to render Akutagawa into English. I made extensive use of various dictionaries including *Kenkyusha's New Japanese-English Dictionary*, *The Compact Nelson Japanese-English Character Dictionary*, and the electronic version of the *Kōjien* Japanese-Japanese dictionary. Full details of all the books I referred to are provided in the bibliography on page 240.

Giles Murray

NATSUME SŌSEKI
(1867–1916)

Natsume Sōseki was born in Tokyo in 1867, just one year before the Meiji Restoration. The eighth and final child in the family, his father, Natsume Kohe Naokatsu, was nearly fifty, and his mother forty, at the time of his birth. The baby Sōseki was brought up by foster parents for eight years, but was returned to his original home at the age of eight, when his foster parents divorced. The name Sōseki is a *nom de plume* he created for himself.

Despite an intense love and affinity for the Chinese classics, the young Sōseki, in tune with the modernizing spirit of the times, chose to specialize in English and became the second-ever student to graduate from the English Literature Department of Tokyo Imperial University.

After graduation, Sōseki worked as an English teacher, first in Tokyo, and then in the provinces, moving from Matsuyama (Shikoku) to Kumamoto (Kyūshū) in 1896. In that same year he also got married, supposedly telling his wife on their wedding day that he was a scholar with no time to fuss over her. Perhaps unsurprisingly, she was emotionally unstable, even trying to kill herself on one occasion. Commentators invariably point out that the marriages depicted in Sōseki's novels are never very happy affairs.

At this time the Japanese government was

grooming homegrown scholars to replace the foreign teachers at universities. Sōseki, who had been selected to follow Lafcadio Hearn at Tokyo Imperial University, was thus sent to England for two years in September of 1900. With an allowance too mean for Oxford or Cambridge, and finding the lecturers at University College London too boring, Sōseki took weekly tutorials from an authority on Shakespeare. The rest of the time he festered in his London lodgings, reading voraciously, and developing his own theory of literature (later published as *Bungakuron*). The isolation may have been painful, but somehow London was the crucible that turned Sōseki, now in his mid-thirties, from a provincial scholar into a prolific best-selling author.

Returning to Tokyo in late 1903, Sōseki worked as a lecturer at the First High School and Tokyo Imperial University. He also started to write. His first novel, *I Am a Cat*, came about by accident, when a satirical short story (narrated by an English teacher's pet cat) had to be spun out due to popular demand. *Botchan* (1905), the tale of a headstrong Tokyoite going forth to teach in the provinces, was another humorous tale loosely based on Sōseki's own experiences in Shikoku. Sōseki was so successful that he gave up his university post in 1907. He then joined the *Asahi Shimbun* on condition of producing one novel per year—a condition he fulfilled, justifying Jay Rubin's description of him as a "word machine [who]

could write anything and keep it going for as long as he liked."*

In 1910 Sōseki vomited blood and was laid low for a year. His productivity hardly declined, though his later novels, such as *Kokoro* (1914) and *Grass by the Wayside* (1915), are more direct, personal and gloomy than their predecessors. He was in the middle of a further novel, *Light and Darkness*, when he died from internal hemorrhaging in December 1916.

Sōseki is revered as the father of modern Japanese literature. He was active just when Japan was opening up to the world, and was the first to chronicle the "loneliness [that] is the price we have to pay for being born in this modern age, so full of freedom, independence, and our own egotistical selves."**

* Jay Rubin, p. 381.
** Natsume Sōseki, *Kokoro,* tr. Edwin McClellan, p. 30.

The First Night

第一夜

Love conquers death

It is tempting to link the female protagonist of this story to Sōseki's sister-in-law, Tose, with whom he was in love until her premature death in 1891. Another more sinister possibility is that Sōseki is here wishing death upon his mentally unstable wife—literally "writing her out of the picture." On the other hand, the story could be just an exercise inspired by the beyond-the-grave love stories of Edgar Allan Poe, such as "Ligeia" and "Eleonora."

This story is available as an MP3 sound file at
www.speaking-japanese.com.

こんな夢を見た。

腕組をして枕元に坐っていると、仰向に寝た女が、静かな声でもう死にますという。女は長い髪を枕に敷いて、輪廓の柔らかな瓜実顔をその中に横たえている。真白な頬の底に温かい血の色が程よく差して、唇の色は無論赤い。到底死にそうには見えない。しかし女は静かな声で、もう死にますとはっきりいった。自分も確にこれは死ぬなと思った。そこで、そうかね、もう死ぬのかね、と上から覗き込むようにして聞いて見た。死にますとも、といいながら、女はぱっちりと眼を開けた。大きな潤のある眼で、長い睫に包まれた中は、ただ一面に真黒であった。その真黒な眸の奥に、自分の姿が鮮に浮かんでいる。

1

こんな this kind of (＝このような)
夢【ゆめ】dream [1510]
見る【みる】see [1615]

2

腕組をする【うでぐみをする】cross one's arms [0687] + [0904]
枕元【まくらもと】bedside [-] + [1226]
坐る【すわる】sit [-]
仰向に【あおむきに】faceup, on one's back [0032] + [1934]
寝る【ねる】sleep, lie down [1503]
女【おんな】woman 愛 [2135]
静かな【しずかな】soft, quiet 愛 [1138]
声【こえ】voice 愛 [1393]
もう soon 愛
死ぬ【しぬ】die 愛 [2194]
いう say 愛
長い【ながい】long 愛 [1626]

髪【かみ】hair [1821]
枕【まくら】pillow [-]
敷く【しく】spread out [1207]
輪廓【りんかく】outline [1067] + [1100]
柔らかな【やわらかな】soft [1325]
瓜実顔【うりざねがお】oval face [-] + [1416] + [1177]
中【なか】within, inside, in, among 愛 [2150]
横たえる【よこたえる】lie down [0733]
真白な【まっしろな】pure white [1337] + [2175]
頬【ほお】cheeks [-]
底【そこ】depths, bottom [1961]
温かい【あたたかい】warm [0442]
血【ち】blood [2196]
色【いろ】color 愛 [1280]
程よく【ほどよく】properly, rightly [0806]
差す【さす】be tinged [2082]
唇【くちびる】lips [1752]
無論【むろん】clearly, undeniably [1351] + [1058]

I had a dream.

I was sitting with my arms crossed by the bedside of a woman. She was lying on her back. In a most gentle voice she said that she was about to die. Her long black hair spread out fanlike over the pillow, framing the soft outlines of her oval face. A sanguine hue tinted the depths of her pure white cheeks, and her lips were a vibrant red. She certainly did not look to be at death's door. But, in that gentle voice, she had told me quite clearly that she was going to die. I too felt sure she would die. So I leaned forward and, gazing down at her, asked her if it could really be so and if truly she was going to die. Whereupon she opened her eyes wide and replied, "Yes, I will die—of that I am certain." Her eyes were large and moist and beneath their long shading lashes were twin expanses of the jettest black. My clearly-mirrored image was floating in the depths of those jet black eyes.

....

赤い【あかい】red [1389]
到底【とうてい】(+ negative) not at all [0848] + [1961]
見える【みえる】look, appear [1615]
しかし but, however
はっきり clearly
自分【じぶん】I, myself, me 憂 [2195] + [1247]
確に【たしかに】certainly [0830]
〜な emphatic sentence-ending particle (masculine)
思う【おもう】think, feel [1633]
〜かね interrogative particle expressing mild doubt 憂
上【うえ】above [2128]
覗き込む【のぞきこむ】gaze into, scrutinize [-] + [1917]
〜ようにする make as if to 〜
聞く【きく】ask [2097]
〜て見る【〜てみる】try to 〜 [1615]
〜とも indeed

〜ながら while, as
ぱっちりと wide open (of eyes)
眼【め】eyes 憂 [0796]
開ける【あける】open [2092]
大きな【おおきな】big [2133]
潤【うるおい】moisture, tenderness [0518]
睫【まつげ】eyelashes [-]
包む【つつむ】wrap, cover [1880]
ただ only, just
一面【いちめん】the whole surface/expanse [2105] + [1324]
真黒【まっくろ】pure black 憂 [1337] + [0689]
眸【ひとみ】pupil (of the eye) [0794]
奥【おく】depths [1806]
姿【すがた】shape, figure [1684]
鮮に【あざやかに】vividly, clearly [1210]
浮かぶ【うかぶ】float, flit [0319]

自分は透き徹るほど深く見えるこの黒眼の色沢を眺めて、これでも死ぬのかと思った。それで、ねんごろに枕の傍へ口を付けて、死ぬんじゃなかろうね、大丈夫だろうね、とまた聞き返した。すると女は黒い眼を眠そうにみはったまま、やっぱり静かな声で、でも、死ぬんですもの、仕方がないわといった。

じゃ、私の顔が見えるかいと一心に聞くと、見えるかいって、そら、そこに、写ってるじゃありませんかと、にこりと笑って見せた。自分は黙って、顔を枕から離した。腕組をしながら、どうしても死ぬのかなと思った。

自分【じぶん】I, myself, me 🐟 [2195] + [1247]

透き徹る【すきとおる】be transparent [1981] + [0510]

〜ほど to the extent that 〜

深い【ふかい】deep [0385]

見える【みえる】seem, appear 🐟 [1615]

黒目【くろめ】black eyes [1754] + [1927]

色沢【つや】glaze, shine [1280] + [0201]

眺める【ながめる】gaze at [0795]

これでも and yet, still

死ぬ【しぬ】die 🐟 [2194]

思う【おもう】think, feel 🐟 [1633]

ねんごろに courteously, warmly, gently

枕【まくら】pillow 🐟 [-]

傍【そば】near, beside [0110]

口【くち】mouth [2119]

付ける【つける】place, put [0019]

死ぬんじゃなかろうね【しぬんじゃなかろうね】＝死なないだろうね

大丈夫【だいじょうぶ】all right [2133] + [2136] + [2157]

また again, once more

聞き返す【ききかえす】ask back, ask again [2097] + [1940]

女【おんな】woman [2135]

黒い【くろい】black [1754]

眼【め】eyes [0796]

眠い【ねむい】sleepy [0782]

みはる open (one's eyes) wide

〜まま still

やっぱり as expected

静かな【しずかな】quiet, soft [1138]

声【こえ】voice [1393]

〜んですもの used for emphasis or to persuade (polite form)

仕方がない【しかたがない】it cannot be helped, that's that [0021] + [1243]

〜 わ sentence-ending particle used to soften one's tone and/or to persuade (feminine)

Gazing into the unclouded depths of her lustrous black eyes, I wondered, would she really die? Tenderly bringing my mouth down to her pillow, I begged her to confirm that she was not going to die now; that she was indeed all right. But the woman, with her sleep-glazed eyes wide open still, tranquilly replied (as I feared she would), "I shall die, and there is nothing we can do about it."

"Can you see my face?" I asked her urgently.

"See it?" she smiled. "It is reflected right here in my eyes, is it not?"

I said nothing, but lifted my face from the pillow. My arms crossed tight on my chest, I wondered if she was truly going to die.

いう say, speak

4

私 【わたし】 I, me [0758]
顔 【かお】 face, expression 𝅘 [1177]
〜かい = 〜か (colloquial form)
一心に 【いっしんに】 intently, wholeheartedly [2105] + [0004]
聞く 【きく】 ask [2097]
そら Why look! (exclamation)
写る 【うつる】 be reflected, be mirrored [1260]
にこりと smilingly
笑う 【わらう】 smile [1692]
〜て見せる 【〜てみせる】 ~ in an exaggerated/ostentatious manner [1615]
黙る 【だまる】 be silent, keep quiet [1833]
離す 【はなす】 remove, take away [1195]
腕組をする 【うでぐみをする】 cross one's arms [0687] + [0904]
〜ながら while, as

どうしても whatever else happens, inevitably
〜かな sentence-ending particle expressing wonder/doubt

　しばらくして、女がまたこういった。

「死んだら、埋めて下さい。大きな真珠貝で穴を掘って。そうして天から落ちて来る星の破片を墓標に置いて下さい。そうして墓の傍に待っていて下さい。また逢いに来ますから」

　自分は、何時逢いに来るかねと聞いた。

「日が出るでしょう。それから日が沈むでしょう。それからまた出るでしょう、そうしてまた沈むでしょう。——赤い日が東から西へ、東から西へと落ちて行くうちに、——あなた、待っていられますか」

　自分は黙って首肯た。女は静かな調子を一段張り上げて、

「百年待っていて下さい」と思い切た声でいった。

しばらくして after a while
女【おんな】woman ☻ [2135]
また again, once more ☻
いう say, speak ☻

死ぬ【しぬ】die [2194]
埋める【うめる】bury [0300]
〜て下さい【〜てください】please 〜 ☻ [2115]
大きな【おおきな】big [2133]
真珠貝【しんじゅがい】pearl oyster shell
　[1337] + [0643] + [1614]
穴【あな】hole, grave [1366]
掘る【ほる】dig [0364]
〜て ＝〜てください
天【てん】the heavens [2148]

落ちる【おちる】fall ☻ [1494]
〜て来る【〜てくる】come to 〜 [2211]
星【ほし】star [1577]
破片【かけ】fragment [0784] + [2158]
墓標【はかじるし】grave marker [1505] + [0730]
置く【おく】place, erect [1671]
墓【はか】grave [1505]
傍【そば】near, beside [0110]
待つ【まつ】wait [0269]
逢う【あう】meet ☻ [-]
来る【くる】come (to do something) ☻ [2211]

自分【じぶん】I, myself, me ☻ [2195] + [1247]
何時【いつ】when [0045] + [0625]
〜かね interrogative particle expressing
　mild doubt

Time passed, and once more the woman spoke: "When I am dead, I want you to bury me. Use a large pearl oyster shell to dig my grave. To mark my resting place, set out a star fragment that has fallen from the sky. Then wait for me at my graveside, for I shall come back to see you again."

"When will you come back?" I inquired.

"The sun rises and thence goes on to set. Once the sun has set, it goes on to rise again, and, having risen, sets once more. As the red orb of the sun sinks from east to west, and from east to west again, will you have the patience to wait for me?"

I said nothing, but nodded my head. Then the woman raised her quiet voice a degree and with sudden intensity said, "Wait for me one hundred years."

. . . .

聞く【きく】ask [2097]

8

日【ひ】sun 象 [1915]
出る【でる】come out, rise 象 [2180]
沈む【しずむ】sink, set 象 [0195]
赤い【あかい】red [1389]
東【ひがし】east [2221]
西【にし】west [2193]
〜て行く【〜てゆく】indicates progression away from the narrator or into the future [0157]
〜うちに while, as
〜ていられる be able to 〜 (potential form of 〜ている)

9

黙る【だまる】be silent, keep quiet [1833]

首肯く【うなずく】nod [1452] + [1567]
静かな【しずかな】quiet, soft [1138]
調子【ちょうし】tone, key, pitch [1051] + [2125]
一段【いちだん】one step, one degree [2105] + [0780]
張り上げる【はりあげる】raise (one's voice) [0348] + [2128]

10

百年【ひゃくねん】one hundred years [1279] + [1284]
思い切た【おもいきった】resolute, firm, determined [1633] + [0015]
声【こえ】voice [1393]

「百年、私<ruby>私<rt>わたくし</rt></ruby>の墓の傍に坐って待っていて下さい。きっと逢いに来ますから」

　自分はただ待っていると答えた。すると、黒い眸のなかに鮮に見えた自分の姿が、ぼうっと崩れて来た。静かな水が動いて写る影を乱したように、流れ出したと思ったら、女の眼がぱちりと閉じた。長い睫の間から涙が頬<ruby>頬<rt>ほお</rt></ruby>へ垂れた。——もう死んでいた。

　自分はそれから庭へ下りて、真珠貝で穴を掘った。真珠貝は大きな滑<ruby>滑<rt>なめら</rt></ruby>かな縁<ruby>縁<rt>ふち</rt></ruby>の鋭どい貝であった。土をすくう度<ruby>度<rt>たび</rt></ruby>に、貝の裏に月の光が差してきらきらした。湿った土の匂<ruby>匂<rt>におい</rt></ruby>もした。穴はしばらくして掘れた。女をその中に入れた。そうして柔らかい土を、上からそっと掛けた。掛ける毎<ruby>毎<rt>たび</rt></ruby>に真珠貝の裏に月の光が差した。

11

百年【ひゃくねん】one hundred years [1279] + [1284]

私【わたくし】I, me [0758]

墓【はか】grave [1505]

傍【そば】near, beside [0110]

坐る【すわる】sit [-]

待つ【まつ】wait ✍ [0269]

〜て下さい【〜てください】please 〜 [2115]

きっと definitely

逢う【あう】meet [-]

来る【くる】come (to do something) [2211]

12

自分【じぶん】I, myself, me ✍ [2195] + [1247]

ただ only, just

答える【こたえる】answer [1722]

黒い【くろい】black [1754]

眸【ひとみ】pupil (of the eye) [0794]

鮮に【あざやかに】vividly, clearly [1210]

見える【みえる】be visible, appear [1615]

姿【すがた】shape, figure [1684]

ぼうっと vaguely, fuzzily

崩れる【くずれる】disintegrate [1478]

〜て来る【〜てくる】begin to 〜 [2211]

静かな【しずかな】tranquil, peaceful, still [1138]

水【みず】water [0003]

動く【うごく】move [1163]

写る【うつる】be reflected, be mirrored [1260]

影【かげ】shadow [1216]

乱す【みだす】mess up, disrupt [0846]

〜ように as, like

流れ出す【ながれだす】flow away, be washed away [0325] + [2180]

思う【おもう】think, feel [1633]

女【おんな】woman ✍ [2135]

眼【め】eyes [0796]

ぱちりと quickly, abruptly

閉じる【とじる】shut [2090]

"Sit at my graveside and wait for one hundred years. I promise I will return to you."

I replied that I would wait. Whereupon my image, which had been mirrored so clearly in those jet black eyes, grew hazy and melted away. It melted away rather as a shadow on a pond breaks up when the water is disturbed. At the very instant this thought occurred to me, the woman's eyes snapped shut. From between her long lashes a single tear slid down her cheek. *She was dead.*

I went down to the garden, and there dug a hole with an oyster shell. The shell was big and smooth and sharp-edged. Each time I scooped up the earth, the moonlight caught the back of the shell, making it glint and sparkle. There was a smell of dank earth. I finally finished digging the grave and placed the woman inside. Tenderly I heaped the soft earth upon her, while the moonlight danced upon the back of the oyster shell with every movement of my arm.

長い【ながい】long [1626]
睫【まつげ】eyelashes [-]
間【あいだ】between [2094]
涙【なみだ】tear [0324]
頬【ほお】cheek [-]
垂れる【たれる】drip, dribble [2219]
もう already
死ぬ【しぬ】die [2194]

13

庭【にわ】garden [1987]
下りる【おりる】descend, go down to [2115]
真珠貝【しんじゅがい】pearl oyster shell ❧ [1337] + [0643] + [1614]
穴【あな】hole, grave ❧ [1366]
掘る【ほる】dig ❧ [0364]
大きな【おおきな】big [2133]
滑かな【なめらかな】smooth [0472]
縁【ふち】edge [0940]
鋭どい【するどい】sharp [1140]
貝【かい】shell, shellfish ❧ [1614]
土【つち】earth ❧ [2127]

すくう scoop up
〜度に【〜たびに】each time (one does something) [1974]
裏【うら】back, back part ❧ [1354]
月【つき】moon ❧ [1876]
光【ひかり】light, glow ❧ [1550]
差す【さす】pour forth, shine ❧ [2082]
きらきらする glint, shine
湿る【しめる】be moist, be damp [0443]
匂【におい】smell [-]
しばらくして after a while
掘れる【ほれる】be dug [0364]
中【なか】inside [2150]
入れる【いれる】put inside [2113]
柔らかい【やわらかい】soft [1325]
上【うえ】above [2128]
そっと softly
掛ける【かける】place over, put on [0361]
〜毎に【〜たびに】each time (one does something) [1283]

それから星の破片の落ちたのを拾って来て、かろく土の上へ乗せた。星の破片は丸かった。長い間大空を落ちている間に、角が取れて滑かになったんだろうと思った。抱き上げて土の上へ置くうちに、自分の胸と手が少し暖くなった。

自分は苔の上に坐った。これから百年の間こうして待っているんだなと考えながら、腕組をして、丸い墓石を眺めていた。そのうちに、女のいった通り日が東から出た。大きな赤い日であった。それがまた女のいった通り、やがて西へ落ちた。赤いまんまでのっと落ちて行った。一つと自分は勘定した。

星【ほし】star 😊 [1577]
破片【かけ】fragment 😊 [0784] + [2158]
落ちる【おちる】fall 😊 [1494]
拾う【ひろう】pick up [0279]
〜て来る【〜てくる】indicates progression in the direction of the narrator [2211]
かろく lightly, gently
土【つち】earth 😊 [2127]
上【うえ】on 😊 [2128]
乗せる【のせる】place upon [2224]
丸い【まるい】circular, round 😊 [2134]
長い【ながい】long [1626]
間【あいだ】time, duration 😊 [2094]
大空【おおぞら】the vast sky overhead [2133] + [1418]
〜間に【〜まに】while [2094]
角【かど】corners, angles [1293]

取れる【とれる】be removed [0847]
滑か【なめらか】smooth [0472]
思う【おもう】think, feel [1633]
抱き上げる【だきあげる】clasp and lift up [0227] + [2128]
置く【おく】place, put [1671]
〜うちに while, as
自分【じぶん】I, myself, me 😊 [2195] + [1247]
胸【むね】chest [0647]
手【て】hands [2155]
少し【すこし】a little [2163]
暖い【あたたかい】warm [0690]

苔【こけ】moss [-]
坐る【すわる】sit [-]
百年【ひゃくねん】one hundred years [1279] + [1284]
こうして in this way

Thereafter I went and found a fallen star fragment and set it carefully upon the ground. The star fragment was rounded. I imagined that its sharp angles had been worn to smoothness during its long fall from the sky. As I held it against me while setting it on the ground, I found my chest and hands had grown a little warmer.

I sat upon the moss. And now to wait for one hundred years, I thought, as I crossed my arms and looked at the rounded gravestone. As I sat there, the sun rose from the east, just as the woman had said it would. It was a huge, red sun. But in the end, just as the woman had said, its red mass slid down in the west. I counted one day.

....

待つ【まつ】wait [0269]
〜だな emotionally tinged expression indicating the narrator's supposition about something
考える【かんがえる】think [2039]
〜ながら while, as
腕組をする【うでぐみをする】cross one's arms [0687] + [0904]
墓石【はかいし】gravestone [1505] + [1884]
眺める【ながめる】gaze at, look at [0795]
そのうちに before long
女【おんな】woman 愛 [2135]
いう say, speak 愛
〜通り【〜とおり】in accordance with, just as 愛 [1982]
日【ひ】sun 愛 [1915]
東【ひがし】east [2221]
出る【でる】come out, rise [2180]

大きな【おおきな】big [2133]
赤い【あかい】red 愛 [1389]
また again
やがて by and by, finally
西【にし】west [2193]
〜まんま still, the same (colloquial form of 〜まま)
のっと suddenly (variant of ぬっと)
〜て行く【〜ていく】indicates progression away from the narrator or into the future [0157]
一つ【ひとつ】one [2105]
勘定する【かんじょうする】count, reckon [1162] + [1420]

しばらくするとまた唐紅の天道がのそりと上って来た。
そうして黙って沈んでしまった。二つとまた勘定した。
　自分はこういう風に一つ二つと勘定して行くうちに、赤
い日をいくつ見たか分らない。勘定しても、勘定しても、
しつくせないほど赤い日が頭の上を通り越して行った。そ
れでも百年がまだ来ない。しまいには、苔の生えた丸い石
を眺めて、自分は女に欺されたのではなかろうかと思い出
した。

しばらくすると after a while
また again, once again 桑
唐紅【からくれない】crimson [1988] + [0857]
天道【てんとう】sun [2148] + [2000]
のそりと lazily, sluggishly
上る【のぼる】rise [2128]
〜て来る【〜てくる】indicates progres-
　sion in the direction of the narrator or
　up to a point [2211]
黙る【だまる】be silent [1833]
沈む【しずむ】sink, set [0195]
〜てしまう expresses completion of an
　action
二つ【ふたつ】two 桑 [1224]
勘定する【かんじょうする】count, reckon
　桑 [1162] + [1420]

自分【じぶん】I, myself, me 桑 [2195] + [1247]
こういう such
風【ふう】way, manner [1908]
一つ【ひとつ】one [2105]
〜て行く【〜てゆく／いく】go and 〜 桑 [0157]

〜うちに while, as
赤い【あかい】red 桑 [1389]
日【ひ】sun 桑 [1915]
見る【みる】see [1615]
分る【わかる】understand, know [1247]
しつくす carry through, complete
〜ほど to the extent that 〜
頭【あたま】head [1073]
上【うえ】above [2128]
通り越す【とおりこす】pass over [1982] + [2085]
百年【ひゃくねん】one hundred years [1279] +
　[1284]
来る【くる】come [2211]
しまいに finally, in the end
苔【こけ】moss [-]
生える【はえる】grow, sprout [2179]
丸い【まるい】round [2134]
石【いし】stone [1884]
眺める【ながめる】gaze at, look at [0795]
女【おんな】woman [2135]
欺す【だます】trick, deceive [1119]
〜ではなかろうか ＝〜ではないだろうか

Time passed, and once again the crimson sun rose sluggish in the sky. Then it set in silence. And I counted two days.

And in this way I counted first one, then two, until finally I lost track of how many red suns I had seen. It did not matter how carefully I counted and counted, the red suns that passed over my head were numerous beyond tallying. Yet still one hundred years had not yet passed. And in the end, as I gazed at the round, moss-covered gravestone, it occurred to me that perhaps I had been deceived by the woman.

· ·

思い出す【おもいだす】start to think [1633] +
 [2180]

　すると石の下から斜に自分の方へ向いて青い茎が伸びて来た。見る間に長くなって丁度自分の胸のあたりまで来て留まった。と思うと、すらりと揺ぐ茎の頂に、心持首を傾けていた細長い一輪の蕾が、ふっくらと瓣を開いた。真白な百合が鼻の先で骨に徹えるほど匂った。そこへ遥の上から、ぽたりと露が落ちたので、花は自分の重みでふらふらと動いた。自分は首を前へ出して冷たい露の滴る、白い花瓣に接吻した。自分が百合から顔を離す拍子に思わず、遠い空を見たら、暁の星がたった一つ瞬いていた。

　「百年はもう来ていたんだな」とこの時始めて気が付いた。

....

すると whereupon
石【いし】stone [1884]
下【した】beneath [2115]
斜に【はすに】slantwise, obliquely [0999]
自分【じぶん】I, myself, me 🐾 [2195] + [1247]
方【ほう】direction [1243]
向く【むく】face, point toward [1934]
青い【あおい】blue, green [1573]
茎【くき】stalk 🐾 [1432]
伸びる【のびる】stretch, grow [0051]
〜て来る【〜てくる】indicates progression in the direction of the narrator [2211]
見る間に【みるまに】instantly [1615] + [2094]
長い【ながい】long [1626]
丁度【ちょうど】exactly [2106] + [1974]
胸【むね】chest [0647]
あたり level, the region of
来る【くる】come, reach [2211]
留まる【とまる】come to a standstill [1646]
思う【おもう】think, feel, be aware of [1633]
すらりと smoothly, gently

揺ぐ【ゆらぐ】shake, tremble [0434]
頂【いただき】top, tip [0108]
心持【こころもち】slightly [0004] + [0275]
首【くび】neck, head [1452]
傾ける【かたぶける】tilt, incline [0114]
細長い【ほそながい】long and thin [0900] + [1626]
一輪【いちりん】a single flower [2105] + [1067]
蕾【つぼみ】bud [-]
ふっくらと fully, luxuriantly
瓣【はなびら】petals [-]
開く【ひらく】open [2092]
真白な【まっしろな】pure white [1337] + [2175]
百合【ゆり】lily 🐾 [1279] + [1274]
鼻【はな】nose [1739]
先【さき】tip [1552]
骨【ほね】bones [1699]
徹える【こたえる】penetrate, go through [0510]
〜ほど to the extent that 〜
匂う【におう】be fragrant [-]
遥【はるか】far away [2007]

Then, from beneath the stone, a green stalk appeared. It was pointing at me. Even as I watched, the stalk grew longer and longer, only stopping when it was touching my chest. From its gently quivering tip, a long slender bud tilted ever so slightly to one side and opened its luxuriant petals before my nose. The fragrance of that pure white lily penetrated to my very bones. From far above a drop of dew fell, making the flower sway to and fro with its own weight. I craned forward and pressed my lips to the cool whiteness of the dew-moist petals. When I drew my face back from the lily I looked up unthinkingly at the distant sky. A single dawn star was shining there.

It was only then that I understood that a hundred years had passed.

....

上 【うえ】 above [2128]

ぽたりと suddenly (of raindrops falling)

露 【つゆ】 dew 义 [1803]

落ちる 【おちる】 fall [1494]

花 【はな】 flower [1405]

自分 【じぶん】 it (refers to the flower) [2195] + [1247]

重み 【おもみ】 weight [2223]

ふらふらと with a light side-to-side motion

動く 【うごく】 move [1163]

首 【くび】 neck, head [1452]

前 【まえ】 forward [1453]

出す 【だす】 put forward, stick out [2180]

冷たい 【つめたい】 cold [0057]

滴る 【したたる】 drip [0499]

白い 【しろい】 white [2175]

花瓣 【はなびら】 petals [1405] + [-]

接吻する 【せっぷんする】 kiss [0368] + [-]

顔 【かお】 face [1177]

離す 【はなす】 remove, take away [1195]

拍子 【ひょうし】 moment [0225] + [2125]

思わず 【おもわず】 involuntarily, unthinkingly [1633]

遠い 【とおい】 far-off [2013]

空 【そら】 sky [1418]

見る 【みる】 look at [1615]

暁 【あかつき】 dawn, daybreak [0669]

星 【ほし】 star [1577]

たった only

一つ 【ひとつ】 one [2105]

瞬く 【またたく】 twinkle, flicker [0841]

19

百年 【ひゃくねん】 one hundred years [1279] + [1284]

もう already

来る 【くる】 come [2211]

～ だな emotionally tinged expression indicating the narrator's supposition about something

時 【とき】 time, moment [0625]

始めて 【はじめて】 for the first time [0211]

気が付く 【きがつく】 realize, become aware [2037] + [0019]

The Third Night

第三夜

Guilt made manifest

Despite its jaunty, conversational tone, this is the most harrowingly nightmarish of the Sōseki tales in this selection. Before starting this story, it is helpful to be aware that in ancient Japan blind people customarily had shaved heads and were often trained to practice specific professions such as massage, acupuncture and music.

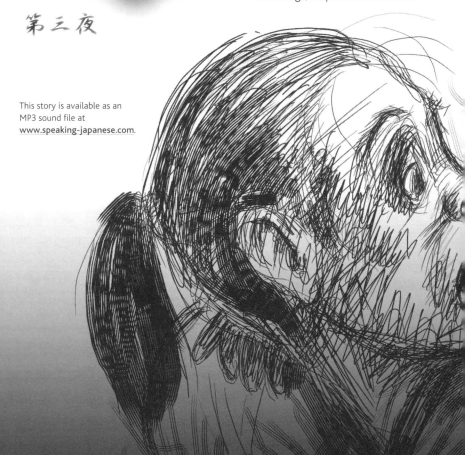

こんな夢を見た。

　六つになる子供を負ってる。慥に自分の子である。ただ不思議な事には何時の間にか眼が潰れて、青坊主になっている。自分が御前の眼は何時潰れたのかいと聞くと、なに昔からさと答えた。声は子供の声に相違ないが、言葉つきはまるで大人である。しかも対等だ。

　左右は青田である。路は細い。鷺の影が時々闇に差す。

「田圃へ掛ったね」と脊中でいった。

「どうして解る」と顔を後ろへ振り向けるようにして聞いたら、

「だって鷺が鳴くじゃないか」と答えた。

　すると鷺が果して二声ほど鳴いた。

1

こんな this kind of (＝このような)
夢【ゆめ】dream [1510]
見る【みる】see [1615]

2

六つ【むっつ】six (years old) [1244]
子供【こども】child 🐸 [2125] + [0066]
負う【おぶう】carry on one's back, bear [1327]
慥に【たしかに】certainly, for sure [-]
自分【じぶん】I, myself, me 🐸 [2195] + [1247]
子【こ】child [2125]
ただ but
不思議な【ふしぎな】strange, extraordinary [2141] + [1633] + [1087]
事【こと】thing [2220]
何時の間にか【いつのまにか】at some point [0045] + [0625] + [2094]
眼【め】eyes 🐸 [0796]

潰れる【つぶれる】lose (of vision, etc.), stop working (of a body organ) 🐸 [-]
青坊主【あおぼうず】shaved head, person with a shaved head [1573] + [0171] + [1231]
御前【おまえ】you [0422] + [1453]
何時【いつ】when [0045] + [0625]
〜かい ＝〜か (colloquial form)
聞く【きく】ask 🐸 [2097]
昔【むかし】a long time ago [1574]
〜さ emphatic particle
答える【こたえる】answer, reply 🐸 [1722]
声【こえ】voice 🐸 [1393]
〜に相違ない【〜にそういない】without doubt [0609] + [2014]
言葉つき【ことばつき】way of talking [1233] + [1497]
まるで completely, utterly
大人【おとな】adult [2133] + [2111]
しかも moreover

I had a dream.

I was carrying a six-year-old child on my back. I am sure that it was my own child. The extraordinary thing was that at some point it had gone blind, and its head had been shaved. I asked it when it had gone blind, to which its casual reply was, "Oh ages back." The voice was, without doubt, the voice of a child, but the way it talked was wholly grown-up. Moreover, it spoke to me as an equal.

On both sides of us there were rice paddies. The path was narrow. From time to time the shadowy shapes of herons punctured the darkness.

"So we've reached the rice paddies then," said the thing on my back.

"How can you tell?" I asked, turning my head.

"Because a heron is squawking, that's why," it replied.

At which moment, sure enough, a heron squawked twice.

....

対等【たいとう】equal (of a relationship) [0556] + [1723]

3

左右【さゆう】left and right, both sides [1887] + [1888]
青田【あおた】green rice paddies [1573] + [1925]
路【みち】road, path [1031]
細い【ほそい】narrow [0900]
鷺【さぎ】heron 爰 [-]
影【かげ】shadow [1216]
時々【ときどき】sometimes [0625]
闇【やみ】darkness [-]
差す【さす】flicker, appear and disappear [2082]

4

田圃【たんぼ】rice paddy [1925] + [-]
掛る【かかる】come to, reach [0361]
脊中【せなか】back [-] + [2150]

いう say, speak

5

解る【わかる】understand, know [1017]
顔【かお】face [1177]
後ろ【うしろ】behind [0267]
～ようにする make as if to ~

6

だって because (colloquial form)
鳴く【なく】sing, cry, squawk 爰 [0481]

7

果して【はたして】sure enough, as expected [2217]
二声【ふたこえ】two cries [1224] + [1393]
～ほど about ~, as much as ~

　自分は我子ながら少し怖くなった。こんなものを脊負っていては、この先どうなるか分らない。どこかうっちゃる所はなかろうかと向うを見ると闇の中に大きな森が見えた。あすこならばと考え出す途端に、脊中で、

「ふふん」という声がした。

「何を笑うんだ」

　子供は返事をしなかった。ただ

「御父さん、重いかい」と聞いた。

「重かあない」と答えると

「今に重くなるよ」といった。

8

自分【じぶん】I, myself, me 👤 [2195] + [1247]
我子【わがこ】my own child [2208] + [2125]
〜ながら while, for all that
少し【すこし】a little [2163]
怖い【こわい】fearful, afraid [0219]
こんな such, this kind of (=このような)
脊負う【しょう】carry on one's back [-] + [1327]
この先【このさき】the future [1552]
分る【わかる】know, understand [1247]
うっちゃる get rid of
所【ところ】opportune place [0568]
なかろうか =ないだろうか
向う【むこう】beyond, ahead [1934]
見る【みる】look, see [1615]
闇【やみ】darkness [-]
中【なか】in, inside [2150]
大きな【おおきな】big [2133]

森【もり】woods, forest [1602]
見える【みえる】be visible, appear [1615]
あすこ =あそこ (colloquial form)
考え出す【かんがえだす】start to think [2039] + [2180]
〜途端に【〜とたんに】at the very instant, no sooner than [1980] + [0826]
脊中【せなか】back [-] + [2150]

9

ふふん ha-ha (onomatopoeic expression that describes a scornful laugh)
声【こえ】voice, utterance [1393]

10

何【なに】what [0045]
笑う【わらう】laugh, jeer, deride [1692]

11

子供【こども】child [2125] + [0066]
返事【へんじ】reply [1940] + [2220]
ただ but, only, merely

For all it was my own child, I began to feel afraid. Carrying this thing on my back, I had no idea what might happen to me. I looked ahead, searching for a place where I could get rid of it, and, in the darkness, saw a large forest. "That's the place!" No sooner had the thought occurred to me than from my back I heard a sniggering sound.

"What are you laughing at?"

The child did not reply.

It just asked, "Heavy am I then, father?"

"You are not heavy" was my reply.

"Well, I am going to get heavier and heavier," it said.

....

12

御父さん【おとっさん】father (colloquial
　form of おとうさん) [0422] + [1248]
重い【おもい】heavy ♨ [2223]
〜かい =〜か (colloquial form)
聞く【きく】ask [2097]

13

重かあない【おもかあない】not heavy
　(colloquial form of 重くない) [2223]
答える【こたえる】respond, answer [1722]

14

今に【いまに】from now, before long [1246]
いう say, speak

自分は黙って森を目標にあるいて行った。田の中の路が不規則にうねってなかなか思うように出られない。しばらくすると二股になった。自分は股の根に立って、ちょっと休んだ。

「石が立ってるはずだがな」と小僧がいった。

なるほど八寸角の石が腰ほどの高さに立っている。表には左り日ケ窪、右堀田原とある。闇だのに赤い字が明かに見えた。赤い字は井守の腹のような色であった。

15

自分【じぶん】I, myself, me 🏃 [2195] + [1247]
黙る【だまる】keep quiet, be silent [1833]
森【もり】woods, forest [1602]
目標【めじるし】sign, landmark [1927] + [0730]
あるく walk
〜て行く【〜ていく】~ away [0157]
田【た】rice paddy [1925]
中【なか】among [2150]
路【みち】road, path [1031]
不規則に【ふきそくに】irregularly [2141] + [0067] + [0967]
うねる meander
なかなか (+ negative) not really, not quite
思う【おもう】think, expect [1633]
〜ように as
出る【でる】emerge [2180]
しばらくすると after a while
二股【ふたまた】fork in the road [1224] + [-]
股【また】fork [-]
根【ね】center, root [0631]
立つ【たつ】stand 🏃 [1257]

ちょっと a bit, a while
休む【やすむ】rest [0036]

16

石【いし】stone 🏃 [1884]
〜はずだ must/should be, ought to be
小僧【こぞう】boy [0002] + [0119]
いう say, speak

17

なるほど sure enough
八寸角【はっすんかく】eight *sun* square (1 *sun* = 3 cm) [1859] + [1864] + [1293]
腰【こし】waist, middle of the body [0711]
〜ほど to the extent of
高さ【たかさ】height [1330]
表【おもて】front [1572]
左り【ひだり】left [1887]
日ケ窪【ひがくぼ】Higakubo (place name) [1915] + [-] + [-]
右【みぎ】right [1888]
堀田原【ほったはら】Hottahara (place name) [0342] + [1925] + [1910]
闇【やみ】darkness [-]
〜だのに despite (＝〜なのに)

36　第三夜

I said nothing, but walked on, making for the forest. The path between the rice paddies snaked so wildly that I could not get across as I had imagined. After a while there was a fork in the path. I stood at the point where the paths met and rested a moment.

"There should be a milestone around here," said the child.

Sure enough, there was an eight-inch-square marker stone that reached to my waist. On the front it said that Higakubo was to the left, Hottahara to the right. It was dark, but the red letters were clearly visible. The red letters were the color of the underbelly of a newt.

....

赤い 【あかい】 red 湿 [1389]
字 【じ】 letters 湿 [1374]
明かに 【あきらかに】 brightly, clearly, dis-
tinctly [0572]
見える 【みえる】 be visible [1615]
井守 【いもり】 newt [2153] + [1375]
腹 【はら】 stomach, belly [0710]
〜のような like, similar to
色 【いろ】 color [1280]

18

「左が好いだろう」と小僧が命令した。左を見ると最先の森が闇の影を、高い空から自分らの頭の上へ拋げかけていた。自分はちょっと躊躇した。

19

「遠慮しないでもいい」と小僧がまたいった。自分は仕方なしに森の方へ歩き出した。腹の中では、よく盲目のくせに何でも知ってるなと考えながら一筋道を森へ近づいてくると、脊中で、「どうも盲目は不自由で不可いね」といった。

20

「だから負ってやるから可いじゃないか」

21

「負ぶってもらって済まないが、どうも人に馬鹿にされて不可い。親にまで馬鹿にされるから不可い」

18

左【ひだり】 left 👤 [1887]
好い【いい】 good [0155]
小僧【こぞう】 boy 👤 [0002] + [0119]
命令する【めいれいする】 order [1303] + [1259]
見る【みる】 look [1615]
最先【さっき】 a little while ago [1599] + [1552]
森【もり】 woods, forest 👤 [1602]
闇【やみ】 darkness [-]
影【かげ】 shadow [1216]
高い【たかい】 high [1330]
空【そら】 the sky [1418]
自分ら【じぶんら】 ourselves [2195] + [1247]
頭【あたま】 head [1073]
上【うえ】 above [2128]
拋げかける【なげかける】 throw upon [-]
自分【じぶん】 I, myself, me 👤 [2195] + [1247]
ちょっと a bit
躊躇する【ちゅうちょする】 hesitate [-] + [-]

19

遠慮する【えんりょする】 hesitate, be diffi-
dent [2013] + [2057]
また again
いう say 👤
仕方なしに【しかたなしに】 reluctantly [0021] + [1243]
方【ほう】 direction [1243]
歩き出す【あるきだす】 start to walk [1566] + [2180]
腹【はら】 stomach, mind [0710]
中【なか】 inside [2150]
盲目【めくら】 blind person 👤 (NOTE: now pejorative; do not use) [1298] + [1927]
〜のくせに in spite of, despite
何でも【なんでも】 anything, everything [0045]
知る【しる】 know [0768]
〜な sentence-ending particle expressing emotion (masculine)
考える【かんがえる】 think, reflect [2039]
〜ながら while, as
一筋【ひとすじ】 without diversion, straight, earnestly [2105] + [1719]

"We want to go left, of course," ordered the boy. I looked to the left and there was the same forest rearing skyward and casting its dark shadow upon our heads. I hesitated for an instant.

"Don't dillydally," chided the child once more. Reluctantly I set off toward the forest. As I headed straight for the forest, I was wondering to myself how a miserable blind brat could know so much, when the thing on my back said, "Yes, blindness is a despicable inconvenience, is it not?"

"I'm carrying you, so it is no trouble at all."

"I'm very much obliged to you for carrying me, but I really do not like being looked down on by people. And I *particularly* do not like being looked down on by my own father."

....

道 【みち】 road [2000]
近づく 【ちかづく】 get closer to, approach [1941]
〜てくる indicates progression up to a point
背中 【せなか】 back [-] + [2150]
どうも somehow, no matter how you view it
不自由 【ふじゆう】 inconvenience, handicap [2141] + [2195] + [2181]
不可い 【いけない】 won't do 変 [2141] + [1882]

20

負う 【おぶう】 carry on one's back 変 [1327]
〜てやる do something for someone
可い 【いい】 good, okay [1882]

21

〜てもらう have someone 〜
済まない 【すまない】 unpardonable, inexcusable [0383]
どうも especially, particularly
人 【ひと】 people
馬鹿にする 【ばかにする】 mock, make a fool of [2073] + [1996]

親 【おや】 father, parent [1172]
まで even

何だか厭になった。早く森へ行って捨ててしまおうと思って急いだ。

「もう少し行くと解る。——丁度こんな晩だったな」と脊中で独言のようにいっている。

「何が」と際どい声を出して聞いた。

「何がって、知ってるじゃないか」と子供は嘲けるように答えた。すると何だか知ってるような気がし出した。けれどもはっきりとは分らない。ただこんな晩であったように思える。そうしてもう少し行けば分るように思える。分っては大変だから、分らないうちに早く捨ててしまって、安心しなくってはならないように思える。自分はますます足を早めた。

何だか【なんだか】somehow or other, indefinably 🕱 [0045]
厭になる【いやになる】get sick of, get fed up with [-]
早い【はやい】quick 🕱 [1549]
森【もり】woods, forest [1602]
行く【いく】go 🕱 [0157]
捨てる【すてる】get rid of, throw away 🕱 [0369]
〜てしまう thoroughly 〜 🕱
思う【おもう】think, feel 🕱 [1633]
急ぐ【いそぐ】hurry [1328]

もう少し【もうすこし】a little further 🕱 [2163]
解る【わかる】understand [1017]

丁度【ちょうど】exactly [2106] + [1974]
こんな like this (＝このような) 🕱
晩【ばん】evening, night 🕱 [0668]
〜な sentence-ending particle expressing emotion (masculine)
脊中【せなか】back [-] + [2150]
独言【ひとりごと】talking to oneself [0293] + [1233]
〜のように as if
いう say, speak

何【なに】what 🕱 [0045]
際どい【きわどい】desperate [0503]
声【こえ】voice [1393]
出す【だす】emit (a sound) [2180]
聞く【きく】ask [2097]

Why I am not sure, but suddenly I felt disgusted. I hastened to get to the woods so I could get rid of it once and for all.

"Go a little further, then you will understand. It was a night just like this," muttered the thing on my back, as if talking to itself.

"Understand what?" I asked, my voice almost hysterical.

"What? You know very well what," sneered the child in reply.

I had a vague sense that I did know what it was talking about. But I didn't fully understand. I did feel that, whatever it was, it might have happened on a night like this. I did feel that if I went on a bit further, I might understand. And I did feel that to understand would be a terrible thing, so I should keep my peace of mind by disposing of the child quickly while I was still in ignorance. I quickened my pace.

....

25

知る【しる】know, be aware of 💀 [0768]
子供【こども】child [2125] + [0066]
嘲ける【あざける】mock, scoff [-]
答える【こたえる】answer [1722]
〜ような like, as if
気がし出す【きがしだす】start to feel [2037] + [2180]
はっきり clearly
分る【わかる】understand 💀 [1247]
ただ but
〜ように as if
大変【たいへん】terrible [2133] + [1311]
〜うちに while, as long as
安心する【あんしんする】feel at ease [1373] + [0004]

自分【じぶん】I, myself, me [2195] + [1247]
ますます all the more [1468]
足【あし】legs, feet, pace [1386]
早める【はやめる】speed up [1549]

雨は最先^{さっき}から降っている。路はだんだん暗くなる。殆んど夢中である。ただ脊中に小さい小僧がくっついていて、その小僧が自分の過去、現在、未来を悉^{ことごと}く照^{てら}して、寸分の事実も洩^もらさない鏡のように光っている。しかもそれが自分の子である。そうして盲目である。自分は堪^{たま}らなくなった。

「此処^{ここ}だ、此処だ。丁度^{ちょうど}その杉の根の所だ」

雨の中で小僧の声ははっきり聞えた。自分は覚えず留^{とま}った。何時^{いつ}しか森の中へ這入^{はい}っていた。一間ばかり先にある黒いものは慥^{たしか}に小僧のいう通り杉の木と見えた。

....

26

雨【あめ】rain ☻ [2218]
最先【さっき】before [1599] + [1522]
降る【ふる】fall [0335]
路【みち】road, path [1031]
だんだん slowly, gradually
暗い【くらい】dark [0689]
殆んど【ほとんど】almost, virtually [-]
夢中【むちゅう】in a trance, desperate, frantic [1510] + [2150]
ただ just
脊中【せなか】back [-] + [2150]
小さい【ちいさい】small [0002]
小僧【こぞう】boy ☻ [0002] + [0119]
くっつく cling/stick to
自分【じぶん】I, myself, me ☻ [2195] + [1247]
過去【かこ】past [2003] + [1364]
現在【げんざい】present [0657] + [1896]
未来【みらい】future [2185] + [2211]

悉く【ことごとく】fully, utterly [-]
照す【てらす】shed light on, illuminate [1809]
寸分【すんぶん】the littlest bit [1864] + [1247]
事実【じじつ】fact, event, instance [2220] + [1416]
洩らす【もらす】leave out, omit [-]
鏡【かがみ】mirror [1157]
〜のように like, resembling
光る【ひかる】shine [1550]
しかも moreover
子【こ】child [2125]
盲目【めくら】blind person (NOTE: now pejorative; do not use) [1298] + [1927]
堪らない【たまらない】be unbearable [0409]

27

此処【ここ】here ☻ [-] + [1918]
丁度【ちょうど】exactly [2106] + [1974]
杉【すぎ】cedar ☻ [0557]
根【ね】root [0631]

The rain had been falling a while now. The path grew darker and darker. I was almost in a trance. But there was a little child stuck to my back, and that child was flooding my past, my present and my future with a merciless light, like a mirror that overlooks nothing, no matter how small. But it was my child; and it was blind. I could not bear it.

"Here! It is here! Here, just at the root of that cedar."

The voice of the child rang out above the sound of the rain. Without thinking I stopped. At some point we had entered the forest. The dark mass just six feet in front of me was a cedar tree, just as the boy had said.

所【ところ】place, spot [0568]

28

中【なか】in, into 炙 [2150]
声【こえ】voice [1393]
はっきり clearly
聞える【きこえる】be audible [2097]
覚えず【おぼえず】unconsciously, una-
　wares [1668]
留る【とまる】stop [1646]
何時しか【いつしか】at some point [0045] +
　[0625]
森【もり】woods, forest [1602]
這入る【はいる】enter [-] + [2113]
一間【いっけん】one *ken* (= 1.82 m) [2105] +
　[2094]
〜ばかり about 〜
先【さき】ahead, in front [1552]
黒い【くろい】dark, black [1754]
慥に【たしかに】certainly, for sure [-]
いう say, speak

〜通り【〜とおり】in accordance with, just
　as [1982]
木【き】tree [2149]
見える【みえる】look like, appear [1615]

「御父さん、その杉の根の所だったね」

「うん、そうだ」と思わず答えてしまった。

「文化五年辰年だろう」

なるほど文化五年辰年らしく思われた。

「御前がおれを殺したのは今から丁度百年前だね」

自分はこの言葉を聞くや否や、今から百年前文化五年の辰年のこんな闇の晩に、この杉の根で、一人の盲目を殺したという自覚が、忽然として頭の中に起った。おれは人殺であったんだなと始めて気が附いた途端に、脊中の子が急に石地蔵のように重くなった。

"Father, it was here! It was at the root of that cedar, was it not?"

"Yes, so it was," came my automatic reply.

"It was 1808, the year of the dragon, was it not?"

Come to think of it, I suppose it had been 1808, the year of the dragon.

"You murdered me a hundred years ago to the day, didn't you?"

And as I heard him say those words, the knowledge suddenly welled up inside me that a hundred years ago to the day, on just such a dark night as this, at the root of this very cedar, I had indeed killed a man. The instant I realized that I was a murderer, the child on my back suddenly grew as heavy as a stone image of Jizō himself.

盲目【めくら】blind person (NOTE: now pejorative; do not use) [1298] + [1927]

自覚【じかく】self-awareness, consciousness [2195] + [1668]

忽然として【こつぜんとして】suddenly, unexpectedly [-] + [1779]

頭【あたま】head [1073]

中【なか】inside [2150]

起る【おきる】arise, come into being, spring up [2079]

人殺【ひとごろし】murderer [2111] + [0889]

〜んだな expresses emotion (masculine)

始めて【はじめて】for the first time [0211]

気が附く【きがつく】realize [2037] + [0257]

〜途端に【〜とたんに】as soon as [1980] + [0826]

脊中【せなか】back [-] + [2150]

子【こ】child [2125]

急に【きゅうに】suddenly [1328]

石地蔵【いしじぞう】stone statue of Kṣiti-garbha (the bodhisattva Jizō, guardian deity of children) [1884] + [0152] + [1530]

〜のように like

重い【おもい】heavy [2223]

The Fifth Night 第五夜

A warrior's romantic last wish

Despite its heroic cast of warriors and lovers, this story is whimsical and ironic in tone. The twentieth-century narrator may find himself in a dire situation in his dream, but still manages to look at the uncouth garb and toilet of his primitive captors with mocking detachment. The motif of the cock may be a deliberate echo of Jesus on the night of his arrest: "I tell thee, Peter, the cock shall not crow this day, before thou shalt thrice deny that thou knowest me." Note that in true Sōseki style, the lovers do not end up living happily ever after.

This story is available as an MP3 sound file at **www.speaking-japanese.com**.

こんな夢を見た。

何でもよほど古い事で、神代に近い昔と思われるが、自分が軍をして運悪く敗北たために、生擒になって、敵の大将の前に引き据えられた。

その頃の人はみんな脊が高かった。そうして、みんな長い髯を生やしていた。革の帯を締めて、それへ棒のような剣を釣るしていた。弓は藤蔓の太いのをそのまま用いたように見えた。漆も塗ってなければ磨きも掛けてない。極めて素樸なものであった。

1

こんな this kind of (＝このような)
夢【ゆめ】dream [1510]
見る【みる】see [1615]

2

何でも【なんでも】probably, likely [0045]
よほど very, greatly
古い【ふるい】old [1262]
事【こと】thing, event [2220]
神代【かみよ】age of the gods, age of myth [0615] + [0018]
近い【ちかい】near, close to [1941]
昔【むかし】long time ago [1574]
思う【おもう】think, imagine [1633]
自分【じぶん】I, myself, me [2195] + [1247]
軍【いくさ】battle, campaign, army [1318]
運悪く【うんわるく】unluckily [2006] + [1758]
敗北る【まける】be defeated, lose [0991] + [0147]
〜ため because, on account of
生擒【いけどり】captured alive [2179] + [-]

敵【てき】enemy [1204]
大将【たいしょう】leader, chief [2133] + [0336]
前【まえ】in front of, before [1453]
引き据える【ひきすえる】drag and force to sit down [0133] + [0365]

3

頃【ころ】time, period [-]
人【ひと】people [2111]
みんな all, everybody 🐾
脊が高い【せがたかい】tall [-] + [1330]
長い【ながい】long [1626]
髯【ひげ】sideburns [-]
生やす【はやす】grow, have (hair) [2179]
革【かわ】leather [1582]
帯【おび】belt [1648]
締める【しめる】tighten, wear (a belt) [0945]
棒【ぼう】pole, stick [0671]
〜のような like 🐾
剣【つるぎ】sword [1096]
釣るす【つるす】suspend, hang [1098]
弓【ゆみ】bow [2120]

I had a dream.

It must have been ancient times, far back enough, perhaps, to be near the age of the gods. I had been in battle, but, having had the ill luck to be defeated, I had been captured and dragged before the enemy captain.

Back in those days people were all very tall. And they all had long sideburns. They wore belts of leather, from which hung pole-like swords. For their bows they appeared to use thick shafts of natural wisteria. They were neither lacquered nor polished. All in all, things were exceedingly primitive.

....

藤蔓【ふじづる】wisteria vine [1544] + [-]
太い【ふとい】thick, fat [1360]
そのまま as is, just like that
用いる【もちいる】use [1889]
見える【みえる】appear, seem [1615]
漆【うるし】lacquer [0497]
塗る【ぬる】paint, brush with [1818]
磨きを掛ける【みがきをかける】shine, pol-
    ish [2033] + [0361]
極めて【きわめて】very, exceedingly [0695]
素樸な【そぼくな】artless, unsophisticated
    [1590] + [-]

4

　敵の大将は、弓の真中を右の手で握って、その弓を草の上へ突いて、酒甕を伏せたようなものの上に腰を掛けていた。その顔を見ると、鼻の上で、左右の眉が太く接続っている。その頃髪剃というものは無論なかった。

5

　自分は虜だから、腰を掛ける訳に行かない。草の上に胡坐をかいていた。足には大きな藁沓を穿いていた。この時代の藁沓は深いものであった。立つと膝頭まで来た。その端の所は藁を少し編残して、房のように下げて、歩くとばらばら動くようにして、飾りとしていた。

4

敵【てき】enemy [1204]
大将【たいしょう】leader, chief [2133] + [0336]
弓【ゆみ】bow ☙ [2120]
真中【まんなか】middle [1337] + [2150]
右【みぎ】right [1888]
手【て】hand [2155]
握る【にぎる】grip, hold [0427]
草【くさ】grass ☙ [1450]
上【うえ】on, upon ☙ [2128]
突く【つく】stick into [1421]
酒甕【さかがめ】pot, jar for saké [0328] + [-]
伏せる【ふせる】turn over, put facedown [0029]
～ような like, resembling ☙
腰を掛ける【こしをかける】sit, take a seat ☙ [0711] + [0361]
顔【かお】face, expression [1177]
見る【みる】look at, see [1615]
鼻【はな】nose [1739]
左右【さゆう】left and right [1887] + [1888]

眉【まゆ】eyebrows [2050]
太い【ふとい】thick, dense [1360]
接続る【つながる】be joined [0368] + [0921]
頃【ころ】time, period [-]
髪剃【かみそり】razor [1821] + [-]
無論【むろん】of course, naturally [1351] + [1058]

5

自分【じぶん】I, myself, me [2195] + [1247]
虜【とりこ】prisoner [2055]
～訳に行かない【～わけにゆかない】un-reasonable/impossible to ~ [0989] + [0157]
胡坐をかく【あぐらをかく】sit cross-legged [0623] + [-]
足【あし】feet [1386]
大きな【おおきな】big [2133]
藁沓【わらぐつ】straw boots ☙ [-] + [-]
穿く【はく】wear (shoes) [-]
時代【じだい】age, period [0625] + [0018]
深い【ふかい】deep, long, tall [0385]
立つ【たつ】stand up [1257]

The enemy captain clasped the middle of his bow in his right hand, thrust it into the grass, and sat down upon something like an upturned sake jar. Looking at his face, I saw that his left and right eyebrows joined in a single thick line above his nose. In those days, of course, they did not have razors.

Since I was a prisoner, it was out of the question for me to sit on anything. So I sat cross-legged on the grass. I was wearing huge straw boots on my feet. Straw boots in those times were very high indeed. When you stood up, they reached to your knees. At the top a little straw was left unwoven. It was ornamental, and made so it hung down like a tassel and bounced up and down when you walked.

....

膝頭【ひざがしら】kneecaps [-] + [1073]
来る【くる】reach, come up to [2211]
端【はし】end, extremity, tip [0826]
所【ところ】place [0568]
藁【わら】straw [-]
少し【すこし】a bit, slightly [2163]
編残す【あみのこす】leave unwoven [0941] + [0640]
房【ふさ】fringe, tassel, tuft [1237]
〜のように like
下げる【さげる】hang down [2115]
歩く【あるく】walk [1566]
ばらばら here and there
動く【うごく】move [1163]
〜ようにする make so that
飾り【かざり】decoration [1129]
〜として as, for

大将は篝火で自分の顔を見て、死ぬか生きるかと聞いた。これはその頃の習慣で、捕虜にはだれでも一応はこう聞いたものである。生きると答えると降参した意味で、死ぬというと屈服しないという事になる。自分は一言死ぬと答えた。大将は草の上に突いていた弓を向うへ拋げて、腰に釣るした棒のような剣をするりと抜き掛けた。それへ風に靡いた篝火が横から吹きつけた。自分は右の手を楓のように開いて、掌を大将の方へ向けて、眼の上へ差し上げた。待てという相図である。大将は太い剣をかちゃりと鞘に収めた。

6

大将【たいしょう】leader, chief 寒 [2133] + [0336]

篝火【かがりび】campfire 寒 [-] + [2159]

自分【じぶん】I, myself, me 寒 [2195] + [1247]

顔【かお】face, expression [1177]

見る【みる】look at, see, watch [1615]

死ぬ【しぬ】die 寒 [2194]

生きる【いきる】live 寒 [2179]

聞く【きく】ask 寒 [2097]

頃【ころ】time, period [-]

習慣【しゅうかん】custom [1711] + [0487]

捕虜【とりこ】prisoner [0315] + [2055]

だれでも anybody

一応【いちおう】tentatively, just as a formality [2105] + [1946]

答える【こたえる】reply 寒 [1722]

降参する【こうさんする】surrender [0335] + [1308]

意味【いみ】meaning [1352] + [0206]

いう say, speak

屈服する【くっぷくする】submit [1958] + [0591]

事【こと】thing, act, result [2220]

一言【ひとこと】single word [2105] + [1233]

草【くさ】grass [1450]

上【うえ】on, upon 寒 [2128]

突く【つく】stick into [1421]

弓【ゆみ】bow [2120]

向う【むこう】over there [1934]

拋げる【なげる】fling, throw [-]

腰【こし】waist, middle of the body [0711]

釣るす【つるす】suspend, hang [1098]

棒【ぼう】pole, stick [0671]

〜のような like

剣【けん】sword 寒 [1096]

するりと smoothly, swiftly

抜き掛ける【ぬきかける】start to draw out [0183] + [0361]

風【かぜ】wind [1908]

The captain looked at me keenly by the light of the campfire and asked me if I chose to live or to die. This was a custom in those times and the question was put to every prisoner as a matter of course. If you replied that you would live, it meant that you surrendered. If you said that you would die, it meant that you refused to submit. I replied simply that I chose to die. The leader flung his bow, which had been thrust into the ground, to one side and briskly drew the polelike sword which hung at his waist. The fire, driven by the wind, flared toward it. I opened up my hand like a maple leaf and, turning my palm toward the captain, lifted it up above my eyes. This was a signal meaning "wait." The captain thrust his rattling sword back into its scabbard.

....

靡く【なびく】sway with the wind [-]
横【よこ】side [0733]
吹きつける【ふきつける】blow against [0170]
右【みぎ】right [1888]
手【て】hand [2155]
楓【かえで】maple leaf [-]
〜のように like
開く【ひらく】open [2092]
掌【たなごころ】palm, hollow of the hand [-]
方【ほう】direction [1243]
向ける【むける】direct toward [1934]
眼【め】eyes [0796]
差し上げる【さしあげる】lift up, raise [2082] +
　　[2128]
待つ【まつ】wait
〜て ＝〜てください
相図【あいず】sign [0609] + [1951]
太い【ふとい】thick, hefty [1360]
かちゃりと with a rattle

鞘【さや】scabbard [-]
収める【おさめる】put back, sheathe [0017]

その頃でも恋はあった。自分は死ぬ前に一目思う女に逢いたいといった。大将は夜が明けて鶏が鳴くまでなら待つといった。鶏が鳴くまでに女を此処へ呼ばなければならない。鶏が鳴いても女が来なければ、自分は逢わずに殺されてしまう。

　大将は腰を掛けたまま、篝火を眺めている。自分は大きな藁沓を組み合わしたまま、草の上で女を待っている。夜は段々更ける。

　時々篝火が崩れる音がする。崩れる度に狼狽たように焰が大将になだれかかる。真黒な眉の下で、大将の眼がぴかぴかと光っている。すると誰やら来て、新しい枝を沢山火の中へ抛げ込んで行く。しばらくすると、火がぱちぱちと鳴る。暗闇を弾き返すような勇ましい音であった。

7

頃【ころ】 time, period [-]

恋【こい】 love [1331]

自分【じぶん】 I, myself, me 🐤 [2195] + [1247]

死ぬ【しぬ】 die [2194]

〜前に【〜まえに】 before [1453]

一目【ひとめ】 at first sight [2105] + [1927]

思う【おもう】 feel for [1633]

女【おんな】 woman 🐤 [2135]

逢う【あう】 meet [-]

いう say, speak 🐤

大将【たいしょう】 leader, chief 🐤 [2133] + [0336]

夜が明ける【よがあける】 dawn, turn to daylight [1301] + [0572]

鶏【とり】 cock, chicken 🐤 [1158]

鳴く【なく】 crow, sing 🐤 [0481]

待つ【まつ】 wait 🐤 [0269]

此処【ここ】 here [-] + [1918]

呼ぶ【よぶ】 summon [0205]

来る【くる】 come, arrive 🐤 [2211]

逢わずに【あわずに】 without meeting [-]

殺す【ころす】 kill [0889]

〜てしまう expresses completion of an action with regret

8

腰を掛ける【こしをかける】 sit, take a seat [0711] + [0361]

〜まま still, just as before 🐤

篝火【かがりび】 campfire 🐤 [-] + [2159]

眺める【ながめる】 gaze at [0795]

大きな【おおきな】 big [2133]

藁沓【わらぐつ】 straw boots [-] + [-]

組み合わす【くみあわす】 cross (one's legs) [0904] + [1274]

草【くさ】 grass [1450]

上【うえ】 on [2128]

夜【よ】 night [1301]

段々【だんだん】 gradually [0780]

There was love even back in those days. I explained that before I died, if only for a moment, I wanted to see the woman I loved. The captain agreed to wait, but only until the night turned to dawn and the cock crowed. I had to summon her thither before the cock crowed. If the woman had not reached us when the cock crowed, then I would be killed without having seen her.

The captain was still sitting, gazing into the campfire. I sat cross-legged on the grass in my great straw boots, waiting for the woman. The night grew later.

From time to time the fire made a sound as it settled. And each time it settled, the fretful flames flooded toward the captain. Beneath his dark brows, the captain's eyes glimmered. Someone came, threw a heap of fresh branches onto the fire, then went on his way. After a while the fire began to make a crackling sound. It was a spirited sound that seemed to drive back the darkness.

....

更ける【ふける】grow late [2205]

9

時々【ときどき】at times, sometimes [0625]
崩れる【くずれる】collapse, break up 🐾 [1478]
音【おと】sound 🐾 [1312]
〜度に【〜たびに】each time (something happens) [1974]
狼狽る【うろたえる】be confused, be flustered [-] + [-]
〜ように as though 🐾
焔【ほのお】flames [-]
なだれかかる rush upon, surge toward
真黒な【まっくろな】pitch-black [1337] + [1754]
眉【まゆ】eyebrows [2050]
下【した】beneath, underneath [2115]
眼【め】eyes [0796]
ぴかぴかと (+ verb) sparkle, glisten, shine
光る【ひかる】shine [1550]
誰やら【だれやら】somebody or other [-]

新しい【あたらしい】new, fresh [1166]
枝【えだ】branches, twigs [0579]
沢山【たくさん】many [0201] + [1867]
火【ひ】fire 🐾 [2159]
中【なか】into, in [2150]
抛げ込む【なげこむ】throw into [-] + [1917]
〜て行く【〜ていく】go and 〜 [0157]
しばらくすると after a while
ぱちぱちと (+ verb) crackle, snap
鳴る【なる】make a sound [0481]
暗闇【くらやみ】darkness [0689] + [-]
弾き返す【はじきかえす】drive back [0418] + [1940]
〜のような like
勇ましい【いさましい】brave [1326]

　この時女は、裏の楢の木に繋いである、白い馬を引き出した。鬣を三度撫でて高い脊にひらりと飛び乗った。鞍もない鐙もない裸馬であった。長く白い足で、太腹を蹴ると、馬は一散に駆け出した。誰かが篝りを継ぎ足したので、遠くの空が薄明るく見える。馬はこの明るいものを目懸て闇の中を飛んで来る。鼻から火の柱のような息を二本出して飛んで来る。それでも女は細い足でしきりなしに馬の腹を蹴ている。馬は蹄の音が宙で鳴るほど早く飛んで来る。女の髪は吹流しのように闇の中に尾を曳いた。それでもまだ篝のある所まで来られない。

時【とき】time, moment [0625]
女【おんな】woman 🔥 [2135]
裏【うら】back, behind (a house) [1354]
楢の木【ならのき】Japanese oak tree [-] + [2149]
繋ぐ【つなぐ】be tied, be fastened [-]
白い【しろい】white 🔥 [2175]
馬【うま】horse 🔥 [2073]
引き出す【ひきだす】pull out, lead forth [0133] + [2180]
鬣【たてがみ】mane [-]
三度【さんど】three times [1225] + [1974]
撫でる【なでる】stroke [-]
高い【たかい】tall, high [1330]
脊【せ】back [-]
ひらりと nimbly, lightly
飛び乗る【とびのる】leap onto, mount [2222] + [2224]

鞍【くら】saddle [-]
鐙【あぶみ】stirrups [-]
裸馬【はだかうま】bareback horse [0819] + [2073]
長い【ながい】long [1626]
足【あし】legs 🔥 [1386]
太腹【ふとばら】flanks [1360] + [0710]
蹴る【ける】kick 🔥 [-]
一散に【いっさんに】at top speed [2105] + [1118]
駆け出す【かけだす】dash forth [1185] + [2180]
誰か【だれか】someone [-]
篝（り）【かが（り）】fire 🔥 [-]
継ぎ足す【つぎたす】add to, supplement [0919] + [1386]
遠い【とおい】far [2013]
空【そら】sky [1418]
薄明るい【うすあかるい】faintly bright [1534] + [0572]

Now it was that the woman led out a white horse which had been tied to the Japanese oak behind her house. She stroked its mane three times before springing lightly onto its tall back. The horse was bare, without saddle or bridle. The woman kicked its flanks with her long white legs, and the horse dashed off. Someone had fed the fire, which imparted a dim glow to the distant sky. The horse set his head for the light and galloped through the darkness. From its nose it shot twin streams of breath that looked like pillars of fire as it came galloping on. Even so, the woman kept kicking the flanks of the horse with her graceful feet. The horse was galloping so fast that the clatter of its hooves echoed in the skies. Like a pennant the woman's hair streamed behind her in the darkness. But she still could not reach the place where the fire burned.

見える【みえる】appear [1615]

明るい【あかるい】bright [0572]

目懸る【めがける】aim at [1927] + [1855]

闇【やみ】darkness 㐧 [-]

中【なか】in, inside, through 㐧 [2150]

飛ぶ【とぶ】fly, move quickly 㐧 [2222]

〜て来る【〜てくる】indicates progression in the direction of the narrator 㐧 [2211]

鼻【はな】nose, nostrils [1739]

火【ひ】fire [2159]

柱【はしら】pillar [0603]

〜のような like

息【いき】breath [1693]

二本【にほん】two columns/pillars [1224] + [2183]

出す【だす】emit, send out [2180]

細い【ほそい】delicate, slender, fine [0900]

しきりなしに without pause

腹【はら】belly, flanks [0710]

蹄【ひづめ】hoof [-]

音【おと】sound [1312]

宙【ちゅう】air, heavens [1413]

鳴る【なる】thunder, echo, resound [0481]

〜ほど to the extent that

早い【はやい】swift, speedy [1549]

髪【かみ】hair [1821]

吹流し【ふきながし】streamer, pennant [0170] + [0325]

〜のように like

尾【お】tail [1942]

曳く【ひく】drag [-]

所【ところ】place [0568]

来る【くる】come, reach, arrive [2211]

すると真闇（まっくら）な道の傍（はた）で、忽（たちま）ちこけこっこうという鶏（とり）の声がした。女は身を空様（そらざま）に、両手に握った手綱をうんと控えた。馬は前足の蹄（ひづめ）を堅い岩の上に発矢（はっし）と刻み込んだ。

こけこっこうと鶏がまた一声（ひとこえ）鳴いた。

女はあっといって、緊（し）めた手綱を一度に緩（ゆる）めた。馬は諸膝（もろひざ）を折る。乗った人と共に真向（まとも）へ前へのめった。岩の下は深い淵（ふち）であった。

蹄の跡はいまだに岩の上に残っている。鶏の鳴く真似（まね）をしたものは天探女（あまのじゃく）である。この蹄の痕（あと）の岩に刻みつけられている間、天探女は自分の敵（かたき）である。

真闇な【まっくらな】pitch-black [1337] + [-]
道【みち】road, path [2000]
傍【はた】side [0110]
忽ち【たちまち】suddenly, in an instant [-]
こけこっこう cock-a-doodle-doo 🔊
鶏【とり／にわとり】cock, rooster 🔊 [1158]
声【こえ】voice, cry [1393]
女【おんな】woman 🔊 [2135]
身【み】body [2213]
空様【そらざま】arching backward [1418] + [0723]
両手【りょうて】both hands [2191] + [2155]
握る【にぎる】clasp, hold [0427]
手綱【たづな】reins 🔊 [2155] + [0928]
うんと vigorously
控える【ひかえる】pull back [0363]

馬【うま】horse 🔊 [2073]
前足【まえあし】forelegs [1453] + [1386]
蹄【ひづめ】hooves 🔊 [-]
堅い【かたい】hard [1805]
岩【いわ】rock 🔊 [1423]
上【うえ】on, upon 🔊 [2128]
発矢と【はっしと】with a loud clack [1634] + [2189]
刻み込む【きざみこむ】carve/cut deeply into [0851] + [1917]

また once more
一声【ひとこえ】one cry [2105] + [1393]
鳴く【なく】crow, sing 🔊 [0481]

あっ ah!
いう say, speak

Then suddenly, from the side of the pitch-black road, came the sound of the cock crowing *cock-a-doodle-doo*. The woman arched her body skyward and, with both hands, pulled the reins back hard. The horse drove its forehooves deep into a hard rock with a great clash.

The cock crowed once more, *cock-a-doodle-doo*.

The woman gasped in surprise and for an instant loosened her hold on the reins she was holding so tight. The horse had tucked in its forelegs. It pitched forward together with its rider. Below the rock there was a deep abyss.

The hoof marks are still upon the rock even now. It was the devil who imitated the crowing of the cock. And for as long as these hoof marks remain graven on the rock, it is that devil who will be my true enemy.

- -

緊める 【しめる】 hold/pull tight [1816]
一度に 【いちどに】 all at once [2105] + [1974]
緩める 【ゆるめる】 relax, loosen [0943]
諸膝 【もろひざ】 both knees [1061] + [-]
折る 【おる】 bend [0189]
乗る 【のる】 ride, mount [2224]
人 【ひと】 person [2111]
〜と共に 【〜とともに】 together with [1551]
真向 【まとも】 straight ahead [1337] + [1934]
前 【まえ】 in front [1453]
のめる fall forward
下 【した】 below, beneath [2115]
深い 【ふかい】 deep [0385]
淵 【ふち】 abyss [-]

14

蹄 【ひづめ】 hoof
跡 【あと】 trace, mark [1032]

いまだに even now
残る 【のこる】 remain, be left [0640]
真似 【まね】 imitation, impersonation [1337] + [0043]
天探女 【あまのじゃく】 Amanojaku (a supernatural, devil-like creature who deceives by impersonation and acts in various ways against the wishes of others; the *kanji* is usually read "Amanosagume," a reference to the female [Shinto] deity whose characteristics Amanojaku has come to assume in popular folklore) [2148] + [0374] + [2135]
痕 【あと】 trace [-]
刻みつける 【きざみつける】 carve/etch into [0851]
間 【あいだ】 while [2094]
自分 【じぶん】 I, myself, me [2195] + [1247]
敵 【かたき】 enemy [1204]

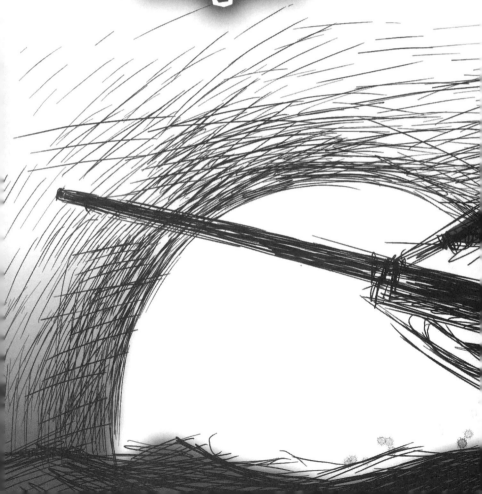

The Seventh Night 第七夜

A traveler in the doldrums

This story is based on Sōseki's own voyage to London in 1900, in the course of which he was tormented by seasickness, insecurity and proselytizing missionaries. In his diary (which he wrote in English), he spoke of the "lifeless tranquility" of the sea, where "infinity and eternity seem to swallow one."* When reading this story, keep in mind that Sōseki was prone to depression throughout his life, that his wife attempted suicide and that even now Japan's suicide rate is double that of the United States and three times that of England.

This story is available as an MP3 sound file at
www.speaking-japanese.com.

* Van C. Gessel, p. 39.

何でも大きな船に乗っている。

この船が毎日毎夜すこしの絶間なく黒い煙を吐いて浪を切って進んで行く。凄じい音である。けれども何処へ行くんだか分らない。ただ波の底から焼火箸のような太陽が出る。それが高い帆柱の真上まで来てしばらくかかっているかと思うと、何時の間にか大きな船を追い越して、先へ行ってしまう。そうして、しまいには焼火箸のようにじゅっといってまた波の底に沈んで行く。その度に蒼い波が遠くの向うで、蘇枋の色に沸き返る。すると船は凄じい音を立ててその跡を追掛けて行く。けれども決して追附かない。

1

何でも【なんでも】probably, seemingly [0045]
大きな【おおきな】big 🦌 [2133]
船【ふね】boat, ship 🦌 [0906]
乗る【のる】travel on, ride [2224]

2

毎日【まいにち】every day [1283] + [1915]
毎夜【まいよ】every night [1283] + [1301]
すこし a little
絶間なく【たえまなく】without pause [0917] + [2094]
黒い【くろい】black [1754]
煙【けぶり】smoke (classical form of けむり) [0700]
吐く【はく】emit, puff out [0151]
浪【なみ】billows, waves [0323]
切る【きる】cut, cross, move across [0015]
進む【すすむ】advance, progress [1991]
〜て行く【〜てゆく】indicates progression

into the future 🦌 [0157]
凄じい【すさまじい】prodigious, extra-ordinary 🦌 [-]
音【おと】sound 🦌 [1312]
何処【どこ】where [0045] + [1918]
行く【ゆく／いく】go [0157]
分る【わかる】know, understand [1247]
ただ only, just [-]
波【なみ】waves 🦌 [0245]
底【そこ】bottom, depths 🦌 [1961]
焼火箸【やけひばし】blazing tongs 🦌 [0681] + [2159] + [-]
〜のような like
太陽【たいよう】sun [1360] + [0453]
出る【でる】come out, rise [2180]
高い【たかい】tall, high [1330]
帆柱【ほばしら】mast [0156] + [0603]
真上【まうえ】right on top [1337] + [2128]
来る【くる】come [2211]

62　第七夜

Why I don't know, but I found myself on board a huge ship.

The ship pressed forward relentlessly, by day and by night, belching black smoke as it cut through the waves. The noise was tremendous. I had no idea whither we were bound. From the depths of the sea the sun rose in a sky red like metal tongs taken from the fire. The sun rose directly above the high mast until I thought it was impaled there. But before I knew it, it had passed over the ship and gone on ahead. Finally, with a sullen, steamy hiss, it sank back once more below the waves. The distant azure waves seethed and boiled crimson-red. And the ship, with its monstrous thunder sound, followed after. But we were doomed never to catch up with the sun.

<hr />

しばらく for a little while
かかる be suspended, hang over [0361]
思う【おもう】think, feel [1633]
何時の間にか【いつのまにか】before one becomes aware of it [0045] + [0625] + [2094]
追い越す【おいこす】pass, overtake [1971] + [2085]
先【さき】ahead [1552]
〜てしまう expresses completion of an action with regret
しまいに finally
〜ように like
じゅっ hiss, crackle
また once again
沈む【しずむ】sink [1991]
その度に【そのたんびに】whenever, every time (colloquial form of そのたびに) [1974]
蒼い【あおい】blue [1512]

遠い【とおい】far-away, distant [2013]
向う【むこう】beyond, over yonder [1934]
蘇枋【すおう】dark red [-] + [-]
色【いろ】color [1280]
沸き返る【わきかえる】seethe, boil [0244] + [1940]
立てる【たてる】make (a noise) [1257]
跡【あと】trace, track, trail [1032]
追掛ける【おっかける】chase, follow (emphatic form of おいかける) [1971] + [0361]
決して【けっして】(+ negative) definitely not, by no means [0197]
追附く【おっつく】catch up with (colloquial form of おいつく) [1971] + [0257]

ある時自分は、船の男を捕まえて聞いて見た。

「この船は西へ行くんですか」

　船の男は怪訝な顔をして、しばらく自分を見ていたが、やがて、

「何故」と問い返した。

「落ちて行く日を追懸るようだから」

　船の男は呵々と笑った。そうして向うの方へ行ってしまった。

「西へ行く日の、果は東か。それは本真か。東出る日の、御里は西か。それも本真か。身は波の上。楫枕。流せ流せ」と囃している。舳へ行って見たら、水夫が大勢寄って、太い帆綱を手操っていた。

....

I once grabbed hold of a crewman and asked him if indeed the ship was heading west.

The crewman looked suspicious. He stared at me a while before bluntly asking, "Why?"

"Because it seems that we are pursuing the setting sun" was my reply.

The crewman laughed dryly and went away, leaving me alone.

I ventured to the prow of the vessel where a group of sailors were pulling on a length of thick rigging and singing:

Is it true that the final goal
Of the west-tending sun is the east?
Is it true that the ancient home
Of the east-rising sun is the west?
On the sea
This boat is our home.
Roll on. Roll on.

....

8
呵々【からから】loudly (of a laugh) [-]
笑う【わらう】laugh [1692]
向う【むこう】over there [1934]
方【ほう】direction [1243]
〜てしまう indicates completion of an action with regret

9
果【はて】end, limit, bounds [2217]
東【ひがし】east [2221]
本真【ほんま】true (Kansai dialect) 🐍 [2183] + [1337]
出る【でる】come out, rise [2180]
御里【おさと】home [0422] + [2206]
身【み】body [2213]
波【なみ】waves [0245]

上【うえ】above [2128]
楫枕【かじまくら】voyage [-] + [-]
流せ流せ【ながせながせ】roll on, roll on [0325] + [0325]
囃す【はやす】sing (to pass time) [-]
舳【へさき】prow, bow [-]
水夫【すいふ】sailor [0003] + [2157]
大勢【おおぜい】many [2133] + [1829]
寄る【よる】approach, gather [1473]
太い【ふとい】thick, fat [1360]
帆綱 【ほづな】halyard (rope used for raising/lowering a sail) [0156] + [0928]
手操る【たぐる】pull on [2155] + [0531]

自分は大変心細くなった。何時陸へ上がれる事か分らない。そうして何処へ行くのだか知れない。ただ黒い煙を吐いて波を切って行く事だけは慥かである。その波は頗る広いものであった。際限もなく蒼く見える。時には紫にもなった。ただ船の動く周囲だけは何時でも真白に泡を吹いていた。自分は大変心細かった。こんな船にいるより一層身を投て死んでしまおうかと思った。

自分【じぶん】I, myself, me 🐚 [2195] + [1247]

大変【たいへん】very, exceedingly 🐚 [2133] + [1311]

心細い【こころぼそい】forlorn, lonely 🐚 [0004] + [0900]

何時【いつ】when [0045] + [0625]

陸【おか】land [0399]

上がる【あがる】reach, climb onto [2128]

事【こと】fact, situation 🐚 [2220]

分る【わかる】know, understand [1247]

何処【どこ】where [0045] + [1918]

行く【ゆく】go 🐚 [0157]

知れる【しれる】know naturally, be knowable [0768]

ただ only, just 🐚

黒い【くろい】black [1754]

煙【けぶり】smoke (classical form of けむり) [0700]

吐く【はく】emit, puff out [0151]

波【なみ】waves 🐚 [0245]

切る【きる】cut, cross, move across [0015]

〜て行く【〜てゆく】indicates progression into the future [0157]

慥か【たしか】certain [-]

頗る【すこぶる】very, exceedingly [-]

広い【ひろい】broad, expansive, vast [1921]

際限【さいげん】bounds, limits, end [0503] + [0296]

蒼い【あおい】blue [1512]

見える【みえる】look, seem [1615]

時には【ときには】at times [0625]

紫【むらさき】purple, violet [1728]

船【ふね】boat, ship [0906]

動く【うごく】move 🐚 [1163]

周囲【まわり】area around, surrounding area [1903] + [1949]

何時でも【いつでも】always [0045] + [0625]

真白【まっしろ】pure white [1337] + [2175]

泡【あわ】bubbles, foam [0249]

吹く【ふく】blow [0170]

こんな this kind of, such (＝このような)

一層【いっそ】rather, all the more (variant of いっそう) [2105] + [2021]

身を投る【みをなげる】throw one's body (overboard) [2213] + [0192]

死ぬ【しぬ】die [2194]

〜てしまう thoroughly 〜

思う【おもう】feel, think [1633]

I felt utterly forlorn. I did not know when we would reach land. And I did not even know where we were headed. All I knew was that the ship would press on and on, belching black smoke as it cut through the waves. The wave-furrowed sea was oppressively vast: an infinite-seeming expanse of blue that turned at times to purple. Only in the environs of the moving ship was the bubbling foam always purest white. I felt so utterly forlorn. Better perhaps to throw myself overboard and die, I thought, than to stay here on this vessel.

....

乗合は沢山いた。大抵は異人のようであった。しかし色々な顔をしていた。空が曇って船が揺れた時、一人の女が欄に倚りかかって、しきりに泣いていた。眼を拭く半巾の色が白く見えた。しかし身体には更紗のような洋服を着ていた。この女を見た時に、悲しいのは自分ばかりではないのだと気が附いた。

　ある晩甲板の上に出て、一人で星を眺めていたら、一人の異人が来て、天文学を知ってるかと尋ねた。自分は詰らないから死のうとさえ思っている。天文学などを知る必要がない。黙っていた。するとその異人が金牛宮の頂にある七星の話をして聞かせた。そうして星も海もみんな神の作ったものだといった。最後に自分に神を信仰するかと尋ねた。自分は空を見て黙っていた。

....

11

乗合【のりあい】fellow passengers [2224] + [1274]

沢山【たくさん】many [0201] + [1867]

大抵【たいてい】for the most part [2133] + [0239]

異人【いじん】foreigner 🐾 [1651] + [2111]

〜のようである seem/appear to be

しかし but, however 🐾

色々な【いろいろな】various [1280]

顔【かお】faces [1177]

空【そら】the sky 🐾 [1418]

曇る【くもる】cloud over [1610]

船【ふね】boat, ship [0906]

揺れる【ゆれる】shake [0434]

時【とき】when 🐾 [0625]

一人【ひとり】one person 🐾 [2105] + [2111]

女【おんな】woman 🐾 [2135]

欄【てすり】handrail [0754]

倚りかかる【よりかかる】lean on [-]

しきりに at frequent intervals

泣く【なく】cry [0253]

眼【め】eyes [0796]

拭く【ふく】wipe [-]

半巾【ハンケチ】handkerchief [2182] + [-]

色【いろ】color [1280]

白い【しろい】white [2175]

見える【みえる】look, seem [1615]

身体【からだ】body [2213] + [0052]

更紗【さらさ】printed cotton, chintz [2205] + [0878]

〜のような like, resembling

洋服【ようふく】clothes [0292] + [0591]

着る【きる】wear [2086]

見る【みる】see 🐾 [1615]

悲しい【かなしい】sad [1775]

自分【じぶん】I, myself, me 🐾 [2195] + [1247]

〜ばかり only, just

My fellow passengers were numerous. Most of them seemed to be foreign, but they all looked different from one another. When the sky clouded over and the ship shuddered, a woman leaned upon the rail and wept endlessly. How white was the handkerchief with which she wiped her eyes! She was wearing some chintz-like garment. When I saw her I understood that I was not alone in my sorrow.

One evening when I had gone up on deck and was looking in solitude at the stars, one of the foreigners approached me and asked me what I knew of astronomy. I was so very bored that I was thinking of taking my own life. What was the point of knowing astronomy? I said nothing. The foreigner then made some tedious speech about the Seven Stars in the head of Taurus, before going on to say that the stars and the sea, nay, everything was the work of God. He finished by asking me if I believed in God. I said nothing, only looked up at the sky.

....

気が附く【きがつく】realize [2037] + [0257]

12

ある晩【あるばん】a certain evening [0668]
甲板【かんぱん】deck [2169] + [0575]
上【うえ】on [2128]
出る【でる】come out [2180]
一人で【ひとりで】alone, by oneself [2105] + [2111]
星【ほし】star 爱 [1577]
眺める【ながめる】look at, gaze at [0795]
来る【くる】come [2211]
天文学【てんもんがく】astronomy 爱 [2148] + [1242] + [1625]
知る【しる】know [0768]
尋ねる【たずねる】ask, inquire 爱 [1498]
詰らない【つまらない】bored, fed up [1021]
死ぬ【しぬ】die [2194]
～さえ even
思う【おもう】think, feel [1633]

～など such things as
必要【ひつよう】need, necessity [0006] + [1683]
黙る【だまる】be silent, keep quiet 爱 [1833]
金牛宮【きんぎゅうきゅう】Taurus [1302] + [2151] + [1459]
頂【いただき】tip [0108]
七星【しちせい】"Seven Stars" (here refers to Pleiades) [2109] + [1577]
話【はなし】talk, speech [1027]
聞かせる【きかせる】explain, talk about [2097]
海【うみ】the sea [0284]
神【かみ】God 爱 [0615]
作る【つくる】make [0049]
いう say, speak
最後に【さいごに】finally [1599] + [0267]
信仰する【しんこうする】believe, have faith in [0075] + [0032]

或時サローンに這入ったら派出な衣裳を着た若い女が向うむきになって、洋琴を弾いていた。その傍に脊の高い立派な男が立って、唱歌を唄っている。その口が大変大きく見えた。けれども二人は二人以外の事にはまるで頓着していない様子であった。船に乗っている事さえ忘れているようであった。

自分はますます詰らなくなった。とうとう死ぬ事に決心した。それである晩、あたりに人のいない時分、思い切って海の中へ飛び込んだ。

或時【あるとき】a certain time [-] + [0625]

サローン saloon

這入る【はいる】go in, enter [-] + [2113]

派出な【はでな】fancy, extravagant, opulent [0281] + [2180]

衣裳【いしょう】clothes [1270] + [-]

着る【きる】wear [2086]

若い【わかい】young [1430]

女【おんな】woman [2135]

向うむき【むこうむき】facing the other way [1934]

洋琴【ピアノ】piano [0292] + [1778]

弾く【ひく】play [0418]

傍【そば】nearby [0110]

脊の高い【せいのたかい】tall [-] + [1330]

立派な【りっぱな】splendid, handsome [1257] + [0281]

男【おとこ】man [1613]

立つ【たつ】stand [1257]

唱歌【しょうか】song [0338] + [1187]

唄う【うたう】sing [0297]

口【くち】mouth [2119]

大変【たいへん】very, exceedingly [2133] + [1311]

大きい【おおきい】big [2133]

見える【みえる】appear, seem [1615]

二人【ふたり】two people, both of them 象 [1224] + [2111]

〜以外【〜いがい】except for, outside of [0025] + [0135]

事【こと】things, matters 象 [2220]

まるで utterly

頓着する【とんじゃくする】pay heed to, notice [-] + [2086]

様子【ようす】appearance [0723] + [2125]

船【ふね】boat, ship [0906]

乗る【のる】travel on, ride [2224]

〜さえ even

忘れる【わすれる】forget [1285]

〜ようである be like, be as if

Once I went into the saloon where a luxuriously dressed young woman was playing the piano with her back to me. At her side stood a tall, handsome man singing a song. How monstrously big his mouth seemed! The two of them, however, were wholly unaware of anything outside of themselves. They seemed to have even forgotten that they were on board a ship.

How meaningless everything felt to me! I finally made up my mind to die. And so one evening when there was nobody about, I did it. I flung myself into the sea.

14

自分【じぶん】 I, myself, me [2195] + [1247]
ますます more and more [1468]
詰らない【つまらない】 bored, fed up [1021]
とうとう at last, finally
死ぬ【しぬ】 die [2194]
決心する【けっしんする】 decide, resolve [0197] + [0004]
ある晩【あるばん】 a certain evening [0668]
あたり nearby, around, about
人【ひと】 person, people [2111]
時分【じぶん】 moment [0625] + [1247]
思い切って【おもいきって】 resolutely [1633] + [0015]
海【うみ】 the sea [0284]
中【なか】 into [2150]
飛び込む【とびこむ】 jump into [2222] + [1917]

ところが──自分の足が甲板を離れて、船と縁が切れたその刹那（せつな）に、急に命が惜（お）しくなった。心の底からよせばよかったと思った。けれども、もう遅い。自分はいやでも応でも海の中へ這入らなければならない。ただ大変高く出来ていた船と見えて、身体は船を離れたけれども、足は容易に水に着かない。しかし捕まえるものがないから、次第々々に水に近附いて来る。いくら足を縮めても近附いて来る。水の色は黒かった。

However … as my feet left the deck—at the very instant when I had broken the bonds which bound me to the vessel—suddenly at that instant life seemed so precious, so desirable a thing that from the depths of my heart I regretted what I had done. But it was too late. Whether I wished to or not, I had no choice but to plunge into that sea. How very high the ship's sides had been built! I had leapt off the vessel, but my feet seemed never to meet the water. But there was nothing for me to grab hold of, so gradually, inevitably, I fell closer and closer down to the sea. No matter how much I squirmed and crushed my legs up against my chest I still sank toward the water, the pitch-black water.

....

縮める【ちぢめる】squeeze, contract [0955]
色【いろ】color [1280]
黒い【くろい】black [1754]

そのうち船は例の通り黒い煙を吐いて、通り過ぎてしまった。自分は何処へ行くんだか判らない船でも、やっぱり乗っている方がよかったと始めて悟りながら、しかもその悟りを利用する事が出来ずに、無限の後悔と恐怖とを抱いて黒い波の方へ静かに落ちて行った。

そのうち before long, meanwhile

船【ふね】boat, ship 🖼 [0906]

例の通り【れいのとおり】just like before, as before [0067] + [1982]

黒い【くろい】black 🖼 [1754]

煙【けぶり】smoke (classical form of けむり) [0700]

吐く【はく】emit, puff out [0151]

通り過ぎる【とおりすぎる】pass by [1982] + [2003]

〜てしまう expresses completion of an action with regret

自分【じぶん】I, myself, me [2195] + [1247]

何処【どこ】where [0045] + [1918]

行く【ゆく】go [0157]

判る【わかる】know, understand [0765]

やっぱり after all

乗る【のる】travel on, ride [2224]

〜の方が【〜のほうが】rather (link for comparisons) [1243]

始めて【はじめて】for the first time [0211]

悟る【さとる】realize, become aware [0312]

〜ながら while, as

しかも moreover, also

悟り【さとり】knowledge, awareness [0312]

利用する【りょうする】take advantage of, make use of [0757] + [1889]

〜事が出来ずに【〜ことができずに】without being able to 〜 [2220] + [2180] + [2211]

無限の【むげんの】boundless, infinite [1351] + [0296]

後悔【こうかい】regret [0267] + [0270]

恐怖【きょうふ】fear [1696] + [0219]

抱く【いだく】have, hold, harbor [0227]

波【なみ】waves [0245]

方【ほう】direction [1243]

静かに【しずかに】silently [1138]

落ちる【おちる】fall [1494]

〜て行く【〜ていく】indicates progression toward a point [0157]

Meanwhile the ship, still belching black smoke, continued on its way and passed me by. It was only then that I realized I should have stayed on board that ship; yes, even if I did not know where it was headed. But now it was too late for me to act on that realization, and it was in the grip of endless regret and infinite fear that I slipped silently toward the black, black waves.

....

AKUTAGAWA RYŪNOSUKE
(1892-1927)

Akutagawa Ryūnosuke was born in the Tsukiji district of Tokyo in March 1892. The eldest son of Niihara Toshizo, he was adopted by his uncle, Akutagawa Michiaki, when his mother went mad only a few months after his birth. The boy felt remote from both his real and his adopted parents, though the insanity of his mother—a silent, pallid figure who lived on in his father's house, obsessively sketching fox-people—was to cast a shadow over his entire life.

As a child, Akutagawa was an avid reader of popular ghost stories. As a young student, his reading grew to cover the Chinese classics, contemporary Japanese authors such as Mori Ōgai and Natsume Sōseki, as well as Guy de Maupassant, Anatole France, Rudyard Kipling, Edgar Allan Poe and other masters of the short story.

Entering Tokyo Imperial University in 1913 as an English literature major, Akutagawa lost no time in producing original work. He had his first short story published in 1914, while "Rashōmon," his best-known tale and the title story of his first collection, came out the following year. The year 1916, when "Hana" ("The Nose") was praised by Sōseki and literary magazines began to court the young writer, marked his breakthrough.

The early stories are often based on old collections of tales, such as *Konjaku monogatari* (*Tales of Times Now Past*), but with psychological insight and dramatic narrative techniques providing depth and credibility for a modern audience. One should not, however, suggest that Akutagawa is a realist. His stories are perfect expressions of the decadent aesthetic, with the gorgeous and the grotesque, the splendid and the sordid, intertwining in highly polished prose.

After graduating in 1916, Akutagawa began teaching English at the Naval Engineering School in Yokosuka, but resigned in 1919, having secured a contract (just as Sōseki had done a decade earlier) to produce fiction for a newspaper. Now married, Akutagawa was a popular and successful author publishing new collections of his work every year.

In March, 1921, Akutagawa was sent to China by the newspaper for which he worked. His health took a dramatic turn for the worse while in Shanghai. The remainder of his life was a tormented cocktail of insomnia, gastric problems and paranoia about having inherited his mother's mental disorder. When he sought new modes of expression outside the short story, his popularity sagged, while his extensive family responsibilities were also burdensome.

On July 24, 1927, a physically and mentally exhausted Akutagawa killed himself with an overdose of barbiturates. The signs of despair are plain to see in *Kappa*, a superficially playful fable about little amphibious creatures (called *kappa*) which he wrote just a few months prior to his death. The human narrator is a patient in a mental hospital; a *kappa* embryo begs to be aborted out of fear that he will succumb to hereditary insanity; and Tok— the depressive *kappa* poet who finally commits suicide—is regarded by many commentators as a self-portrait.

Akutagawa's life was short, but his oeuvre of over one hundred short stories was nonetheless enough to establish him as the uncontested master of the short story in modern Japanese literature.

In a Grove 藪の中

Sex, lies and violent rape

This story was the favorite of the assassin character played by Forest Whitaker in Jim Jarmusch's 1999 film *Ghost Dog*. Told by seven different people, it is for the reader to build up a composite picture of what actually happened. A similar narrative technique is used in *Murder in the Orient Express*, where twelve passengers provide evidence to the Belgian detective, Hercule Poirot. What distinguishes Akutagawa from Agatha Christie (apart from the level of literary craft) is his introduction of supernatural elements and a refusal to tie up loose ends. We have no idea which of the unreliable narrators is telling the truth. But it is this very ambiguity that endows the story with its resonance. Readers who are interested in stories told by unreliable narrators might also enjoy William Faulkner's *The Sound and the Fury* or Ford Maddox Ford's *The Good Soldier*.

This story is available as an MP3 sound file at
www.speaking-japanese.com. To reduce download times, the audio version has been divided into
seven chapters. These correspond with the testimony
of the various characters and are (1) The Woodcutter,
(2) The Priest, (3) The Police Officer, (4) The Old
Woman, (5) The Robber, (6) The Young Woman and
(7) The Dead Man. The chapters are numbered and
marked with an ◀) MP3 icon in the left margin of the
page containing the Japanese text.

検非違使に問われたる木樵りの物語

　さようでございます。あの死骸を見つけたのは、わたしに違いございません。わたしは今朝何時もの通り、裏山の杉を伐りに参りました。すると山陰の藪の中に、あの死骸があったのでございます。あった処でございますか？　それは山科の駅路からは、四、五町ほど隔たっておりましょう。竹の中に痩せ杉の交った、人気のない所でございます。

··

検非違使【けびいし】police chief with judicial powers [0674] + [0598] + [2014] + [0068]

問う【とう】ask, question, interrogate [2091]

木樵り【きこり】woodchopper [2149] + [-]

物語【ものがたり】account, tale, story [0587] + [1040]

1

さよう so, in this way (＝そのよう)

〜でございます ＝〜です (polite form) 👤

死骸【しがい】dead body, corpse 👤 [2194] + [-]

見つける【みつける】find [1615]

〜に違いございません【〜にちがいございません】certainly, no doubt (polite form of 〜にちがいない) [2014]

今朝【けさ】this morning [1246] + [1114]

何時もの【いつもの】usual [0045] + [0625]

〜通り【〜とおり】just as, in accordance with [1982]

裏山【うらやま】hill/mountain behind one's home [1354] + [1867]

杉【すぎ】cedar [0557]

伐る【きる】chop down [0026]

参る【まいる】go (polite/humble form of いく) [1308]

山陰【やまかげ】shady part of the mountain [1867] + [0397]

処【ところ】place [1918]

山科【やましな】Yamashina (place name) [1867] + [0775]

駅路【えきろ】postal road, staging road [1184] + [1031]

四五町【しごちょう】four or five *chō* (1 *chō* = 110 m) [1928] + [2142] + [0756]

〜ほど extent of, rough distance of

隔たる【へだたる】be distant from [0480]

〜ておる ＝〜ている (polite form)

竹【たけ】bamboo [0168]

痩せ杉【やせすぎ】thin cedar [-] + [0557]

交る【まじる】be mixed with [1272]

人気のない【ひとけのない】desolate [2111] + [2037]

所【ところ】place [0568]

The Testimony of the Woodcutter Questioned by the Chief of Police

Yes, that's right. It was indeed I who found the body. This morning, just as I always do, I went off to cut down cedars on the mountainside. And that's when I came upon the body, in a thicket in a remote part of the mountain. Where exactly was it? I suppose it would be at a distance of about five or six hundred yards from the Yamashina road: a deserted spot where the bamboo is mixed with cedar.

....

死骸は縹の水干に、都風のさび烏帽子をかぶったまま、仰向けに倒れておりました。何しろ一刀とは申すものの、胸もとの突き傷でございますから、死骸のまわりの竹の落葉は、蘇芳に滲みたようでございます。いえ、血はもう流れてはおりません。傷口も乾いておったようでございます。おまけに其処には、馬蠅が一匹、わたしの足音も聞えないように、べったり食いついておりましたっけ。

死骸【しがい】corpse 👣 [2194] + [-]

縹【はなだ】pale blue [-]

水干【すいかん】everyday garment worn by commoners [0003] + [2116]

都風【みやこふう】the style of the capital (Kyoto) [1106] + [1908]

さび烏帽子【さびえぼし】crumpled hat worn by men [-] + [0416] + [2125]

かぶる wear (on the head)

〜まま still

仰向けに【あおむけに】faceup, on one's back [0032] + [1934]

倒れる【たおれる】fall over, collapse [0093]

〜ておる ＝〜ている (polite form) 👣

何しろ【なにしろ】anyhow, in any event [0045]

一刀【ひとかたな】a single sword blow [2105] + [1856]

申す【もうす】say (humble form of いう) [2186]

〜ものの despite, although

胸もと【むなもと】chest [0647]

突き傷【つききず】stab wound [1421] + [0118]

〜でございます ＝〜です (polite form) 👣

まわり around, near to

竹【たけ】bamboo [0168]

落葉【おちば】fallen leaves [1494] + [1497]

蘇芳【すおう】dark red (refers to a sappan-wood dye) [-] + [1404]

滲みる【しみる】be stained [-]

〜ようでございます seem/appear to be 👣

血【ち】blood [2196]

流れる【ながれる】flow, pour [0325]

傷口【きずぐち】wound [0118] + [2119]

乾く【かわく】be dry [1101]

おまけに in addition, furthermore

其処【そこ】there, that place [-] + [1918]

馬蠅【うまばえ】horsefly [2073] + [-]

一匹【いっぴき】one (of animals) [2105] + [1878]

足音【あしおと】sound of footsteps [1386] + [1312]

聞こえる【きこえる】be audible [2097]

〜ように as if

べったり closely and stickily

食いつく【くいつく】feed on, fasten one's teeth on [1316]

The dead man was lying on his back. He had a light blue coat on—with one of those crumpled hats still stuck on his head. Anyway, although he had only been stabbed once, the stab wound was in the chest, so the dead bamboo leaves around the body were stained a deep crimson color. No, the blood had stopped running. I imagine that the wound had dried. But as if all that wasn't enough, there was a horsefly feasting so greedily on the wound that it didn't even hear the sound of me coming up.

....

太刀か何かは見えなかったか？　いえ、何もございません。唯その側の杉の根がたに、縄が一筋落ちておりました。それから、──そうそう、縄の外にも櫛が一つございました。死骸のまわりにあったものは、この二つぎりでございます。が、草や竹の落葉は、一面に踏み荒されておりましたから、きっとあの男は殺される前に、よほど手痛い働きでも致したのに違いございません。何、馬はいなかったか？あそこは一体馬なぞには、はいれない所でございます。何しろ馬の通う路とは、藪一つ隔たっておりますから。

3

太刀【たち】sword [1360] + [1857]
何か【なにか】something, anything [0045]
見える【みえる】be visible [1615]
何も【なにも】(+ negative) nothing [0045]
ございます ＝ある (polite form) ☘
唯【ただ】just, only [0339]
側【そば】nearby, beside [0105]
杉【すぎ】cedar [0557]
根がた【ねがた】trunk [0631]
縄【なわ】rope ☘ [0942]
一筋【ひとすじ】one line/length [2105] + [1719]
落ちる【おちる】fall, drop [1494]
〜ておる ＝〜ている (polite form) ☘
それから in addition
〜の外に【〜のほかに】as well as, in addition to [0135]
櫛【くし】comb [-]
一つ【ひとつ】one [2105]
死骸【しがい】corpse [2194] + [-]
まわり around, near to

二つ【ふたつ】two [1224]
〜ぎり just, only
〜でございます ＝〜です (polite form) ☘
草【くさ】grass [1450]
竹【たけ】bamboo [0168]
落葉【おちば】fallen leaves [1494] + [1497]
一面に【いちめんに】all over [2105] + [1324]
踏み荒らす【ふみあらす】trample on violently [1066] + [1447]
きっと surely, certainly
男【おとこ】man [1613]
殺す【ころす】kill [0889]
〜前に【〜まえに】before, prior to [1453]
よほど very, greatly
手痛い【ていたい】severe, horrible [2155] + [2065]
働き【はたらき】action, activity [0113]
致す【いたす】＝する (humble form) [1883]
〜に違いございません【〜にちがいございません】certainly, no doubt (polite form of 〜にちがいない) [2014]
何【なに】what [0045]

Didn't I see a sword or any sort of weapon? No, there was nothing like that. There was just a single length of rope lying at the bottom of a nearby cedar tree. And—oh yes, I remember now—apart from the rope, there was a comb. These were the only two things near the body. But all around, the grass and the bamboo leaves had been messed up and trampled, so I'm quite sure that before the fellow was killed he put up quite a struggle. Wasn't there a horse there? No, it's the sort of place that horses can't get into. After all, there was a thicket separating it from the road that horses use.

馬【うま】horse 🐎 [2073]

一体【いったい】indeed (exclamation) [2105] + [0052]

〜なぞ and other such things (colloquial form of 〜など)

はいる enter

所【ところ】place [0568]

何しろ【なにしろ】anyhow, in any event [0045]

通う【かよう】go to and fro, pass [1982]

路【みち】road [1031]

藪一つ【やぶひとつ】one thicket [-] + [2105]

隔たる【へだたる】be distant from [0480]

検非違使に問われたる旅法師の物語

　あの死骸の男には、確かに昨日遇っております。昨日の、——さあ、午頃でございましょう。場所は関山から山科へ、参ろうという途中でございます。あの男は馬に乗った女と一しょに、関山の方へ歩いて参りました。女は牟子を垂れておりましたから、顔はわたしにはわかりません。見えたのは唯萩重ねらしい、衣の色ばかりでございます。馬は月毛の、——確か法師髪の馬のようでございました。

検非違使【けびいし】police chief with judicial powers [0674] + [0598] + [2014] + [0068]

問う【とう】ask, question, interrogate [2091]

旅法師【たびほうし】traveling priest [0624] + [0248] + [0892]

物語【ものがたり】account, tale, story [0587] + [1040]

死骸【しがい】corpse [2194] + [-]

男【おとこ】man [1613]

確かに【たしかに】certainly [0830]

昨日【きのう】yesterday [0601] + [1915]

遇う【あう】encounter [2001]

〜ておる ＝〜ている (polite form)

さあ let's see, hmm

午頃【ひるごろ】around noon [1254] + [-]

〜でございます ＝〜です (polite form)

場所【ばしょ】place [0408] + [0568]

関山【せきやま】Sekiyama (place name) [2099] + [1867]

山科【やましな】Yamashina (place name) [1867] + [0775]

参る【まいる】go (polite/humble form of いく) [1308]

途中【とちゅう】on the way to, midpoint [1980] + [2150]

馬【うま】horse [2073]

乗る【のる】ride [2224]

女【おんな】woman [2135]

〜と一しょに【〜といっしょに】together with [2105]

方【ほう】direction, way [1243]

歩く【あるく】walk [1566]

〜て参る【〜てまいる】indicates progression away from the speaker (polite/humble form of 〜ていく)

牟子【むし】veil [-] + [2125]

垂れる【たれる】hang, droop [2219]

顔【かお】face [1177]

わかる have knowledge about

見える【みえる】be visible [1615]

唯【ただ】just, only [0339]

萩重ね【はぎがさね】autumn garment (deep red on the outside and blue on the

The Testimony of the Traveling Priest Questioned by the Chief of Police

Yes, I most certainly saw the dead man yesterday. Yesterday at—hmm, let me see, it would probably be about midday. The place was at about the halfway point when you're going from Sekiyama to Yamashina. The man was walking in the direction of Sekiyama leading a woman on a horse. She was wearing a veil, so I didn't see her face. All I noticed was the color of her clothes—the crimson and blue of an autumn kimono. The horse was a sorrel, and, come to think of it, its mane was trimmed.

....

inside) [1495] + [2223]
衣 【きぬ】 clothing, garment [1270]
色 【いろ】 color [1280]
〜ばかり just, only
月毛 【つきげ】 sorrel [1876] + [2152]
確か 【たしか】 certainly
法師髪 【ほうしがみ】 short mane [0248] + [0892] + [1821]
〜のようでございます look/appear to be

丈(たけ)でございますか？　丈は四寸(よき)もございましたか？——何しろ沙門(しゃもん)の事でございますから、その辺(へん)ははっきり存じません。男は、——いえ、太刀も帯(お)びておれば、弓矢も携えておりました。殊(こと)に黒い塗(ぬ)り箙(えびら)へ、二十あまり征矢(そや)をさしたのは、唯今(ただいま)でもはっきり覚えております。

5

あの男がかようになろうとは、夢にも思わずにおりましたが、真(まこと)に人間の命なぞは、如露亦如電(にょろやくにょでん)に違いございません。やれやれ、何とも申しようのない、気の毒な事を致しました。

丈【たけ】height [2136]
～でございます =～です (polite form) ☠
四寸【よき】four *sun* (refers to the horse being four *sun* [4 x 3 cm] above the normal four *shaku* [4 x 30 cm] height, and so means 132 cm) [1928] + [1864]
ございます =ある (polite form)
何しろ【なにしろ】anyhow, in any event [0045]
沙門【しゃもん】monk [0199] + [0597]
事【こと】circumstance, situation ☠ [2220]
辺【へん】aspect, side, matter [1916]
はっきり clearly ☠
存ずる【ぞんずる】know (humble/polite form of しる) [1894]
男【おとこ】man ☠ [1613]
太刀【たち】sword [1360] + [1857]
帯びる【おびる】wear (on the waist), have belted on [1648]
～ておる =～ている (polite form) ☠
弓矢【ゆみや】bow and arrows [2120] + [1267]
携える【たずさえる】carry [0465]
殊に【ことに】distinctly, especially [0639]
黒い【くろい】black [1754]
塗り箙【ぬりえびら】lacquered quiver [1818] + [-]
二十【にじゅう】twenty [1224] + [2110]
～あまり more than ~
征矢【そや】arrows [0218] + [1267]
さす stick in
唯今【ただいま】now [0339] + [1246]
覚える【おぼえる】remember [1668]

5

かようにin this way (=このように)
夢にも思わず【ゆめにもおもわず】not even in one's wildest dreams [1510] + [1633]
おる =いる (polite form)
真に【まことに】truly, verily [1337]
人間【にんげん】human being [2111] + [2094]
命【いのち】life [1303]
～なぞ such things as (colloquial form of ～など)

Its height? The horse was about a hand taller than the average. The truth is that, as a priest, I really don't know too much about that sort of thing. The man—No, he was wearing a sword, but he had a bow and arrow too. One thing I remember now with complete clarity is his black-lacquered quiver with twenty or more arrows in it.

I would never have dreamed that he would meet a fate such as this. Truly the life of man is as fleeting as the dew or the lightning. Ah, Lord bless us! The utter pathos of what has happened leaves me quite at a loss for words.

....

如露亦如電【にょろやくにょでん】 like dew or lightning, gone in a flash [0154] + [1803] + [1268] + [0154] + [1784]

〜に違いございません【〜にちがいございません】 certainly, no doubt (polite form of 〜にちがいない)

やれやれ Poor fellow!, Lord bless us! (exclamation)

何とも申しようのない【なんとももうしようのない】 it is difficult to say, no words will suffice (申す is the humble form of いう) [0045] + [2186]

気の毒な【きのどくな】 sad, pitiful [2037] + [1571]

致す【いたす】 = する (humble form) [0883]

検非違使に問われたる放免の物語

　わたしが搦め取った男でございますか？　これは確かに多襄丸という、名高い盗人でございます。尤もわたしが搦め取った時には、馬から落ちたのでございましょう、粟田口の石橋の上に、うんうん呻っておりました。時刻でございますか？　時刻は昨夜の初更頃でございます。何時ぞやわたしが捉え損じた時にも、やはりこの紺の水干に、打出しの太刀を佩いておりました。唯今はその外にも御覧の通り、弓矢の類さえ携えております。さようでございますか？　あの死骸の男が持っていたのも、──では人殺しを働いたのは、この多襄丸に違いございません。

....

検非違使【けびいし】 police chief with judicial powers [0674] + [0598] + [2014] + [0068]

問う【とう】 ask, question, interrogate [2091]

放免【ほうめん】 released prisoner working for the police chief [0570] + [1309]

物語【ものがたり】 account, tale, story [0587] + [1040]

6

搦め取る【からめとる】 arrest ☠ [-] + [0847]

男【おとこ】 man ☠ [1613]

〜でございます ＝〜です (polite form) ☠

確かに【たしかに】 certainly [0830]

多襄丸【たじょうまる】 Tajōmaru (person's name) ☠ [1372] + [-] + [2134]

名高い【なだかい】 famous, notorious [1371] + [1330]

盗人【ぬすびと】 robber [1714] + [2111]

尤も【もっとも】 but, even so [-]

時【とき】 when ☠ [0625]

馬【うま】 horse [2073]

落ちる【おちる】 fall [1494]

粟田口【あわだぐち】 Awadaguchi (place name) [-] + [1925] + [2119]

石橋【いしばし】 stone bridge [1884] + [0738]

上【うえ】 on, upon [2128]

うんうん ugh (onomatopoeic expression that describes the sound of someone groaning)

呻る【うなる】 groan [-]

〜ておる ＝〜ている (polite form) ☠

時刻【じこく】 time ☠ [0625] + [0851]

昨夜【さくや】 last night [0601] + [1301]

初更【しょこう】 first watch of the night (7:00–9:00 P.M.) [0759] + [2205]

The Testimony of the Police Officer Questioned by the Chief of Police

The man that I arrested? Why, it is most definitely the notorious highwayman, Tajōmaru. When I caught him—I suppose it was because he'd been thrown by his horse—he was moaning and groaning on the stone bridge at Awadaguchi. What time was it? It was about first watch last night. The other day when I just failed to catch him, he was wearing this same blue kimono and had the same long embossed sword. This time around, as you can see, he has added a bow and arrows to his little arsenal. Is that the case? If they belonged to the murdered man, then that proves beyond doubt that it was Tajōmaru who committed this murder.

~頃 【～ごろ】 about ~ [-]

何時ぞや 【いつぞや】 the other day [0045] + [0625]

捉える 【とらえる】 catch [-]

~損じる 【～そんじる】 fail to ~ [0468]

やはり sure enough

紺 【こん】 deep blue, navy blue [0899]

水干 【すいかん】 everyday garment worn by commoners [0003] + [2116]

打出しの 【うちだしの】 embossed [0142] + [2180]

太刀 【たち】 sword [1360] + [1857]

佩く 【はく】 wear (of swords) [-]

唯今 【ただいま】 now, this time [0339] + [1246]

外に 【ほかに】 in addition, besides [0135]

御覧の通り 【ごらんのとおり】 as you can see, as you saw [0422] + [1827] + [1982]

弓矢 【ゆみや】 bow and arrows [2120] + [1267]

類 【るい】 thing with the same characteristics as something else, similar-looking thing [1176]

~さえ also, even

携える 【たずさえる】 carry [0465]

さよう so, in this way (＝そのよう)

死骸 【しがい】 corpse [2194] + [-]

持つ 【もつ】 carry [0275]

では in this case, if that is the case

人殺し 【ひとごろし】 murder, homicide [2111] + [0889]

働く 【はたらく】 carry out, perform [0113]

~に違いございません 【～にちがいございません】 certainly, no doubt (polite form of ～にちがいない) [2014]

革を巻いた弓、黒塗りの箙、鷹の羽の征矢が十七本、──これは皆、あの男が持っていたものでございましょう。はい。馬もおっしゃる通り、法師髪の月毛でございます。その畜生に落されるとは、何かの因縁に違いございません。それは石橋の少し先に、長い端綱を引いたまま、路ばたの青芒を食っておりました。

　この多襄丸というやつは、洛中に徘徊する盗人の中でも、女好きのやつでございます。昨年の秋鳥部寺の賓頭盧の後の山に、物詣でに来たらしい女房が一人、女の童と一しょに殺されていたのは、こいつの仕業だとか申しておりました。その月毛に乗っていた女も、こいつがあの男を殺したとなれば、何処へどうしたかわかりません。差出がましゅうございますが、それも御詮議下さいまし。

7

革【かわ】leather [1582]
巻く【まく】wind, roll, wrap [1691]
弓【ゆみ】bow [2120]
黒塗り【くろぬり】black-lacquer coating [1754] + [1818]
箙【えびら】quiver [-]
鷹【たか】hawk [2036]
羽【はね】feather [0167]
征矢【そや】arrows [0218] + [1267]
十七本【じゅうななほん】seventeen (of long, thin objects) [2110] + [2109] + [2183]
皆【みな】everything, all of it [1581]
男【おとこ】man 愛 [1613]
持つ【もつ】carry, have [0275]
〜でございます ＝〜です (polite form) 愛
馬【うま】horse [2073]
おっしゃる say (honorific form of いう)
〜通り【〜とおり】just as, in accordance with [1982]
法師髪【ほうしがみ】short mane [0248] +

[0892] + [1821]
月毛【つきげ】sorrel 愛 [1876] + [2152]
畜生【ちくしょう】beast, animal [1329] + [2179]
落す【おとす】drop, throw off [1494]
何かの【なにかの】a certain, a kind of [0045]
因縁【いんねん】karma, destiny [1936] + [0940]
〜に違いございません【〜にちがいございません】certainly, no doubt (polite form of 〜にちがいない) [2014]
石橋【いしばし】stone bridge [1884] + [0738]
少し先【すこしさき】some distance ahead [2163] + [1552]
長い【ながい】long [1626]
端綱【はづな】reins [0826 + [0928]
引く【ひく】drag, trail [0133]
〜まま still
路ばた【みちばた】roadside [1031]
青芒【あおすすき】eulalia [1573] + [-]
食う【くう】eat [1316]
〜ておる ＝〜ている (polite form) 愛

The leather-wrapped bow, the black-lacquered quiver, seventeen arrows with hawk feathers—Tajōmaru had, I believe, all these things in his possession. Yes, his horse was, as you say, a sorrel with a trimmed mane. Myself, I do believe that the fates had a hand in it when he was thrown by the beast. It was grazing at the roadside a little beyond the bridge, with the long reins dangling on the ground.

Even by the standards of the thieves who infest Kyoto, this Tajōmaru fellow was a real women's man. Last autumn a married woman—apparently on a pilgrimage to the mountain behind the Piṇḍola of Toribedera temple—was killed together with a young girl. Word was that this was his handiwork. And if Tajōmaru did indeed murder this man, then we have no idea about where the woman on the sorrel is, or what's become of her. If I may be so bold, I urge you to take this point into consideration.

7

多襄丸【たじょうまる】Tajōmaru (person's name) [1372] + [-] + [2134]
～という called ～
やつ fellow
洛中【らくちゅう】in the capital (Kyoto) [-] + [2150]
徘徊する【はいかいする】loiter, prowl around [-] + [-]
盗人【ぬすびと】robber [1714] + [2111]
中【なか】among [2150]
女好き【おんなずき】womanizer [2135] + [0155]
昨年【さくねん】last year [0601] + [1284]
秋【あき】autumn, fall [0776]
鳥部寺【とりべでら】Toribedera temple [2083] + [1099] + [1367]
賓頭盧【びんずる】(statue of) Piṇḍola-bhâravâja (one of Buddha's disciples) [-] + [1073] + [-]
後【うしろ】behind [0267]
山【やま】mountain [1867]
物詣で【ものもうで】visiting a temple [0587] + [-]

来る【くる】come (to do something) [2211]
女房【にょうぼう】wife [2135] + [1237]
一人【ひとり】one person [2105] + [2111]
女の童【めのわらわ】child, young girl [2135] + [1348]
～と一しょに【～といっしょに】together with [2105]
殺す【ころす】kill 🐾 [0889]
こいつ this fellow 🐾
仕業【しわざ】deed, doing [0021] + [1674]
申す【もうす】say (polite form of いう) [2186]
乗る【のる】ride [2224]
女【おんな】woman [2135]
何処【どこ】where [0045] + [1918]
わかる know
差出がましゅうございます【さしでがましゅうございます】forward, impertinent (polite form of 差し出がましい) [2082] + [2180]
御【ご】honorific prefix [0422]
詮議【せんぎ】consideration, examination, deliberation [-] + [1087]
～下さいまし【～くださいまし】please ～ (polite form of ～ください) [2115]

検非違使に問われたる媼の物語

　はい、あの死骸は手前の娘が、片附いた男でございます。が、都のものではございません。若狭の国府の侍でございます。名は金沢の武弘、年は二十六歳でございました。いえ、優しい気立でございますから、遺恨なぞ受けるはずはございません。

　娘でございますか？　娘の名は真砂、年は十九歳でございます。これは男にも劣らぬ位、勝気の女でございますが、まだ一度も武弘の外には、男を持った事はございません。顔は色の浅黒い、左の眼尻に黒子のある、小さい瓜実顔でございます。

検非違使【けびいし】police chief with judicial powers [0674] + [0598] + [2014] + [0068]

問う【とう】ask, question, interrogate [2091]

媼【おうな】old woman [-]

物語【ものがたり】account, tale, story [0587] + [1040]

8

死骸【しがい】corpse [2194] + [-]

手前の【てまえの】my (humble form of わたしの) [2155] + [1453]

娘【むすめ】daughter 💀 [0302]

片附く【かたづく】be married to [2158] + [0257]

男【おとこ】man 💀 [1613]

〜でございます＝〜です (polite form) 💀

都【みやこ】the capital (Kyoto) [1106]

もの person

若狭【わかさ】Wakasa (name of a province) [1430] + [0294]

国府【こくぶ】public office [1964] + [1960]

侍【さむらい】samurai [0062]

名【な】name 💀 [1371]

金沢の武弘【かなざわのたけひろ】Takehiro of Kanazawa (person's name) 💀 [1302] + [0201] + [2046] + [0141]

年【とし】age 💀 [1284]

二十六歳【にじゅうろくさい】twenty-six years old [1224] + [2110] + [1244] + [1605]

優しい【やさしい】kind [0130]

気立【きだて】disposition, nature, temper [2037] + [1257]

遺恨【いこん】grudge, ill will, hatred [2023] + [0272]

〜なぞ and such things (colloquial form

The Testimony of the Old Woman Questioned by the Chief of Police

Yes, the dead man is the man to whom my daughter was married. But he doesn't come from Kyoto. He was a samurai, an official from Wakasa. His name was Kanazawa no Takehiro, and he was twenty-six years old. No, he had a very gentle nature, so it's unlikely that anyone had any sort of grudge against him.

My daughter? My daughter's name is Masago, and she's nineteen years old. She's a woman every bit as headstrong as a man, but never once has she consorted with anyone but Takehiro. Her complexion is dusky; her oval face is petite, with a mole by the left eye.

----

of ～など)

受ける 【うける】 receive [1569]

～はずはございません it is unlikely that (polite form of ～はずはない)

9

真砂 【まさご】 Masago (person's name) [1337] + [0772]

十九歳 【じゅうきゅうさい】 nineteen years old [2110] + [2112] + [1605]

劣らぬ 【おとらぬ】 not be inferior to, not yield to [1553]

～位 【～くらい】 to the degree that [0042]

勝気 【かちき】 strong temperament [0686] + [2037]

女 【おんな】 woman [2135]

一度も 【いちども】 (+ negative) not even once [2105] + [1974]

～の外に 【～のほかに】 other than, except for [0135]

持つ 【もつ】 have (relations with) [0275]

事 【こと】 experience, instance [2220]

ございます ＝ある (polite form)

顔 【かお】 face [1177]

色 【いろ】 color [1280]

浅黒い 【あさぐろい】 dark, swarthy [0289] + [1754]

左 【ひだり】 left [1887]

眼尻 【めじり】 corner of the eye [1927] + [-]

黒子 【ほくろ】 mole [1754] + [2125]

小さい 【ちいさい】 small [0002]

瓜実顔 【うりざねがお】 oval face [-] + [1416] + [1177]

武弘は昨日娘と一しょに、若狭へ立ったのでございますが、こんな事になりますとは、何という因果でございましょう。しかし娘はどうなりましたやら、婿の事はあきらめましても、これだけは心配でなりません。どうかこの姥が一生のお願いでございますから、たとい草木を分けましても、娘の行方をお尋ね下さいまし。何に致せ憎いのは、その多襄丸とか何とか申す、盗人のやつでございます。婿ばかりか、娘までも……（跡は泣き入りて言葉なし。）

* * * * *

武弘【たけひろ】Takehiro (person's name) [2046] + [0141]

昨日【きのう】yesterday [0601] + [1915]

娘【むすめ】daughter ✿ [0302]

〜と一しょに【〜といっしょに】together with [2105]

若狭【わかさ】Wakasa (name of a province) [1430] + [0294]

立つ【たつ】set out [1257]

〜でございます ＝〜です (polite form) ✿

事【こと】state of affairs, situation ✿ [2220]

何という【なんという】horribly unexpected [0045]

因果【いんが】cause and effect, fate, destiny [1936] + [2217]

しかし but, however

〜やら expresses uncertainly

婿【むこ】son-in-law ✿ [0414]

あきらめる give up on, lose hope for

心配【しんぱい】worry, anxiety [0004] + [0981]

どうか please

姥【うば】old woman [-]

一生のお願い【いっしょうのおねがい】the greatest wish of one's life (used when pleading with someone) [2105] + [2179] + [1199]

たとい〜ても even if

草木【くさき】vegetation, grass and trees [1450] + [2149]

分ける【わける】divide, split [1247]

行方【ゆきがた】direction, whereabouts [0157] + [1243]

尋ねる【たずねる】investigate [1498]

〜下さいまし【〜くださいまし】please 〜 (polite form of 〜ください) [2115]

何に致せ【なにいたせ】in any event (humble form of 何にせよ／何にしても) [0045] + [0883]

憎い【にくい】hateful [0489]

Yesterday Takehiro and my daughter set out for Wakasa. What had they done to deserve this dreadful fate? Even if I accept that I have lost my son-in-law for good, I'm still worried sick about what might have happened to my daughter. This is the desperate plea of an old woman. Leave no stone unturned, but please, please find out where she's gone. Oh how I hate that damned robber, that Tajōmaru or whatever his stupid name is. As if my son-in-law wasn't enough, he has to take my daughter too ... [*At this point her testimony was drowned out in tears.*]

....

多襄丸【たじょうまる】Tajōmaru (person's name) [1372] + [-] + [2134]

〜とか何とか【〜とかなんとか】or whatever [0045]

〜と申す【〜ともうす】called (polite form of 〜という) [2186]

盗人【ぬすびと】robber [1714] + [2111]

やつ fellow

〜ばかりか〜までも not only ~ but also ~

跡【あと】the rest [1032]

泣き入る【なきいる】burst into tears [0253] + [2113]

言葉なし【ことばなし】no words, no speech [1233] + [1497]

多襄丸の白状

11

MP3
5.
The
Robber
12:01

12

　あの男を殺したのはわたしです。しかし女は殺しはしません。では何処へ行ったのか？　それはわたしにもわからないのです。まあ、お待ちなさい。いくら拷問にかけられても、知らない事は申されますまい。その上わたしもこうなれば、卑怯な隠し立てはしないつもりです。

　わたしは昨日の午少し過ぎ、あの夫婦に出会いました。その時風の吹いた拍子に、牟子の垂絹が上ったものですから、ちらりと女の顔が見えたのです。ちらりと、——見えたと思う瞬間には、もう見えなくなったのですが、一つにはそのためもあったのでしょう、わたしにはあの女の顔が、女菩薩のように見えたのです。わたしはその咄嗟の間に、たとい男は殺しても、女は奪おうと決心しました。

....

多襄丸【たじょうまる】Tajōmaru (person's
　name) [1372] + [-] + [2134]
白状【はくじょう】confession [2175] + [0204]

11

男【おとこ】man 🈁 [1613]
殺す【ころす】kill 🈁 [0889]
しかし but, however
女【おんな】woman 🈁 [2135]
何処【どこ】where [0045] + [1918]
行く【いく】go [0157]
わかる know, understand
まあ oh, hey
待つ【まつ】wait [0269]
拷問【ごうもん】torture [0274] + [2091]
かける apply

知る【しる】know [0768]
事【こと】thing, fact, event [2220]
申す【もうす】say, speak (humble form of
　いう) [2186]
〜まい will not 〜
その上【そのうえ】in addition [2128]
卑怯な【ひきょうな】cowardly [1688] + [-]
隠し立て【かくしだて】secrecy, conceal-
　ment [0502] + [1257]
〜つもり intend to 〜

12

昨日【きのう】yesterday [0601] + [1915]
午【ひる】midday [1254]
〜少し過ぎ【〜すこしすぎ】a little after 〜
　[2163] + [2003]

The Confession of Tajōmaru

It is I who killed that man. But I did not kill the woman. Where's she gone then? That I do not know. Whoa, hold on a minute! No matter how much I'm tortured by you, I can't very well tell you what I don't know, can I? Anyway, the way things are now, I don't intend to try anything underhand or keep anything back.

I ran into that couple a little after midday yesterday. Right at that moment there was a gust of wind that lifted her long veil, and I caught a glimpse of her face—just for a second. Just a brief instant—"Now you see it, now you don't." Perhaps that's one reason why she looked so like a goddess to me. But it was in that fraction of a second that I made up my mind to take that woman, even if I had to kill the man to do so.

....

夫婦【ふうふ】husband and wife, couple [2157] + [0343]
出会う【であう】meet by chance, encounter [2180] + [1275]
時【とき】time, moment, occasion [0625]
風【かぜ】wind [1908]
吹く【ふく】blow [0170]
拍子【ひょうし】instant [0225] + [2125]
牟子【むし】veil [-] + [2125]
垂絹【たれぎぬ】hanging silk [2219] + [0920]
上る【あがる】rise [2128]
ちらりと momentarily 奥
顔【かお】face [1177]
見える【みえる】be visible 奥 [1615]
思う【おもう】think [1633]

瞬間【しゅんかん】moment [0841] + [2094]
一つ【ひとつ】one (reason) [2105]
そのため for that reason 奥
女菩薩【にょぼさつ】female bodhisattva, goddess [2135] + [-] + [-]
～のように like
咄嗟の間【とっさのあいだ】space of an instant [-] + [-] + [2094]
たとい～ても even if
奪う【うばう】sieze, carry off [1517]
決心する【けっしんする】resolve (to do something) [0197] + [0004]

何、男を殺すなぞは、あなた方の思っているように、大した事ではありません。どうせ女を奪うとなれば、必、男は殺されるのです。唯わたしは殺す時に、腰の太刀を使うのですが、あなた方は太刀は使わない。唯権力で殺す、金で殺す、どうかするとお為ごかしの言葉だけでも殺すでしょう。なるほど血は流れない、男は立派に生きている、――しかしそれでも殺したのです。罪の深さを考えて見れば、あなた方が悪いか、わたしが悪いか、どちらが悪いかわかりません。（皮肉なる微笑）

しかし男を殺さずとも、女を奪う事が出来れば、別に不足はない訳です。いや、その時の心もちでは、出来るだけ男を殺さずに、女を奪おうと決心したのです。

何【なに】what, no [0045]

男【おとこ】man [1613]

殺す【ころす】kill [0889]

〜なぞ and other such things (colloquial form of 〜など)

あなた方【あなたがた】you people [1243]

思う【おもう】think, feel [1633]

〜ように as

大した【たいした】significant [2133]

事【こと】thing, act, matter [2220]

どうせ after all

女【おんな】woman [2135]

奪う【うばう】sieze, carry off [1517]

必【かならず】certainly, without fail [0006]

唯【ただ】just, only [0339]

時【とき】when [0625]

腰【こし】waist [0711]

太刀【たち】sword [1360] + [1857]

使う【つかう】use [0068]

権力【けんりょく】power [0731] + [2114]

金【かね】money [1302]

どうかすると sometimes, occasionally

お為ごかし【おためごかし】self-interest posing as kindness [2225]

言葉【ことば】words, language [1233] + [1497]

なるほど of course, indeed

血【ち】blood [2196]

流れる【ながれる】flow [0325]

立派に【りっぱに】splendidly [1257] + [0281]

生きる【いきる】live, be alive [2179]

Oh, killing a man is not—despite what you people may think—a very serious matter. After all, if you're going to make off with the woman, it's just a matter of course for the man to get killed. But when I kill someone, I use the sword here at my side. You may not use the sword, but you kill your victims with your authority; you kill them with money; sometimes you even manage to kill them with pure hypocrisy. Of course, no blood is spilled and your victim is still wonderfully alive—but you have murdered him nonetheless. When it comes to the heinousness of the crime, then I really don't know who is the more wicked, you lot or me. [*Ironic smile.*]

Still, I would be quite happy to be able to get the woman without having to kill the man. No, what I felt then was a determination to get my hands on the girl, while doing my best not to kill the man.

....

しかし but, however 愛
罪【つみ】crime, sin [1673]
深さ【ふかさ】depth, turpitude [0385]
考える【かんがえる】think, consider [2039]
〜て見る【〜てみる】try to 〜 [1615]
悪い【わるい】bad, wicked 愛 [1758]
どちらが which (of us)
わかる understand, know
皮肉なる【ひにくなる】ironic [1923] + [2042]
微笑【びしょう】smile [0461] + [1692]

14

殺さず【ころさず】not kill 愛 [0889]
〜事が出来る【〜ことができる】be able to 〜 [2220] + [2180] + [2211]
別に【べつに】(+ negative) not particularly [0760]

不足【ふそく】dissatisfaction [2141] + [1386]
訳【わけ】reason, matter, case [0989]
心もち【こころもち】mood, frame of mind [0004]
出来るだけ【できるだけ】as much as possible [2180] + [2211]
決心する【けっしんする】resolve (to do something) 愛 [0197] + [0004]

が、あの山科の駅路では、とてもそんな事は出来ません。そこでわたしは山の中へ、あの夫婦をつれこむ工夫をしました。

これも造作はありません。わたしはあの夫婦と途づれになると、向うの山には古塚がある、この古塚を発いて見たら、鏡や太刀が沢山出た、わたしは誰も知らないように、山の陰の藪の中へ、そういう物を埋めてある、もし望み手があるならば、どれでも安い値に売り渡したい、――という話をしたのです。男は何時かわたしの話に、だんだん心を動かし初めました。それから、――どうです、慾というものは恐しいではありませんか？　それから半時もたたない内に、あの夫婦はわたしと一しょに、山路へ馬を向けていたのです。

15

山科【やましな】Yamashina (place name) 🕱[1867] + [0775]
駅路【えきろ】postal road, staging road [1184] + [1031]
とても (+ negative) by no means
そんな that kind of (＝そのような)
事【こと】act, feat [2220]
出来る【できる】be capable of [2180] + [2211]
そこで so, at that point
山【やま】mountains, hills 🕱[1867]
中【なか】in, inside 🕱[2150]
夫婦【ふうふ】husband and wife, couple 🕱[2157] + [0343]
つれこむ lead into
工夫【くふう】scheme, plan, measure [2118]+ [2157]

15

造作【ぞうさ】difficulty, trouble [1983] + [0049]
途づれ【みちづれ】traveling companion [1980]
向う【むこう】over there, over yonder [1934]
古塚【ふるづか】mound, tumulus 🕱[1262] + [0406]
発く【あばく】dig up [1634]
〜て見る【〜てみる】try to 〜 [1615]
鏡【かがみ】mirror [1157]
太刀【たち】sword [1360] + [1857]
沢山【たくさん】many [0201] + [1867]
出る【でる】emerge, appear [2180]
誰も【だれも】(+ negative) no one [-]
知る【しる】know [0768]
〜ように so that

On the Yamashina road that was quite simply impossible. That's why I devised a plan to lure the couple into the mountains.

It wasn't difficult at all. First I got to be their traveling companion, then I spun them a yarn that there was an ancient mound on the mountain yonder, and that when I'd dug around, I'd discovered loads of mirrors and swords. I said that to make sure no one else found them, I'd buried them in a thicket in a remote part of the mountain, but that if anyone was interested, I was ready to sell any of the things at a low price. At some point the man found himself getting sucked in and excited by my story. And then—Oh, isn't greed a fearful thing? And then, in less than an hour, the couple were with me and turning their horse toward the mountain road.

陰【かげ】shade, shady part [0397]
藪【やぶ】grove [-]
物【もの】thing, object [0587]
埋める【うずめる】bury [0300]
もし (+ conditional) if
望み手【のぞみて】buyer, interested party [1756] + [2155]
安い【やすい】cheap [1373]
値【ね】price [0081]
売り渡す【うりわたす】sell [1391] + [0445]
話【はなし】tale, pitch, yarn ☠ [1027]
男【おとこ】man [1613]
何時か【いつか】at some point [0045] + [0625]
だんだん gradually
心を動かす【こころをうごかす】get excited about [0004] + [1163]
〜初める【〜はじめる】begin to ~ [0759]
慾【よく】greed [-]
恐しい【おそろしい】fearful, terrifying [1696]
半時【はんとき】about one hour [2182] + [0625]
たつ pass (of time)
〜内に【〜うちに】(after a negative) before [2162]
〜と一しょに【〜といっしょに】together with [2105]
山路【やまみち】mountain road [1867] + [1031]
馬【うま】horse [2073]
向ける【むける】direct, point toward [1934]

わたしは藪の前へ来ると、宝はこの中に埋めてある、見に来てくれといいました。男は慾に渇いていますから、異存のあるはずはありません。が、女は馬も下りずに、待っているというのです。またあの藪の茂っているのを見ては、そういうのも無理はありますまい。わたしはこれも実をいえば、思う壺にはまったのですから、女一人を残したまま、男と藪の中へはいりました。

藪は少時の間は竹ばかりです。が、半町ほど行った処に、やや開いた杉むらがある、──わたしの仕事を仕遂げるのには、これほど都合の好い場所はありません。わたしは藪を押し分けながら、宝は杉の下に埋めてあると、尤もらしい嘘をつきました。

16

藪【やぶ】grove 愛 [-]
前【まえ】front, before [1453]
来る【くる】come, arrive 愛 [2211]
宝【たから】treasure 愛 [1415]
中【なか】in, inside 愛 [2150]
埋める【うずめる】bury 愛 [0300]
見る【みる】see 愛 [1615]
〜てくれ please 〜 (blunt form of 〜てください)
いう say, speak 愛
男【おとこ】man 愛 [1613]
慾に渇く【よくにかわく】feel thirsty for, lust after [-] + [0379]
異存【いぞん】objection [1651] + [1894]
〜はずはない it is unlikely that

女【おんな】woman 愛 [2135]
馬【うま】horse [2073]
下りずに【おりずに】without dismounting [2115]
待つ【まつ】wait [0269]
また then, again
茂る【しげる】grow thickly [1435]
無理はありますまい【むりはありますまい】no wonder [1351] + [0659]
実をいえば【じつをいえば】to tell the truth [1416]
思う壺【おもうつぼ】wish, strategy, trick [1633] + [-]
はまる get wrapped up in
一人【ひとり】one person, alone [2105] + [2111]
残す【のこす】leave behind [0640]

When we were level with the thicket, I told them that the treasure was buried in there, and they should come in and look it over. The man was in a frenzy of greed so had no objections whatsoever to my proposal. The woman, however, remained on the horse and said she would wait. This was only natural considering how thick the undergrowth was. To tell you the truth, things were turning out just as I hoped, so I left the woman by herself, and went off into the thicket with the man.

For a while the thicket was nothing but bamboo, but after about sixty yards, there was a reasonably open spot in a patch of cedar trees. It was the ideal spot for me to do the business. So as I pushed my way through the thicket, I fed him some convincing lie about the treasure being buried under the cedars.

～まま still
はいる go in, enter

17

少時の間【しばらくのあいだ】a little while
[2163] + [0625] + [2094]
竹【たけ】bamboo [0168]
～ばかり only, just
半町【はんちょう】half a *chō* (1 *chō* = 110 m)
[2182] [0756]
～ほど to the extent of 愛
行く【いく】go [0157]
処【ところ】place [1918]
やや somewhat
開く【ひらく】open [2092]
杉むら【すぎむら】patch of cedars 愛 [0557]
仕事【しごと】work, task [0021] + [2220]

仕遂げる【しとげる】carry out, execute
[0021] + [2004]
都合の好い【つごうのいい】convenient,
handy [1106] + [1274] + [0155]
場所【ばしょ】place [0408] + [0568]
押し分ける【おしわける】push apart [0234] +
[1247]
杉【すぎ】cedar [0557]
下【した】below, beneath [2115]
尤もらしい【もっともらしい】plausible [-]
嘘をつく【うそをつく】tell a lie [-]

男はわたしにそういわれると、もう痩せ杉が透いて見える方へ、一生懸命に進んで行きます。その内に竹が疎らになると、何本も杉が並んでいる、──わたしは其処へ来るが早いか、いきなり相手を組み伏せました。男も太刀を佩いているだけに、力は相当にあったようですが、不意を打たれてはたまりません。忽ち一本の杉の根がたへ、括りつけられてしまいました。縄ですか？　縄は盗人の有難さに、何時塀を越えるかわかりませんから、ちゃんと腰につけていたのです。勿論声を出させないためにも、竹の落葉を頬張らせれば、外に面倒はありません。

男【おとこ】man [1613]

いう say, speak

痩せ杉【やせすぎ】thin cedar [-] ÷ [0557]

透く【すく】be few and far between (*lit.*, "be transparent") [1981]

見える【みえる】be visible [1615]

方【ほう】direction [1243]

一生懸命【いっしょうけんめい】diligently [2105] + [2179] + [1855] + [1303]

進む【すすむ】go forward [1911]

～て行く【～てゆく】indicates progression away from the speaker [0157]

その内【そのうち】after a little while [2162]

竹【たけ】bamboo [0168]

疎ら【まばら】sporadic, sparse [0799]

何本も【なんぼんも】many (of long, thin objects) [0045] + [2183]

杉【すぎ】cedar [0557]

並ぶ【ならぶ】stand in a row, be lined up [1436]

其処【そこ】there [-] + [1918]

来る【くる】come, reach [2211]

～が早いか【～がはやいか】as soon as [1549]

いきなり suddenly

相手【あいて】counterpart, the other person [0609] + [2155]

組み伏せる【くみふせる】pin down [0904] + [0029]

太刀【たち】sword [1360] + [1857]

佩く【はく】wear (of swords) [-]

力【ちから】strength, power [2114]

相当に【そうとうに】sufficiently, plenty [0609] + [1378]

～ようです appear to be, seem to be

不意を打つ【ふいをうつ】take by surprise [2141] + [1352] + [0142]

～たまらない be unable to endure, be unable to stand up to

忽ち【たちまち】in a moment, in an instant [-]

Upon being told this, the man thrust energetically on toward where the cedars could be seen through the foliage. After a while the bamboo thinned out, and there were a great number of cedars. No sooner had we reached this place than I pinned the unsuspecting fellow to the ground. He was a sword-bearing samurai, so he was very powerful. Still, he had been taken completely by surprise and soon I had him trussed up to the root of a cedar. The rope? I thank my lucky stars that I'm a robber! I never know when I might have to scale a wall, so I had the thing tied to my waist. To make sure he couldn't cry out, I stuffed dead leaves into his mouth. And that was that. Problem solved!

....

一本【いっぽん】one (of long, thin objects) [2105] + [2183]
根がた【ねがた】trunk [0631]
括りつける【くくりつける】tie to [0276]
〜てしまう thoroughly 〜
縄【なわ】rope 夒 [0942]
盗人【ぬすびと】robber, thief [1714] + [2111]
有難さ【ありがたさ】blessing [1895] + [1196]
何時【いつ】when [0045] + [0625]
塀【へい】wall [0407]
越える【こえる】climb, get over [2085]
わかる know, understand
ちゃんと duly, properly
腰【こし】waist, middle of the body [0711]
つける attach, tie
勿論【もちろん】of course [-] + [1058]
声を出す【こえをだす】shout, make a sound [1393] + [2180]
〜ために so that
竹【たけ】bamboo [0168]

落葉【おちば】fallen leaves [1494] + [1497]
頬張る【ほおばる】stuff in the mouth [-] + [0348]
外に【ほかに】otherwise [0135]
面倒【めんどう】trouble, problem [1324] + [0093]

わたしは男を片附けてしまうと、今度はまた女の所へ、男が急病を起したらしいから、見に来てくれといいに行きました。これも図星に当ったのは、申し上げるまでもありますまい。女は市女笠を脱いだまま、わたしに手をとられながら、藪の奥へはいって来ました。ところが其処へ来て見ると、男は杉の根に縛られている、――女はそれを一目見るなり、何時の間に懐から出していたか、きらりと小刀を引き抜きました。わたしはまだ今までに、あの位気性の烈しい女は、一人も見た事がありません。もしその時でも油断していたらば、一突きに脾腹を突かれたでしょう。いや、それは身を躱した所が、無二無三に斬り立てられる内には、どんな怪我も仕兼ねなかったのです。

18

男【おとこ】man 🕱 [1613]

片附ける【かたづける】deal with, take care of [1243] + [0257]

〜てしまう thoroughly 〜

今度【こんど】next [1246] + [1974]

また again

女【おんな】woman 🕱 [2135]

所【ところ】place [0568]

急病を起す【きゅうびょうをおこす】suddenly fall ill, have a sudden attack [1328] + [2059] + [2079]

見る【みる】see 🕱 [1615]

来る【くる】come 🕱 [1615]

〜てくれ please 〜 (blunt form of 〜てください)

いう tell, say

行く【ゆく】go (to do something) [0157]

図星に当る【ずぼしにあたる】hit the bull's-eye [1951] + [1577] + [1378]

申し上げるまでもありますまい【もうしあげるまでもありますまい】needless to say (superhumble form of いうまでもない) [2186] + [2128]

市女笠【いちめがさ】straw hat worn by women for sunshade and/or to conceal the face [1258] + [2135] + [-]

脱ぐ【ぬぐ】take off [0663]

〜まま still

手をとる【てをとる】take by the hand [2155]

藪【やぶ】grove [-]

奥【おく】depths [1806]

はいる enter

〜て来る【〜てくる】indicates progression in the direction of the speaker or up to a point [1615]

ところが but

其処【そこ】there [-] + [1918]

〜て見る【〜てみる】try to 〜 [1615]

杉【すぎ】cedar [0557]

Having dealt with the man, I went back to where the woman was to tell her that the man had had a sudden attack and she should come and see. No need to say that this little ruse was yet another bull's-eye. The woman, her hat off and hand in hand with yours truly, came on into the grove. When we got there, there was her husband tied to the trunk of the cedar. The instant the woman caught sight of him—she must have drawn it very fast from the breast of her kimono—she'd pulled a glistening little dagger on me. I have never seen a woman so fierce and fiery in my life. Any slipup on my part, and she'd have stabbed me one in the side. So I dodged and danced about, but while she was slashing and stabbing all over the place, there's no telling what damage I could have sustained.

根【ね】root [0631]
縛る【しばる】tie up [0949]
・目【ひとめ】one glance [2105] + [1927]
〜なり as soon as
何時の間に【いつのまに】before one knows it [0045] + [0625] + [2094]
懐【ふところ】breast [0528]
出す【だす】take out [2180]
きらりと in a flash (onomatopoeic expression that describes a quick flash of light)
小刀【さすが】dagger 夐 [0002] + [1857]
引き抜く【ひきぬく】draw, pull out [0133] + [0183]
今まで【いままで】until now
位【くらい】extent, degree [0042]
気性【きしょう】temper [2037] + [0222]
烈しい【はげしい】violent [1698]
一人【ひとり】one person [2105] + [2111]
事【こと】thing, experience [2220]

もし (+ conditional) if
時【とき】time, moment [0625]
油断する【ゆだんする】be careless [0255] + [1001]
一突き【ひとつき】one stab/thrust [2105] + [1421]
脾腹【ひばら】side, flank [-] + [0710]
突く【つく】stab [1421]
身を躱す【みをかわす】dodge, move one's body [2213] + [-]
〜所が【〜ところが】but [0568]
無二無三に【むにむさんに】recklessly, desperately [1351] + [1224] + [1351] + [1225]
斬り立てる【きりたてる】slash and stab [-] + [1257]
〜内に【〜うちに】while, as [2162]
怪我【けが】wound [0220] + [2208]
仕兼ねる【しかねる】be able, be capable of [0021] + [1469]

が、わたしも多襄丸ですから、どうにかこうにか太刀も抜かずに、とうとう小刀を打ち落しました。いくら気の勝った女でも、得物がなければ仕方がありません。わたしはとうとう思い通り、男の命は取らずとも、女を手に入れる事は出来たのです。

　男の命は取らずとも、──そうです。わたしはその上にも、男を殺すつもりはなかったのです。ところが泣き伏した女を後に、藪の外へ逃げようとすると、女は突然わたしの腕へ、気違いのように縋りつきました。しかも切れ切れに叫ぶのを聞けば、あなたが死ぬか夫が死ぬか、どちらか一人死んでくれ、二人の男に恥を見せるのは、死ぬよりもつらいというのです。

多襄丸【たじょうまる】Tajōmaru (person's name) [1372] + [-] + [2134]

どうにかこうにか somehow or other

太刀【たち】sword [1360] + [1857]

抜かずに【ぬかずに】without drawing [0183]

とうとう finally, in the end 🈛

小刀【さすが】dagger [0002] + [1857]

打ち落す【うちおとす】strike down [0142] + [1494]

気の勝った【きのかった】aggressive [2037] + [0686]

女【おんな】woman 🈛 [2135]

得物【えもの】weapon [0351] + [0587]

仕方がない【しかたがない】helpless [0021] + [1243]

思い通り【おもいどおり】as planned, as expected [1633] + [1982]

男【おとこ】man 🈛 [1613]

命を取らず【いのちをとらず】not take a life, not kill 🈛 [1303] + [0847]

手に入れる【てにいれる】get, rape [2155] + [2113]

〜事が出来る【〜ことができる】be able to 〜 [2220] + [2180] + [2211]

19

その上【そのうえ】more than that [2128]

殺す【ころす】kill [0889]

〜つもり intend to 〜

ところが but

泣き伏す【なきふす】lie down and weep [0253] + [0029]

後にする【あとにする】leave behind [0267]

藪【やぶ】grove [-]

But I am Tajōmaru, so somehow without even drawing my sword, I managed to knock the dagger from her hands. No matter how aggressive a woman she was, without a weapon there was nothing she could do. At last I was able to do exactly what I wanted: to enjoy her without having to take her husband's life.

Without taking her husband's life—yes, that is the truth. After all I had done, I had no intention of killing him. But, as I was about to hightail it out of the grove, leaving the woman sobbing on the ground behind me, she suddenly clutched my arm like a woman possessed. Then I heard her cry out broken-voiced that either I or her husband—one of us—must die: to have had her shame witnessed by two men was more painful than death itself.

. . . .

外【そと】outside [0135]
逃げる【にげる】escape [1970]
突然【とつぜん】suddenly [1421] + [1779]
腕【うで】arm [0687]
気違い【きちがい】maniac (NOTE: now pejorative; do not use) [2037] + [2014]
〜のように like
縋りつく【すがりつく】cling to [-]
しかも moreover, furthermore
切れ切れに【きれぎれに】disconnectedly [0015]
叫ぶ【さけぶ】scream, wail [0149]
聞く【きく】hear [2097]
死ぬ【しぬ】die 愛 [2194]
夫【おっと】husband [2157]
一人【ひとり】one person [2105] + [2111]

〜てくれ please 〜 (blunt form of 〜てくだ さい)
二人【ふたり】two people [1224] + [2111]
恥【はじ】shame [0882]
見せる【みせる】show [1615]
つらい painful
いう say

いや、その内どちらにしろ、生き残った男につれ添いたい、
——そうも喘ぎ喘ぎいうのです。わたしはその時猛然と、
男を殺したい気になりました。(陰鬱なる興奮)

　こんな事を申し上げると、きっとわたしはあなた方より、
残酷な人間に見えるでしょう。しかしそれはあなた方が、
あの女の顔を見ないからです。殊にその一瞬間の、燃える
ような瞳を見ないからです。わたしは女と眼を合せた時、
たとい神鳴に打ち殺されても、この女を妻にしたいと思い
ました。妻にしたい、——わたしの念頭にあったのは、唯
こういう一事だけです。これはあなた方の思うように、卑
しい色慾ではありません。

その内【そのうち】of the two (choices)
[2162]

どちらにしろ whatever one does, whatever option one chooses

生き残る【いきのこる】survive [2179] + [0640]

男【おとこ】man 🐾 [1613]

つれ添う【つれそう】marry [0390]

喘ぎ喘ぎ【あえぎあえぎ】panting and
gasping [-]

いう say, speak

時【とき】time, moment 🐾 [0625]

猛然と【もうぜんと】fiercely, wildly [0393] +
[1779]

殺す【ころす】kill [0889]

気【き】feeling [2037]

陰鬱なる【いんうつなる】gloomy [0397] + [-]

興奮【こうふん】excitement [1852] + [1532]

事【こと】thing [2220]

申し上げる【もうしあげる】say, tell (super-
humble form of いう) [2186] + [2128]

きっと definitely, certainly

あなた方【あなたがた】you people 🐾 [1243]

残酷な【ざんこくな】cruel [0640] + [1048]

人間【にんげん】person, human [2111] +
[2094]

見える【みえる】seem, appear [1615]

しかし but, however

女【おんな】woman 🐾 [2135]

顔【かお】face, expression [1177]

見る【みる】see 🐾 [1615]

殊に【ことに】especially, particularly [0639]

一瞬間【いっしゅんかん】one instant [2105] +
[0841] + [2094]

燃える【もえる】burn [0739]

～ような like

瞳【ひとみ】pupils (of the eyes) [0836]

眼を合わせる【めをあわせる】exchange

I don't care of which of you it is, I shall be wife of the man who survives. This is what she said between her gasping and her panting. It was then that I first felt a furious desire to kill the man. [*Melancholy excitement.*]

When I tell you this, no doubt you think me a crueler man than any of yourselves. But that is only because you cannot see her face: to be exact, because you can't see her eyes which, at that instant, seemed to be burning. When our eyes met, I felt that I wanted her for my wife, even if I were struck dead by lightning for so doing. I want her for my wife—that was the only thought I had. And it wasn't just base, animal lust, as you all assume.

----

looks, meet eyes with [0796] + [1274]

たとい〜ても if

神鳴 【かみなり】 thunderbolt, lightning [0615] + [0481]

打ち殺す 【うちころす】 strike and kill [0142] + [0889]

妻 【つま】 wife 変 [1628]

思う 【おもう】 think, feel 変 [1633]

念頭 【ねんとう】 mind [1304] + [1073]

唯 【ただ】 just, only [0339]

一事 【いちじ】 one thing [2105] + [2220]

〜ように like, as

卑しい 【いやしい】 ignoble, base [1688]

色慾 【しきよく】 lust, sexual desire [1280] + [-]

もしその時色慾の外に、何も望みがなかったとすれば、わたしは女を蹴倒しても、きっと逃げてしまったでしょう。男もそうすればわたしの太刀に、血を塗る事にはならなかったのです。が、薄暗い藪の中に、じっと女の顔を見た刹那、わたしは男を殺さない限り、此処は去るまいと覚悟しました。

しかし男を殺すにしても、卑怯な殺し方はしたくありません。わたしは男の縄を解いた上、太刀打ちをしろといいました。（杉の根がたに落ちていたのは、その時捨て忘れた縄なのです。）男は血相を変えたまま、太い太刀を引き抜きました。と思うと口も利かずに、憤然とわたしへ飛びかかりました。——その太刀打ちがどうなったかは、申し上げるまでもありますまい。

....

もし (+ conditional) if
時【とき】time, moment 🐾 [0625]
色慾【しきよく】lust, sexual desire [1280] + [-]
〜の外に【〜のほかに】other than [0135]
何も【なにも】(+ negative) nothing, no [0045]
望み【のぞみ】hope, desire [1756]
女【おんな】woman [2135]
蹴倒す【けたおす】kick to the ground [-] + [0093]
きっと certainly, surely
逃げる【にげる】flee, get away [1970]
〜てしまう expresses completion of an action with regret
男【おとこ】man 🐾 [1613]
太刀【たち】sword 🐾 [1360] + [1857]
血【ち】blood [2196]
塗る【ぬる】paint [1818]

事【こと】thing, event [2220]
薄暗い【うすぐらい】semidark, dim [1534] + [0689]
藪【やぶ】grove, thicket [-]
中【なか】in, inside [2150]
じっと fixedly
顔【かお】face, expression [1177]
見る【みる】look at [1615]
刹那【せつな】instant, moment [-] + [0564]
殺す【ころす】kill 🐾 [0889]
〜限り【〜かぎり】(after a negative) unless [0296]
此処【ここ】here, this place [-] + [1918]
去る【さる】leave [1364]
〜まい will not 〜
覚悟する【かくごする】resolve (to do something) [1668] + [0312]

If my only thought then had been lust, I would certainly have got away—kicking the woman to the ground if need be—and the man would not have sullied my sword with his blood. But in the murky grove, in the instant when I gazed into her face, I made up my mind that I wouldn't leave the place without first killing her husband.

Maybe I was going to kill him, but that doesn't mean I wanted to kill him in a cowardly way. So, after untying the rope, I told him we were going to fight a duel to the death. (You found this rope, which I threw to one side and forgot about, by the cedar.) The husband, his face an angry mask of fury, drew his massive sword and, without saying a word, sprang furiously upon me. There is, of course, no need for me to tell you how the battle ended.

21

しかし but, however

〜にしても even if

卑怯な【ひきょうな】cowardly, dishonorable [1688] + [-]

殺し方【ころしかた】way of killing [0889] + [1243]

縄【なわ】rope 💥 [0942]

解く【とく】loosen [1017]

〜上【〜うえ】after, upon [2128]

太刀打ち【たちうち】sword fight 💥 [1360] + [1857] + [0142]

しろ imperative form of する

いう say, speak

杉【すぎ】cedar [0557]

根がた【ねがた】trunk [0631]

落ちる【おちる】fall (to the ground) [1494]

捨てる【すてる】throw away [0369]

忘れる【わすれる】forget about [1285]

血相を変える【けっそうをかえる】have a furious expression (*lit.,* "change color") [2196] + [0609] + [1311]

〜まま still

太い【ふとい】thick, fat [1360]

引き抜く【ひきぬく】draw, pull out [0133] + [0183]

思う【おもう】think, feel [1633]

口を利かずに【くちをきかずに】without speaking [2119] + [0757]

憤然と【ふんぜんと】angrily, wrathfully [0512] + [1779]

飛びかかる【とびかかる】spring upon [2222]

申し上げるまでもありますまい【もうしあげるまでもありますまい】It goes without saying, needless to say (superhumble form of いうまでもない) [2186] + [2128]

わたしの太刀は二十三合目に、相手の胸を貫きました。二十三合目に、——どうかそれを忘れずに下さい。わたしは今でもこの事だけは、感心だと思っているのです。わたしと二十合斬り結んだものは、天下にあの男一人だけですから。（快活なる微笑）

わたしは男が倒れると同時に、血に染まった刀を下げたなり、女の方を振り返りました。すると、——どうです、あの女は何処にもいないではありませんか？　わたしは女がどちらへ逃げたか、杉むらの間を探して見ました。が、竹の落葉の上には、それらしい跡も残っていません。また耳を澄ませて見ても、聞えるのは唯男の喉に、断末魔の音がするだけです。

太刀【たち】sword [1360] + [1857]
二十三合目【にじゅうさんごうめ】twenty-third stroke 蜀 [1224] + [2110] + [1225] + [1274] + [1927]
相手【あいて】counterpart, opponent [0609] + [2155]
胸【むね】chest [0647]
貫く【つらぬく】pierce, go through [1593]
どうか please
忘れず【わすれず】not forget [1285]
〜下さい【〜ください】please 〜 [2115]
今でも【いまでも】even now [1246]
事【こと】thing, fact [2220]
感心【かんしん】admirable [1814] + [0004]
思う【おもう】think [1633]
二十合【にじゅうごう】twenty strokes [1224] + [2110] + [1294]

斬り結ぶ【きりむすぶ】exchange blows [-] + [0912]
もの person
天下【てんか】the whole world [2148] + [2115]
男【おとこ】man 蜀 [1613]
一人【ひとり】one person [2105] + [2111]
快活なる【かいかつなる】lively, cheerful [0182] + [0285]
微笑【びしょう】smile [0461] + [1692]

倒れる【たおれる】fall over, collapse [0093]
〜と同時に【〜とどうじに】at the same time [1897] + [0625]
血【ち】blood [2196]
染まる【そまる】be dyed with, change color [1640]

On the twenty-third stroke, my sword pierced the chest of my enemy. The *twenty-third stroke* ... please do not forget that. Even now I am full of admiration for this feat. That man is the only person in the whole wide world to have ever traded more than twenty strokes with me. [*Cheerful smile.*]

As the man fell to the ground, I lowered my blood-stained sword and turned around to face the woman. And—can you believe it?—she wasn't there. I wondered where she had got to and I tried looking among the cedars. There was no trace of her on the dried bamboo leaves. I strained to listen, but the only sound I could hear was the death rattle in her husband's throat.

....

刀【かたな】sword [1857]
下げる【さげる】lower [2115]
〜なり (after a verb in the past tense) having 〜
女【おんな】woman 义 [2135]
方【ほう】direction [1243]
振り返る【ふりかえる】turn around [0316] + [1940]
何処にも【どこにも】(+ negative) anywhere, nowhere [0045] + [1918]
どちら where
逃げる【にげる】flee, run away [1970]
杉むら【すぎむら】cedar patch [0557]
間【あいだ】among, between [2094]
探す【さがす】look for [0374]
〜て見る【〜てみる】try to 〜 义 [1615]
竹【たけ】bamboo [0168]

落葉【おちば】fallen leaves [1494] + [1497]
上【うえ】on, upon [2128]
跡【あと】traces [1032]
残る【のこる】be left behind, remain [0640]
また moreover, again
耳を澄ませる【みみをすませる】prick up one's ears, listen carefully [2190] + [0517]
聞える【きこえる】be audible [2097]
唯【ただ】just, only [0339]
喉【のど】throat [-]
断末魔【だんまつま】dying agony, moment of death [1001] + [2184] + [2035]
音【おと】sound [1312]

　事によるとあの女は、わたしが太刀打を始めるが早いか、人の助けでも呼ぶために、藪をくぐって逃げたのかも知れない。——わたしはそう考えると、今度はわたしの命ですから、太刀や弓矢を奪ったなり、すぐにまたもとの山路（やまみち）へ出ました。其処（そこ）にはまだ女の馬が、静かに草を食っています。その後（ご）の事は申し上げるだけ、無用の口数（くちかず）に過ぎますまい。唯、都へはいる前に、太刀だけはもう手放していました。——わたしの白状はこれだけです。どうせ一度は樗（おうち）の梢（こずえ）に、懸（か）ける首と思っていますから、どうか極刑（ごくけい）に遇（あ）わせて下さい。（昂然（こうぜん）たる態度）

Perhaps the woman had slipped out of the thicket and run off to call for help as soon as we started our duel. When this occurred to me, I realized that now it was my life that was in danger, so I helped myself to his sword, bow and arrows, and rushed back out onto the mountain road. The woman's horse was still there nibbling quietly on the grass. No point in wasting words telling you what happened afterward. Before I came into town, I had already got rid of the sword. That is my whole confession. I always thought my head would end up on top of a stake anyway, so you go ahead and put me to death. [*Attitude of triumph.*]

....

申し上げる【もうしあげる】say, tell (super-humble form of いう) [2186] + [2128]

無用の【むようの】futile, useless [1351] + [1889]

口数【くちかず】number of words [2119] + [1170]

過ぎる【すぎる】exceed [2003]

〜まい not 〜

唯【ただ】just, only [0339]

都【みやこ】the capital (Kyoto) [1106]

はいる enter, go in

前【まえ】before [1453]

手放す【てばなす】get rid of [2155] + [0570]

白状【はくじょう】confession [2175] + [0204]

どうせ anyhow

一度【いちど】just once [2105] + [1974]

樗【おうち】sumac (Japanese bead tree) [-]

梢【こずえ】top (of a tree) [0656]

懸ける【かける】hang [1855]

首【くび】head [1452]

思う【おもう】think [1633]

どうか please

極刑【ごくけい】extreme penalty, execution [0695] + [0555]

遇わせる【あわせる】inflict [2001]

〜て下さい【〜てください】please 〜 [2115]

昂然たる【こうぜんたる】elated, triumphant [1562] + [1779]

態度【たいど】attitude [1822] + [1974]

清水寺に来れる女の懺悔

　　——その紺の水干を着た男は、わたしを手ごめにしてしまうと、縛られた夫を眺めながら、嘲るように笑いました。夫はどんなに無念だったでしょう。が、いくら身悶えをしても、体中にかかった縄目は、一層ひしひしと食い入るだけです。わたしは思わず夫の側へ、転ぶように走り寄りました。いえ、走り寄ろうとしたのです。しかし男は咄嗟の間に、わたしを其処へ蹴倒しました。丁度その途端です。わたしは夫の眼の中に、何ともいいようのない輝きが、宿っているのを覚りました。何ともいいようのない、——わたしはあの眼を思い出すと、今でも身震いが出ずにはいられません。

清水寺【きよみずでら】Kiyomizudera temple [0384] + [0003] + [1367]
来れる【きたれる】come (classical form of くる) [2211]
女【おんな】woman [2135]
懺悔【ざんげ】confession [-] + [0270]

紺【こん】deep blue, navy blue [0899]
水干【すいかん】everyday garment worn by commoners [0003] + [2116]
着る【きる】wear [2086]
男【おとこ】man ⚐ [1613]
手ごめにする【てごめにする】rape [2155]
〜てしまう expresses completion of an action with regret
縛る【しばる】tie up [0949]

夫【おっと】husband ⚐ [2157]
眺める【ながめる】look at [0795]
〜ながら while, as
嘲る【あざける】mock, insult [-]
〜ように like, as if ⚐
笑う【わらう】laugh [1692]
どんなに to what extent, how much (= どのように)
無念【むねん】resentful, mortified [1351] + [1304]
身悶えをする【みもだえをする】squirm, wriggle [2213] + [-]
体中【からだじゅう】all over the body [0052] + [2150]
かかる be covered with, be caught in
縄目【なわめ】knot [0942] + [1927]

The Confession of the Woman Visitor to Kiyomizudera Temple

That man in the blue kimono first raped me. Then he looked at my husband, who was tied up, and laughed with contempt. My poor husband's feelings of humiliation can hardly be imagined! But no matter how much he struggled, the rope just dug deeper into his body. Driven by instinct, I staggered up and rushed over to my husband's side—no, I tried to run over to him, but the man kicked me straight down to the ground. It was precisely then that … I became aware of an indescribable glint in the eyes of my husband. I can't describe it … but when I think about the expression in his eyes, even now I can't stop shaking.

一層【いっそう】only more [2105] + [2021]
ひしひしと tightly
食い入る【くいいる】bite, dig in [1316] + [2113]
思わず【おもわず】instinctively, without thinking [1633]
側【そば】side, beside [0105]
転ぶ【ころぶ】fall, stumble [0995]
走り寄る【はしりよる】run up to [1390] + [1473]
しかし but, however
咄嗟の間【とっさのあいだ】space of an instant [-] + [-] + [2094]
其処【そこ】there [-] + [1918]
蹴倒す【けたおす】kick to the ground [-] + [0093]
丁度【ちょうど】exactly, precisely [2106] + [1974]

途端【とたん】moment, instant [1980] + [0826]
眼【め】eye 🦌 [0796]
中【なか】inside [2150]
何ともいいようのない【なんともいいようのない】indescribable 🦌 [0045]
輝き【かがやき】flicker, gleam [0947]
宿る【やどる】lodge, dwell in [1475]
覚る【さとる】perceive [1668]
思い出す【おもいだす】remember [1633] + [2180]
今でも【いまでも】even now [1246]
身震いが出ず【みぶるいがでず】not shudder/shake [2213] + [1794] + [2180]
いられる potential form of いる

口さえ一言も利けない夫は、その刹那の眼の中に、一切の心を伝えたのです。しかも其処に閃いていたのは、怒りでもなければ悲しみでもない、——唯わたしを蔑んだ、冷たい光だったではありませんか？　わたしは男に蹴られたよりも、その眼の色に打たれたように、我知らず何か叫んだぎり、とうとう気を失ってしまいました。

　その内にやっと気がついて見ると、あの紺の水干の男は、もう何処かへ行っていました。跡には唯杉の根がたに、夫が縛られているだけです。

25

口を利く【くちをきく】speak [2119] + [0757]
～さえ even
一言【いちごん】single word [2105] + [1233]
夫【おっと】husband 愛 [2157]
刹那【せつな】instant, moment [-] + [0564]
眼【め】eye 愛 [0796]
中【なか】in, inside [2150]
一切【いっさい】all, everything [2105] + [0015]
心【こころ】feelings, heart [0004]
伝える【つたえる】communicate, transmit [0028]
しかも moreover, furthermore
其処に【そこに】there, at that point [-] + [1918]
閃く【ひらめく】flash, well up [-]
怒り【いかり】anger [1639]
悲しみ【かなしみ】sorrow [1775]
唯【ただ】just, only 愛 [0339]
蔑む【さげすむ】despise [-]
冷たい【つめたい】cold, icy [0057]
光【ひかり】gleam [1550]

男【おとこ】man 愛 [1613]
蹴る【ける】kick [-]
～よりも more than
色【いろ】expression [1280]
打つ【うつ】hit, strike [0142]
～ように as if, like
我知らず【われしらず】unconsciously, forgetting oneself [2208] + [0768]
何か【なにか】something [0045]
叫ぶ【さけぶ】cry out, shout [0149]
～ぎり expresses finality with no further action expected
とうとう finally, at length
気を失う【きをうしなう】lose consciousness [2037] + [2189]
～てしまう expresses completion of an action with regret

25

その内【そのうち】meanwhile, after a while [2162]
やっと finally, at last
気がつく【きがつく】come to, regain con-

My husband was not able to say anything, but, in that brief instant, the look in his eyes told me everything in his heart. It wasn't anger or sorrow that burned in his eyes—it was a fire of coldest contempt. The expression in those eyes hurt me more than the robber's kicks. I lost control of myself, shrieked wildly, and finally passed out.

Time passed. When I eventually came to, the man in the blue kimono was long gone. All that was left was my husband tied to the trunk of the cedar.

....

sciousness [2037]
〜て見る【〜てみる】try to 〜 [1615]
紺【こん】deep blue, navy blue [0899]
水干【すいかん】everyday garment worn
   by commoners [0003] + [2116]
何処か【どこか】somewhere [0045] + [1918]
行く【いく】go [0157]
跡【あと】aftermath [1032]
杉【すぎ】cedar [0557]
根がた【ねがた】trunk [0631]
夫【おっと】husband [2157]
縛る【しばる】tie up [0949]

わたしは竹の落葉の上に、やっと体を起したなり、夫の顔を見守りました。が、夫の眼の色は、少しもさっきと変りません。やはり冷たい蔑みの底に、憎しみの色を見せているのです。恥しさ、悲しさ、腹立たしさ、──その時のわたしの心の中(うち)は、何といえば好(よ)いかわかりません。わたしはよろよろ立ち上りながら、夫の側へ近寄りました。

「あなた。もうこうなった上は、あなたと御一しょにはおられません。わたしは一思いに死ぬ覚悟です。しかし、──しかしあなたもお死になすって下さい。あなたはわたしの恥を御覧になりました。わたしはこのままあなた一人、お残し申す訳には参りません。」

竹【たけ】bamboo [0168]
落葉【おちば】fallen leaves [1494] + [1497]
上【うえ】on, upon [2128]
やっと finally, at length, with difficulty
体【からだ】body [0052]
起す【おこす】raise, lift up [2079]
〜なり (after a verb in the past tense) having ~
夫【おっと】husband 象 [2157]
顔【かお】face [1177]
見守る【みまもる】look steadily at [1615] + [1375]
眼【め】eyes [0796]
色【いろ】color, expression 象 [1280]
少しも【すこしも】(+ negative) not a bit [2163]
さっき before
変る【かわる】change [1311]

やはり sure enough
冷たい【つめたい】cold, indifferent [0057]
蔑み【さげすみ】contempt [-]
底【そこ】base, bottom [1961]
憎しみ【にくしみ】hate [0489]
見せる【みせる】show, reveal [1615]
恥しさ【はずかしさ】shame, embarrassment [0882]
悲しさ【かなしさ】sorrow, sadness [1775]
腹立たしさ【はらだたしさ】anger [0710] + [1257]
時【とき】time, moment [0625]
心【こころ】heart [0004]
中【うち】in, inside [2150]
何といえば好いか【なんといえばよいか】indescribable [0045] + [0155]
わかる know
よろよろ unsteadily

With difficulty I lifted myself up off the bamboo leaves, and looked long and hard at my husband's face. The expression in his eyes had not changed at all. There was the same cold contempt, with hatred lurking beneath. Shame, sorrow, rage—I cannot describe my emotions at that moment. I clambered unsteadily to my feet and went over to my husband.

"After what has happened today, I cannot stay with you, Takehiro. I have made up my mind and have resolved to die. However— I want you to die with me. You witnessed my humiliation, so I cannot let you live on alone."

立ち上る【たちあがる】stand up [1257] + [2128]

〜ながら while, as

側【そば】side, nearby [0105]

近寄る【ちかよる】approach [1941] + [1473]

26

こうなった上【こうなったうえ】with things in this situation [2128]

〜と御一しょに 【〜とごいっしょに】 together with (honorific form) [2105] + [0422]

おる =いる (polite form)

一思い【ひとおもい】of one mind, of fixed purpose [2105] + [1633]

死ぬ【しぬ】die 🐾 [2194]

覚悟【かくご】determination [1668] + [0312]

しかし but, however 🐾

なする =なさる (polite form of する) [2194]

〜て下さい【〜てください】please 〜 [2115]

恥【はじ】shame [0882]

御覧になる【ごらんになる】see (honorific form of みる) [0422] + [1827]

このまま in this state, with things as they are

一人【ひとり】one person [2105] + [2111]

残す【のこす】leave (alive) [0640]

〜申す訳には参りません【〜もうすわけにはまいりません】be unable to 〜, cannot very well 〜 (humble form of 〜する わけにはいかない) [2186] + [0989] + [1308]

わたしは一生懸命に、これだけの事をいいました。それでも夫は忌わしそうに、わたしを見つめているばかりなのです。わたしは裂けそうな胸を抑えながら、夫の太刀を探しました。が、あの盗人に奪われたのでしょう、太刀は勿論弓矢さえも、藪の中には見当りません。しかし幸い小刀だけは、わたしの足もとに落ちているのです。わたしはその小刀を振り上げると、もう一度夫にこういいました。

「ではお命を頂かせて下さい。わたしもすぐにお供します。」

....

27

一生懸命【いっしょうけんめい】diligently, with all one's effort [2105] + [2179] + [1855] + [1303]

事【こと】thing [2220]

いう say, speak 💀

夫【おっと】husband 💀 [2157]

忌わしい【いまわしい】loathsome, horrible [1401]

見つめる【みつめる】gaze fixedly [1615]

～ばかり just, only

裂ける【さける】burst, split [1727]

胸【むね】chest, breast [0647]

抑える【おさえる】suppress, fight down [0193]

～ながら while, as

太刀【たち】sword 💀 [1360] + [1857]

探す【さがす】look for, find [0374]

盗人【ぬすびと】robber [1714] + [2111]

奪う【うばう】take, steal [1517]

勿論【もちろん】of course [-] + [1058]

弓矢【ゆみや】bow and arrows [2120] + [1267]

～さえ even

藪【やぶ】grove [-]

中【なか】in, inside [2150]

見当る【みあたる】be seen, be found [1615] + [1378]

しかし but, however

幸い【さいわい】fortunately [1408]

小刀【さすが】dagger 💀 [0002] + [1857]

足もと【あしもと】at one's feet [1386]

落ちる【おちる】fall [1494]

振り上げる【ふりあげる】pick up, brandish [0316] + [2128]

もう一度【もういちど】one more time [2105] + [2111]

28

命【いのち】life [1303]

頂く【いただく】take, receive [0108]

～て下さい【～てください】please ～ [2115]

すぐに at once

供をする【ともをする】accompany [0066]

I had forced myself to spell things out. But my husband just kept staring at me with a look of revulsion. I suppressed my feelings—my heart was about to explode—and looked around for my husband's sword. I suppose that the robber must have stolen it. In the grove there was no sign of the sword or the bow and arrows either. Luckily, though, my dagger was still there, lying at my feet. I raised it high, and spoke again to my husband.

"Let me take your life. I shall accompany you presently."

夫はこの言葉を聞いた時、やっと唇を動かしました。勿論口には笹の落葉が、一ぱいにつまっていますから、声は少しも聞えません。が、わたしはそれを見ると、忽ちその言葉を覚りました。夫はわたしを蔑んだまま、『殺せ』と一言いったのです。わたしは殆ど、夢うつつの内に、夫の縹の水干の胸へ、ずぶりと小刀を刺し通しました。

わたしはまたこの時も、気を失ってしまったのでしょう。やっとあたりを見まわした時には、夫はもう縛られたまま、とうに息が絶えていました。その蒼ざめた顔の上には、竹に交った杉むらの空から、西日が一すじ落ちているのです。

夫【おっと】husband 👤 [2157]
言葉【ことば】words, remark 👤 [1233] + [1497]
聞く【きく】hear [2097]
時【とき】time, moment 👤 [0625]
やっと barely, slightly, finally 👤
唇【くちびる】lips [1752]
動かす【うごかす】move [1163]
勿論【もちろん】of course [-] + [1058]
口【くち】mouth [2119]
笹【ささ】bamboo grass [1708]
落葉【おちば】fallen leaves [1494] + [1497]
一ぱい【いっぱい】fully, completely [2105]
つまる be stuffed, be blocked
声【こえ】voice [1393]
少しも【すこしも】(+ negative) not even a little bit [2163]
聞える【きこえる】be audible [2097]
見る【みる】see [1615]

忽ち【たちまち】in a moment, all at once [-]
覚る【さとる】know, understand [1668]
蔑む【さげすむ】despise [-]
～まま still 👤
殺す【ころす】kill [0889]
一言【ひとこと】one word, laconic utterance [2105] + [1233]
いう say, speak
殆ど【ほとんど】almost, more or less [-]
夢うつつ【ゆめうつつ】dreamlike state [1510]
内【うち】in [2162]
縹【はなだ】pale blue [-]
水干【すいかん】everyday garment worn by commoners [0003] + [2116]
胸【むね】chest [0647]
ずぶりと directly, boldly
小刀【さすが】dagger [0002] + [1857]
刺し通す【さしとおす】stab right through [0855] + [1982]

When my husband heard these words, his lips moved ever so slightly. Of course, since his mouth was crammed full of bamboo leaves, I couldn't hear a word he said. But I was watching and I knew straightaway what he had said. "Kill me" was his brief and still contemptuous reply. I was almost in a trance as I plunged the dagger through his light-blue kimono and deep into his chest.

At that point I must have fainted again. When I was able to look around me, my husband was still tied up, but his breathing had stopped a while ago. From the sky up above the bamboo and cedars a single ray of the sinking sun shone upon his ashen face.

30

また once again
気を失う【きをうしなう】faint, lose consciousness [2037] + [2189]
あたり surroundings
見まわす【みまわす】look around [1615]
縛る【しばる】tie up [0949]
とうに some while ago
息【いき】breath, breathing [1693]
絶える【たえる】stop, cease [0917]
蒼ざめる【あおざめる】turn pale/pallid [1512]
顔【かお】face [1177]
上【うえ】above [2128]
竹【たけ】bamboo [0168]
交る【まじる】be mixed with [1272]
杉むら【すぎむら】patch of cedars [0557]
空【そら】the sky [1418]
西日【にしび】western sunlight, sinking sun [2193] + [1915]

一すじ【ひとすじ】one ray [2105]
落ちる【おちる】fall [1494]

わたしは泣き声を呑みながら、死骸の縄を解き捨てました。そうして、――そうしてわたしがどうなったか？　それだけはもうわたしには、申し上げる力もありません。とにかくわたしはどうしても、死に切る力がなかったのです。小刀を喉に突き立てたり、山の裾の池へ身を投げたり、いろいろな事もして見ましたが、死に切れずにこうしている限り、これも自慢にはなりますまい。（寂しき微笑）わたしのように腑甲斐ないものは、大慈大悲の観世音菩薩も、お見放しなすったものかも知れません。しかし夫を殺したわたしは、盗人の手ごめに遇ったわたしは、一体どうすれば好いのでしょう？　一体わたしは、――わたしは、――（突然烈しき歔欷）

Gulping back my sobs, I untied the rope from the body and threw it to one side. And then—then what became of me? Oh, I do not have the energy to tell you that. I suppose I lacked the willpower to kill myself. I stabbed myself in the throat with a dagger; I threw myself into a pond at the foot of the mountain—I tried all sorts of things. But despite it all, I was not able to kill myself, so I have nothing to be proud of. [*Sad smile.*] Even Kannon the Compassionate has probably forsaken a coward like me. But I killed my own husband; I was raped by a common thief. What should I do? In God's name what should I do? [*Sudden burst of sobbing.*]

～のように like
腑甲斐ない【ふがいない】cowardly, faint-hearted [-] + [2169] + [1776]
もの person
大慈大悲【だいじだいひ】very merciful and compassionate [2133] + [1515] + [2133] + [1775]
観世音菩薩【かんぜおんぼさつ】the bodhisattva Avalokiteśvara (Kannon) [1212] + [2178] + [1312] + [-] + [-]
見放す【みはなす】abandon [1615] + [0570]
なする =なさる (polite form of する)
～かも知れない【～かもしれない】maybe, perhaps [0768]
しかし but, however
夫【おっと】husband [2157]
殺す【ころす】kill [0889]
盗人【ぬすびと】robber [1714] + [2111]

手ごめ【てごめ】rape [2155]
遇う【あう】undergo, experience [2001]
一体【いったい】what on earth! (exclamation) 愛 [2105] + [0052]
好い【よい】good, right, proper [0155]
突然【とつぜん】suddenly [1421] + [1779]
烈しき【はげしき】violent, intense (classical form of 烈しい) [1698]
歔欷【すすりなき】sobbing [-] + [-]

巫女の口を借りたる死霊の物語

　　——盗人は妻を手ごめにすると、其処へ腰を下したまま、いろいろ妻を慰め出した。おれは勿論口は利けない。体も杉の根に縛られている。が、おれはその間に、何度も妻へ目くばせをした。この男のいう事を真に受けるな、何をいっても嘘と思え、——おれはそんな意味を伝えたいと思った。しかし妻は悄然と笹の落葉に坐ったなり、じっと膝へ目をやっている。それがどうも盗人の言葉に、聞き入っているように見えるではないか？　おれは妬しさに身悶えをした。が、盗人はそれからそれへと、巧妙に話を進めている。

巫女【みこ】spirit medium [-] + [2135]
口【くち】mouth [2119]
借りたる【かりたる】borrow, make use of (classical form of 借りる) [0091]
死霊【しりょう】ghost [2194] + [1793]
物語【ものがたり】tale, account [0587] + [1040]

31

盗人【ぬすびと】robber [1714] + [2111]
妻【つま】my wife [1628]
手ごめにする【てごめにする】rape [2155]
其処【そこ】there [-] + [1918]
腰を下す【こしをおろす】sit down [0711] + [2115]
〜まま still
いろいろ in many ways
慰め出す【なぐさめだす】begin to console [1835] + [2180]
おれ me, I, myself (masculine)

勿論【もちろん】of course [-] + [1058]
口を利く【くちをきく】speak [2119] + [0757]
体【からだ】body [0052]
杉【すぎ】cedar [0557]
根【ね】root [0631]
縛る【しばる】tie up [0949]
間【あいだ】duration, meantime [2094]
何度も【なんども】many times [0045] + [1974]
目くばせ【めくばせ】glances, winking, eye signals [1927]
男【おとこ】man [1613]
いう say, speak
事【こと】thing [2220]
真に受ける【まにうける】take at face value [1337] + [1569]
〜な do not ~!
何【なに】what, whatever [0045]

The Account of the Ghost as Transmitted Through a Medium

After the robber had raped my wife, he sat near her, and began to say all sorts of comforting things. I, of course, was unable to speak and was lashed to the trunk of the cedar. But, in the meanwhile, I kept giving her looks: "Don't take anything this man says at face value. Whatever he says, it's a lie!" was the message I was trying to send. But my wife just sat dejectedly upon the dead leaves, staring down at her knees. It really looked to me as if she was listening intently to what the robber was saying. Jealousy made me writhe. But the robber craftily steered the conversation from one topic to another.

....

嘘【うそ】lie [-]
思う【おもう】think, feel 灸 [1633]
意味【いみ】meaning [1352] + [0206]
伝える【つたえる】communicate, transmit [0028]
しかし but, however
悄然と【しょうぜんと】dejectedly, despondently [-] + [1779]
笹【ささ】bamboo grass [1708]
落葉【おちば】fallen leaves [1494] + [1497]
坐る【すわる】sit [-]
〜なり (after a verb in the past tense) still, in the unchanged state of
じっと fixedly
膝【ひざ】knees [-]
目をやる【めをやる】look at [1927]
どうも somehow
言葉【ことば】words, remark [1233] + [1497]

聞き入る【ききいる】listen raptly [2097] + [2113]
〜ように as if, like
見える【みえる】seem, appear [1615]
妬しさ【ねたましさ】jealousy [-]
身悶えをする【みもだえをする】writhe, squirm [2213] + [-]
それからそれへ from one thing to the next
巧妙に【こうみょうに】craftily, adroitly [0138] + [0176]
話【はなし】conversation, talk [1027]
進める【すすめる】push forward, drive [1991]

一度でも肌身を汚したとなれば、夫との仲も折り合うまい。そんな夫に連れ添っているより、自分の妻になる気はないか？　自分はいとしいと思えばこそ、大それた真似も働いたのだ、──盗人はとうとう大胆にも、そういう話さえ持ち出した。

　盗人にこういわれると、妻はうっとりと顔を擡げた。おれはまだあの時ほど、美しい妻は見た事がない。しかしその美しい妻は、現在縛られたおれを前に、何と盗人に返事をしたか？　おれは中有に迷っていても、妻の返事を思い出すごとに、嗔恚に燃えなかったためしはない。妻は確かにこういった、──「では何処へでもつれて行って下さい。」（長き沈黙）

一度【いちど】once [2105] + [1974]
肌身【はだみ】body [0553] + [2213]
汚す【けがす】soil, make dirty [0163]
夫【おっと】husband ☙ [2157]
仲【なか】good relations, friendship [0027]
折り合う【おりあう】get along with [0189] + [1274]
〜まい not 〜
連れ添う【つれそう】be married to, live together with [1976] + [0390]
自分【じぶん】me ☙ [2195] + [1247]
妻【つま】wife ☙ [1628]
気【き】wish, inclination [2037]
いとしい dear, beloved
思う【おもう】think, feel [1633]
〜こそ precisely because
大それた【だいそれた】audacious, bold [2133]

真似【まね】behavior, act [1337] + [0043]
働く【はたらく】do, perform [0113]
盗人【ぬすびと】robber ☙ [1714] + [2111]
とうとう finally, at length
大胆に【だいたんに】boldly [2133] + [0622]
話【はなし】talk, proposal [1027]
〜さえ even
持ち出す【もちだす】bring forth, suggest [0275] + [2180]

いう say, speak ☙
うっとりと spellbound, infatuatedly
顔【かお】face [1177]
擡げる【もたげる】lift, raise [-]
おれ me, I, myself (masculine) ☙
まだ not yet
時【とき】time, moment [0625]

"Now that you've been defiled, you'll never be able to reconcile with your husband. So, rather than stick with him, how about becoming my wife? The truth is, it was the love I felt for you that made me do the wicked thing I did." This was the shameless proposal that the robber finally had the gall to make.

After the robber had spoken, my wife lifted her face. She looked rapturous, entranced. I had never seen her look so beautiful as she did then. But what do you think my beautiful wife replied to the robber, right in front of me as I sat tied up there? I may now be floating in limbo, but every single time her answer comes back to me, I am on fire with wrath. For my wife really and truly said, "Take me with you wherever you go." [*Long silence.*]

....

～ほど to the extent of
美しい【うつくしい】beautiful 愛 [1451]
見る【みる】see [1615]
事【こと】experience [2220]
しかし but, however
現在【げんざい】now, at present [0657] + [1896]
縛る【しばる】tie up [0949]
前【まえ】before, in front of [1453]
何と【なんと】what [0045]
返事【へんじ】answer 愛 [1940] + [2220]
中有【ちゅうう】space, limbo [2150] + [1895]
迷う【まよう】wander, stray [1967]
思い出す【おもいだす】recall, remember [1633] + [2180]
～ごとに each time (one does something)
嗔恚【しんい】wrath, anger [-] + [-]

燃える【もえる】burn [0739]
ためし example, instance, experience
確かに【たしかに】for sure, certainly [0830]
何処へでも【どこへでも】anywhere [0045] + [1918]
つれる take (someone)
～て行く【～ていく】~ away [0157]
～て下さい【～てください】please ~ [2115]
長き【ながき】long, lengthy (classical form of 長い) [1626]
沈黙【ちんもく】silence [0195] + [1833]

妻の罪はそれだけではない。それだけならばこの闇の中に、いまほどおれも苦しみはしまい。しかし妻は夢のように、盗人に手をとられながら、藪の外へ行こうとすると、忽ち顔色を失ったなり、杉の根のおれを指さした。「あの人を殺して下さい。わたしはあの人が生きていては、あなたと一しょにはいられません。」──妻は気が狂ったように、何度もこう叫び立てた。「あの人を殺して下さい。」──この言葉は嵐のように、今でも遠い闇の底へ、まっ逆様におれを吹き落そうとする。一度でもこの位憎むべき言葉が、人間の口を出た事があろうか？

妻【つま】wife 💀 [1628]

罪【つみ】sin, crime [1673]

闇【やみ】darkness 💀 [-]

中【なか】in, within [2150]

いま now

〜ほど as much as 〜

おれ me, I, myself (masculine) 💀

苦しみ【くるしみ】suffering [1433]

〜しまい =しない

しかし but, however

夢【ゆめ】dream [1510]

〜のように like, as if 💀

盗人【ぬすびと】thief [1714] + [2111]

手をとる【てをとる】take one's hand [2155]

〜ながら while, as

藪【やぶ】grove [-]

外【そと】outside [0135]

行く【ゆく】go [0157]

忽ち【たちまち】in a moment, all at once [-]

顔色【がんしょく】complexion, facial color [1177] + [1280]

失う【うしなう】lose [2189]

〜なり (after a verb in the past tense) having 〜

杉【すぎ】cedar [0557]

根【ね】root [0631]

指さす【ゆびさす】point at with the finger [0278]

人【ひと】person 💀 [2111]

殺す【ころす】kill 💀 [0889]

〜て下さい【〜てください】please 〜 💀 [2115]

生きる【いきる】live [2179]

〜と一しょに【〜といっしょに】together with [2105]

気が狂う【きがくるう】go crazy [2037] + [0202]

何度も【なんども】many times, repeatedly [0045] + [1974]

叫び立てる【さけびたてる】call out [0149] +

But that was not the extent of her crime. If it were, my suf-ferings in this nether-darkness would not be as sharp as they are now. Just as my wife—dazed, hand in hand with the robber—was about to leave the grove, her face suddenly went white, and she pointed her finger at me there at the base of the cedar. "Kill that man, I beg of you. As long as that man is alive, I cannot be with you," she shrieked, over and over again, like one gone mad. "Kill that man, I beg you." The memory of those words is like a storm that even now can throw me headlong deep down into the abyss of darkness. Have such evil words ever before come forth from human mouth?

- -

[1257]
言葉【ことば】words, remark 💀 [1233] + [1497]
嵐【あらし】storm [1491]
〜のように like
今でも【いまでも】even now [1246]
遠い【とおい】distant [2013]
底【そこ】depths [1961]
まっ逆様に【まっさかさまに】headfirst
[1966] + [0723]
吹き落す【ふきおとす】blow down [0170] +
[1494]
一度【いちど】once 💀 [2105] + [1974]
位【くらい】degree, extent 💀 [0042]
憎むべき【にくむべき】hateful [0489]
人間【にんげん】person, human [2111] +
[2094]
口【くち】mouth [2119]
出る【でる】come out, emerge [2180]
事【こと】thing [2220]

一度でもこの位呪わしい言葉が、人間の耳に触れた事があろうか？　一度でもこの位、──（突然迸る如き嘲笑）その言葉を聞いた時は、盗人さえ色を失ってしまった。「あの人を殺して下さい。」──妻はそう叫びながら、盗人の腕に縋っている。盗人はじっと妻を見たまま、殺すとも殺さぬとも返事をしない。──と思うか思わない内に、妻は竹の落葉の上へ、唯一蹴りに蹴倒された。（再、迸る如き嘲笑）盗人は静かに両腕を組むと、おれの姿へ眼をやった。「あの女はどうするつもりだ？　殺すか、それとも助けてやるか？返事は唯頷けば好い。殺すか？」──おれはこの言葉だけでも、盗人の罪は赦してやりたい。（再、長き沈黙）

一度【いちど】once 🦋 [2105] + [1974]

位【くらい】degree, extent 🦋 [0042]

呪わしい【のろわしい】hateful, accursed [-]

言葉【ことば】words, remark 🦋 [1233] + [2220]

人間【にんげん】person, human [2111] + [2094]

耳【みみ】ear [2190]

触れる【ふれる】touch [1018]

事【こと】thing, event [2220]

突然【とつぜん】suddenly [1421] + [1779]

迸る【ほとばしる】spurt forth, gush out 🦋 [-]

如き【ごとき】like (classical form of ～ような) 🦋 [0154]

嘲笑【ちょうしょう】cold/scornful laugh 🦋 [-] + [1692]

聞く【きく】hear [2097]

時【とき】when [0625]

盗人【ぬすびと】thief 🦋 [1714] + [2111]

～さえ even

色を失う【いろをうしなう】turn pale (with surprise) [1280] + [2189]

～てしまう thoroughly ～

人【ひと】person [2111]

殺す【ころす】kill 🦋 [0889]

～て下さい【～てください】please ～ [2115]

妻【つま】wife 🦋 [1628]

叫ぶ【さけぶ】cry out [0149]

～ながら while, as

腕【うで】arm [0687]

縋る【すがる】cling to [-]

じっと fixedly

見る【みる】look at [1615]

～まま still

Have such cursed words ever before been heard by the human ear? Have ever … [*He bursts into a sudden mocking laugh.*] When he heard her say this, even the robber went pale. "Kill that man, I beg of you," my wife shrieked as she clung to his arm. The robber just stared at her and did not respond as to whether he would kill me or not. I was still wondering what his answer would be when my wife was knocked down to the forest floor with a single kick. [*Once again he bursts into a sudden mocking laugh.*] The robber calmly folded his arms and looked over to me. "What do you want to do with that woman? Kill her? Or let her live? A simple nod is answer enough." These words are enough to make me want to forgive him his crime. [*Another long silence.*]

殺さぬ【ころさぬ】not kill [0889]
返事【へんじ】answer 👤 [1940] + [2220]
思うか思わない内に【おもうかおもわないうちに】even as one thinks, before one knows it, suddenly [1633] + [2162]
竹【たけ】bamboo [0168]
落葉【おちば】fallen leaves [1494] + [1497]
上【うえ】on [2128]
唯【ただ】just, only 👤 [0339]
一蹴り【ひとけり】one kick [2105] + [-]
蹴倒す【けたおす】kick to the ground [-] + [0093]
再【ふたたび】once again 👤 [2192]
静かに【しずかに】quietly [1138]
両腕を組む【りょううでをくむ】cross both arms [2191] + [0687] + [0904]
おれ me, I, myself (masculine) 👤

姿【すがた】shape, body [1684]
眼をやる【めをやる】look at [0796]
女【おんな】woman [2135]
〜つもり intend to ~
助ける【たすける】help, save, let live [0764]
〜てやる do for someone 👤
頷く【うなずく】nod [-]
好い【よい】good, sufficient [0155]
罪【つみ】crime, sin [1673]
赦す【ゆるす】forgive [0993]
長き【ながき】long, lengthy (classical form of 長い) [1626]
沈黙【ちんもく】silence [0195] + [1833]

妻はおれがためらう内に、何か一声叫ぶが早いか、忽ち藪の奥へ走り出した。盗人も咄嗟に飛びかかったが、これは袖さえ捉えなかったらしい。おれは唯幻のように、そういう景色を眺めていた。

盗人は妻が逃げ去った後、太刀や弓矢を取り上げると、一箇所だけおれの縄を切った。「今度はおれの身の上だ。」——おれは盗人が藪の外へ、姿を隠してしまう時に、こう呟いたのを覚えている。その跡は何処も静かだった。いや、まだ誰かの泣く声がする。おれは縄を解きながら、じっと耳を澄ませて見た。が、その声も気がついて見れば、おれ自身の泣いている声だったではないか？（三度、長き沈黙）

34

妻【つま】wife 🐾 [1628]
おれ me, I, myself (masculine) 🐾
ためらう hesitate
〜内に【〜うちに】while, as [2162]
何か【なにか】something [0045]
一声【ひとこえ】a single cry [2105] + [1393]
叫ぶ【さけぶ】shout, cry [0149]
〜が早いか【〜がはやいか】as soon as [1549]
忽ち【たちまち】in an instant, all at once [-]
藪【やぶ】grove [-]
奥【おく】depths, remote part [1806]
走り出す【はしりだす】begin to run off [1390] + [2180]
盗人【ぬすびと】robber 🐾 [1714] + [2111]
咄嗟に【とっさに】promptly, instantaneously [-] + [-]
飛びかかる【とびかかる】spring after [2222]

袖【そで】sleeve [-]
〜さえ even
捉える【とらえる】snatch, grab [0365]
唯【ただ】just, only [0339]
幻【まぼろし】ghost [0132]
〜のように like
景色【けしき】scene, sight [1597] + [1280]
眺める【ながめる】look at, gaze at [0795]

35

逃げ去る【にげさる】run away [1970] + [1364]
〜後【〜のち】after [0267]
太刀【たち】sword [1360] + [1857]
弓矢【ゆみや】bow and arrows [2120] + [1267]
取り上げる【とりあげる】pick up [0847] + [2128]
一箇所【いっかしょ】one point/part [2105] + [1735] + [0568]
縄【なわ】rope 🐾 [0942]

I hesitated. My wife shrieked, then ran deeper into the thicket. The robber sprang after her right away, but could not even get a grip on her sleeve. I just observed the scene like a ghost.

After my wife had fled, the robber picked up my sword and bow and arrows, then cut my rope in one place. "Now it's my life that's on the line," I remember the robber muttering to himself as he disappeared from the grove. After that there was complete silence. I'm wrong, there was the sound of someone crying. As I shuffled off the rope, I strained to listen. It was then that I realized it was the sound of myself weeping. [*For a third time, a long silence.*]

切る【きる】cut [0015]

今度【こんど】now, this time [1246] + [1974]

身の上【みのうえ】lot, fortune, life [2213] + [2128]

外【そと】outside [0135]

姿を隠す【すがたをかくす】disappear (*lit.*, "hide one's figure") [1684] + [0502]

〜てしまう expresses completion of an action with regret

時【とき】when [0625]

呟く【つぶやく】mutter, grumble [-]

覚える【おぼえる】remember [1668]

跡【あと】afterward [1032]

何処も【どこも】everywhere [0045] + [1918]

静か【しずか】quiet, silent [1138]

誰か【だれか】someone [-]

泣く声【なくこえ】weeping [0253] + [1393]

解く【とく】loosen [1017]

〜ながら while, as

じっと fixedly

耳を澄ませる【みみをすませる】prick up one's ears, listen carefully [2190] + [0517]

〜て見る【〜てみる】try to ~ 愛 [1615]

声【こえ】sound 愛 [1393]

気がつく【きがつく】realize, become aware [2037]

自身【じしん】oneself [2195] + [2213]

泣く【なく】weep, cry [0253]

三度【みたび】third time [1225] + [1974]

長き【ながき】long, lengthy (classical form of 長い) [1626]

沈黙【ちんもく】silence [0195] + [1833]

おれはやっと杉の根から、疲れ果てた体を起した。おれの前には妻が落した、小刀《さすが》が一つ光っている。おれはそれを手にとると、一突きにおれの胸へ刺した。何か腥い塊がおれの口へこみ上げて来る。が、苦しみは少しもない。唯《ただ》胸が冷たくなると、一層あたりがしんとしてしまった。ああ、何という静かさだろう。この山陰《やまかげ》の藪の空には、小鳥一羽囀《さえず》りに来ない。唯杉や竹の杪《うら》に、寂しい日影が漂っている。日影が、――それも次第に薄れて来る。もう杉や竹も見えない。おれは其処《そこ》に倒れたまま、深い静かさに包まれている。

おれ me, I, myself (masculine) 💀
やっと finally, with difficulty
杉【すぎ】cedar 💀 [0557]
根【ね】root [0631]
疲れ果てる【つかれはてる】be utterly exhausted [2060] + [2217]
体【からだ】body [0052]
起す【おこす】lift upright [2079]
前【まえ】in front, before [1453]
妻【つま】wife [1628]
落す【おとす】drop [1494]
小刀【さすが】dagger [0002] + [1857]
一つ【ひとつ】one [2105]
光る【ひかる】shine [1550]
手にとる【てにとる】pick up [2155]
一突き【ひとつき】one stab [2105] + [1421]
胸【むね】chest 💀 [0647]
刺す【さす】stab [0855]

何か【なにか】something [0045]
腥い【なまぐさい】rank, raw and bloody [-]
塊【かたまり】lump [0457]
口【くち】mouth [2119]
こみ上げる【こみあげる】come up into [2128]
～て来る【～てくる】begin to ~ [2211]
苦しみ【くるしみ】pain, discomfort [1433]
少しも【すこしも】(+ negative) no ... whatsoever [2163]
唯【ただ】just 💀 [0339]
冷たい【つめたい】cold [0057]
一層【いっそう】all the more [2105] + [2021]
あたり surroundings
しんとする be silent
～てしまう expresses completion of an action with regret
何という【なんという】indescribable [0045]
静かさ【しずかさ】silence 💀 [1138]
山陰【やまかげ】shady part of the mountain [1867] + [0397]

I was exhausted, but with an effort I got up from the root of the cedar. In front of me gleamed the dagger that my wife had dropped. I took it in my hand and drove it into my chest with a single stroke. A reeking gout of blood rose up into my mouth. I felt no pain. Only as my chest grew cold, everything around grew hushed. Ah, what a silence that was! Not a single bird came to sing in the sky above the grove on that remote mountainside. A melancholy sunbeam played on the tips of the branches of the cedars and the bamboo. The sunbeam—that too slowly faded. I could no longer see the cedars or the bamboo. I lay where I had fallen, shrouded in that deep silence.

....

藪【やぶ】grove [-]
空【そら】the sky [1418]
小鳥【ことり】bird [0002] + [2083]
一羽【いちわ】one bird [2105] + [0167]
囀る【さえずる】sing, chirp [-]
来る【くる】come (to do something) [2211]
竹【たけ】bamboo 🐾 [0168]
杪【うら】tip of a branch [-]
寂しい【さびしい】lonely, mournful [1472]
日影【ひかげ】sunshine, light 🐾 [1915] + [1216]
漂う【ただよう】float [0493]
次第に【しだいに】gradually [0038] + [1706]
薄れる【うすれる】grow faint [1534]
〜て来る【〜てくる】expresses progression up to a point [2211]
見える【みえる】be visible, be able to see [1615]
其処に【そこに】there, at that point [-] + [1918]

倒れる【たおれる】collapse, fall to the ground [0093]
--まま still
深い【ふかい】deep [0385]
包む【つつむ】wrap, envelop [1880]

その時誰か忍び足に、おれの側へ来たものがある。おれ
はそちらを見ようとした。が、おれのまわりには、何時か
薄闇が立ちこめている。誰か、——その誰かは見えない手
に、そっと胸の小刀を抜いた。同時におれの口の中には、
もう一度血潮が溢れて来る。おれはそれぎり永久に、中有
の闇へ沈んでしまった。………………………………

37

時【とき】time [0625]

誰か【だれか】someone 🦊 [-]

忍び足【しのびあし】quiet steps [1407] + [1386]

おれ me, I, myself (masculine) 🦊

側【そば】side [0105]

来る【くる】come, approach [2211]

もの thing, person

見る【みる】see [1615]

まわり surroundings

何時か【いつか】at some time [0045] + [0625]

薄闇【うすやみ】twilight [1534] + [-]

立ちこめる【たちこめる】press in [1257]

見える【みえる】be visible, be able to see [1615]

手【て】hand [2155]

そっと quietly, discreetly

胸【むね】chest [0647]

小刀【さすが】dagger [0002] + [1857]

抜く【ぬく】extract, pull out [0183]

同時に【どうじに】at the same time [1897] + [0625]

口【くち】mouth [2119]

中【なか】in, inside [2150]

もう一度【もういちど】one more time [2105] + [1974]

血潮【ちしお】blood [2196] + [0516]

溢れる【あふれる】well up [-]

〜て来る【〜てくる】begin to 〜 [2211]

〜ぎり indicates that no further action is to come

永久に【えいきゅうに】for eternity

中有【ちゅうう】limbo [2150] + [1895]

闇【やみ】darkness [-]

沈む【しずむ】sink [0195]

〜てしまう expresses completion of an action with regret

It was then that someone crept stealthily up to me. I tried to see who it was, but the darkness had pressed in and enveloped me. Someone—someone drew the knife from my chest with a hand I could not see. At the same time, blood welled up into my mouth. And I sank into the darkness of limbo forever.

The Nose

A moral tale from the dawn of plastic surgery

This story first appeared in *Shinshichō* magazine in 1915. Upon its publication, Natsume Sōseki, who was then the grand old man of Japanese letters, wrote a famous letter to Akutagawa in which he praised the younger writer for the "unforced absurdity and concise, controlled style" of the work, and encouraged him to "try and write another twenty or thirty pieces like it so you can carve out your own special niche in the world of letters."* Akutagawa did precisely that and quickly established his reputation as a leading writer of short stories.

This story is available as an MP3 sound file at **www.speaking-japanese.com**. To reduce download times, the audio version has been split into five chapters. These are (1) Naigu's Big Nose, (2) Is it Treatable?, (3) The Operation, (4) Side Effects and (5) Back to Nature. The chapters are numbered and marked with an ◀))) MP3 icon in the left margin of the page containing the Japanese text.

* G. H. Healey, p. 28.

禅智内供の鼻といえば、池の尾で知らない者はない。長さは五六寸あって、上唇の上から頤の下まで下っている。形は元も先も同じように太い。いわば、細長い腸詰めのような物が、ぶらりと顔のまん中からぶら下っているのである。

五十歳を越えた内供は、沙弥の昔から内道場供奉の職にのぼった今日まで、内心では始終この鼻を苦に病んで来た。勿論表面では、今でもさほど気にならないような顔をしてすましている。これは専念に当来の浄土を渇仰すべき僧侶の身で、鼻の心配をするのが悪いと思ったからばかりではない。

1

禅智内供【ぜんちないぐ】Zenchi Naigu (person's name; 内供 is actually part of the man's title, but here it shall be treated as part of his name) 炎 [0708] + [1781] + [2162] + [0066]

鼻【はな】nose 炎 [1739]

〜といえば speaking of 炎

池の尾【いけのお】Ike-no-O (name of an area in Kyoto) [0160] + [1942]

知る【しる】know [0768]

者【もの】person [2047]

長さ【ながさ】length [1626]

五六寸【ごろくすん】five or six *sun* (1 *sun* = 3 cm) [2142] + [1244] + [1864]

上唇【うわくちびる】upper lip [2128] + [1752]

上【うえ】above [2128]

頤【あご】chin 炎 [-]

下【した】below [2115]

下る【さがる】hang down [2115]

形【かたち】shape [0565]

元【もと】root, base [1226]

先【さき】tip, end [1552]

同じ【おなじ】the same [1897]

〜ように like, as

太い【ふとい】fat, thick [1360]

いわば so to speak

細長い【ほそながい】long and thin [0900] + [1626]

腸詰め【ちょうづめ】sausage [0709] + [1021]

〜のような like, similar to

物【もの】thing [0587]

ぶらりと (+ verb) droop, sag

顔【かお】face 炎 [1177]

まん中【まんなか】middle [2150]

ぶら下る【ぶらさがる】hang down, dangle, sag [2115]

2

五十歳【ごじっさい】fifty years of age [2142] + [2110] + [1605]

越える【こえる】exceed [2085]

内供【ないぐ】Naigu (person's name) [0708] + [1781]

沙弥【しゃみ】novice monk [0199] + [0214]

When it came to Zenchi Naigu's nose, there was no one in Ike-no-O who did not know about it. Five or six inches long, it hung over his upper lip and right down to his chin. It was equally thick at the base and the tip. It was as though an object akin to a long, thin sausage was dangling pendulously from the middle of his face.

Naigu was over fifty. In his heart of hearts, his nose had been an unending source of grief to him from the distant past, when he was a novice, up till the present, when he had risen to the position of Palace Minister. Publicly, of course, he pretended that it did not bother him much. This was not only because he thought it wrong for a monk like himself who ought to be praying intently for rebirth in the Pure Land, to worry about his nose.

··

昔【むかし】the old days, long ago [1574]

内道場供奉【ないどうじょうぐぶ】Minister of the Shingon'in temple within the emperor's palace (the title from which Naigu gets his name) [2162] + [2000] + [0408] + [0066] + [1629]

職【しょく】job, work, duty [0960]

のぼる rise to

今日【こんにち】now, the present [1246] + [1915]

内心では【ないしんでは】inwardly, in one's heart of hearts [2162] + [0004]

始終【しじゅう】always, all the time, first to last [0211] + [0903]

苦に病む【くにやむ】worry about, suffer from [1433] + [2059]

～て来る【てくる】indicates continuation of an action up to a point [2211]

勿論【もちろん】of course [-] + [1058]

表面では【ひょうめんでは】on the surface, publicly [1572] + [1324]

今でも【いまでも】even now [1246]

さほど that much (＝それほど)

気になる【きになる】care about, be bothered by [2037]

～ような like 愛

すます handle (a situation), leave the matter as it is

専念に【せんねんに】intently, devotedly [1690] + [1304]

当来【とうらい】afterlife, afterworld [1378] + [2211]

浄土【じょうど】the Pure Land, (Buddhist) Paradise [0282] + [2127]

渇仰する【かつごうする】revere, adore [0379] + [0032]

～べき should ～, ought to ～

僧侶【そうりょ】monk [0119] + [-]

身【み】position, status [2213]

心配【しんぱい】anxiety, worry [0004] + [0981]

悪い【わるい】bad [1758]

思う【おもう】think [1633]

～ばかり only, just

それより寧、自分で鼻を気にしているという事を、人に知られるのが嫌だったからである。内供は日常の談話の中に、鼻という語が出て来るのを何よりも惧れていた。

　内供が鼻を持てあました理由は二つある。――一つは実際的に、鼻の長いのが不便だったからである。第一飯を食う時にも独りでは食えない。独りで食えば、鼻の先が鋺の中の飯へとどいてしまう。そこで内供は弟子の一人を膳の向うへ坐らせて、飯を食う間中、広さ一寸長さ二尺ばかりの板で、鼻を持上げていて貰う事にした。

3

寧【むしろ】rather, more than that [-]
自分【じぶん】himself [2195] + [1247]
鼻【はな】nose ❧ [1739]
気にする【きにする】worry about [2037]
事【こと】fact [2220]
人【ひと】people [2111]
知る【しる】know [0768]
嫌【いや】unpleasant, no good [0459]
内供【ないぐ】Naigu (person's name) ❧ [2162] + [0066]
日常【にちじょう】every day, the ordinary [1915] + [1657]
談話【だんわ】conversation, chat [1053] + [1027]
中【なか】in [2150]
語【ご】word [1040]
出て来る【でてくる】come up, emerge [2180] + [2211]
何より【なにより】more than anything [0045]
惧れる【おそれる】fear, worry about [-]

3

持てあます【もてあます】be at a loss about [0275]
理由【りゆう】reason [0659] + [2181]
二つ【ふたつ】two [1224]
一つ【ひとつ】one [2105]
実際的に【じっさいてきに】in fact, in actuality [1416] + [0503] + [0767]
長い【ながい】long [1626]
不便【ふべん】inconvenient, inconvenience [2141] + [0071]
第一【だいいち】first of all [1706] + [2105]
飯を食う【めしをくう】eat a meal ❧ [1110] + [1316]
時【とき】when [0625]
独りで【ひとりで】by oneself, independently ❧ [0293]
食う【くう】eat ❧ [1316]
先【さき】tip, end [1552]
鋺【かなまり】metal bowl [-]

No, it was rather that he could not stand people knowing that he was bothered by his nose. What frightened Naigu more than anything was the word "nose" popping up in the course of everyday conversation.

There were two reasons that Naigu was so embarrassed about his nose. One was that the length of his nose was a practical inconvenience. In the first place, he was not even able to eat his meals by himself. If he ate by himself, the tip of his nose would end up sticking into the food in his metal bowl. To counter this, Naigu arranged for a disciple to sit on the far side of the table while he was eating and hold his nose up with a wooden board twenty-four inches long and an inch or so wide.

....

中【なか】in, inside [2150]
飯【めし】rice, food [1110]
とどく reach
〜てしまう thoroughly 〜
そこで for this, to deal with this
弟子【でし】disciple [1291] + [2125]
一人【ひとり】one person [2105] + [2111]
膳【ぜん】small dining tray [-]
向う【むこう】far side [1934]
坐る【すわる】sit [-]
〜間中【〜あいだじゅう】for the entire
　duration [2094] + [2150]
広さ【ひろさ】width [1921]
一寸【いっすん】one *sun* (= 3 cm) [2105] +
　[1864]
長さ【ながさ】length [1626]
二尺【にしゃく】two *shaku* (1 *shaku* = 30
　cm) [1224] + [2148]
〜ばかり about 〜
板【いた】board [0575]

持上げる【もちあげる】lift up, hold up
　[0275] + [2128]
〜て貰う【〜てもらう】have someone 〜 [-]
〜事にする【〜ことにする】arrange to 〜,
　decide to 〜 [2220]

しかしこうして飯を食うという事は、持上げている弟子に
とっても、持上げられている内供にとっても、決して容易
な事ではない。一度この弟子の代りをした中童子が、嚔を
した拍子に手がふるえて、鼻を粥の中へ落した話は、当時
京都まで喧伝された。――けれどもこれは内供にとって、
決して鼻を苦に病んだ重な理由ではない。内供は実にこの
鼻によって傷けられる自尊心のために苦しんだのである。

しかし but, however
飯を食う【めしをくう】eat a meal [1110] + [1316]
事【こと】act, thing [2220]
持上げる【もちあげる】lift up, hold up [0275] + [2128]
弟子【でし】disciple [1291] + [2125]
〜にとって for
内供【ないぐ】Naigu (person's name) [2162] + [0066]
決して【けっして】definitely [0197]
容易な【よういな】easy, simple [1462] + [1561]
一度【いちど】once, one time [2105] + [1561]
代り【かわり】substitute, replacement [0018]
中童子【ちゅうどうじ】temple pageboy (twelve- to thirteen-year-old boy who works for a temple as a servant) [2150] + [1348] + [2125]
嚔【くさめ】sneeze [-]
拍子【ひょうし】moment, instant [0225] + [2125]
手【て】hand [2155]
ふるえる shake

鼻【はな】nose [1739]
粥【かゆ】rice porridge [-]
中【なか】into [2150]
落す【おとす】drop, let fall [1494]
話【はなし】story, account, tale [1027]
当時【とうじ】at that time [1378] + [0625]
京都【きょうと】Kyoto [1297] + [1106]
喧伝する【けんでんする】speak/bruit about [-] + [0028]
苦に病む【くにやむ】worry about, suffer from [1433] + [2059]
重な【おもな】main, significant [2223]
理由【りゆう】reason [0659] + [2181]
実に【じつに】in fact [1416]
〜によって by, as a result of
傷く【きずつく】wound, damage [0118]
自尊心【じそんしん】pride, self-esteem [2195] + [1500] + [0004]
〜のために on account of, because of [2225]
苦しむ【くるしむ】suffer [1433]

For neither the disciple who held up the nose, nor for Naigu, whose nose was being held up, was this by any means a simple process. The story of how once a pageboy who was standing in for the disciple, had sneezed, lost his grip, and deposited Naigu's nose into his rice porridge had made a stir as far off as Kyoto at the time. For Naigu, however, this was definitely not the main reason that his nose had been such a source of grief. The truth is that the wounds inflicted on his pride by his nose were what he really suffered from.

4

池の尾の町の者は、こういう鼻をしている禅智内供のた
めに、内供の俗でない事を仕合せだといった。あの鼻では
誰も妻になる女があるまいと思ったからである。中にはま
た、あの鼻だから出家したのだろうと批評する者さえあっ
た。しかし内供は、自分が僧であるために、幾分でもこの
鼻に煩される事が少くなったと思っていない。内供の自尊
心は、妻帯というような結果的な事実に左右されるために
は、余りにデリケイトに出来ていたのである。そこで内供
は、積極的にも消極的にも、この自尊心の毀損を恢復しよ
うと試みた。

The townsfolk of Ike-no-O used to say that with a nose like that, it was lucky for Zenchi Naigu that he wasn't a layman. They were convinced that with that nose, he would never have found a woman to be his wife. There were even those among them who opined that it was probably that nose which had made him become a man of the cloth. As for Naigu himself, he did not think that being a monk had made his nose-inflicted sufferings any less. Naigu's pride was too delicately constituted for it to be affected by such practical eventualities as marriage. However that may be, he sought to patch up the damage to his self-esteem by both active and passive means.

....

～というような such as
結果的な【けっかてきな】eventual, matter-of-course [0912] + [2217] + [0767]
事実【じじつ】fact, reality [2220] + [1416]
左右する【さゆうする】influence, move [1887] + [1888]
余りに【あまりに】excessively, very [1289]
出来る【できる】be constituted, be put together [2180] + [2211]
積極的【せっきょくてき】active, assiduous [0835] + [0695] + [0767]
消極的【しょうきょくてき】halfhearted, passive [0327] + [0695] + [0767]
毀損【きそん】damage [-] + [0468]
恢復する【かいふくする】restore, repair [-] + [0420]
試みる【こころみる】try, attempt [1025]

5

第一に内供の考えたのは、この長い鼻を実際以上に短く見せる方法である。これは人のいない時に、鏡へ向って、いろいろな角度から顔を映しながら、熱心に工夫を凝らして見た。どうかすると、顔の位置を換えるだけでは、安心が出来なくなって、頬杖をついたり頤の先へ指をあてがったりして、根気よく鏡を覗いて見る事もあった。しかし自分でも満足するほど鼻が短く見えた事は、これまでに唯の一度もない。時によると、苦心すればするほど、却て長く見えるような気さえした。内供は、こういう時には、鏡を筥へしまいながら、今更のようにため息をついて、不承不承にまた元の経机へ観音経をよみに帰るのである。

What first occurred to Naigu was to devise ways to make his nose look shorter than it actually was. When no one was around, he would try every trick in the book as he faced the mirror and contemplated his face from every which angle. Sometimes merely altering the position of his face would lead to a crisis in confidence: then he would cup his face in his palms, or plant his fingertips on his chin, and gaze doggedly into the mirror. Up till now, though, never even once had his nose appeared short enough to satisfy him. In fact, at times, the greater the pains he went to, it sometimes felt to him that the thing—most perversely—looked longer. At such times, Naigu would shut the mirror away in a box, sigh all the more deeply, and return dispirited to his devotional table and the Kannon Sutra he had originally been reading.

根気よく【こんきよく】 patiently, with perseverance [0631] + [2037]

覗く【のぞく】 gaze at, peer at [-]

事【こと】 occasion, instance 𒀭 [2220]

しかし but, however

自分【じぶん】 himself [2195] + [1247]

満足する【まんぞくする】 be satisfied [0441] + [1386]

〜ほど to the extent that 〜 𒀭

見える【みえる】 look, seem 𒀭 [1615]

これまでに until now, until this point

唯の【ただの】 simple, mere [0339]

一度【いちど】 once, one time [2105] + [1974]

時によると【ときによると】 on some occasions [0625]

苦心する【くしんする】 take pains, make an effort [1433] + [0004]

却て【かえって】 on the contrary, all the more [0761]

〜ような like, as if

気【き】 feeling, sense [2037]

〜さえ even

こういう this, such

筥【はこ】 box [-]

しまう shut up in, put in order

今更のように【いまさらのように】 all the more, at this late stage [1246] + [2205]

ため息をつく【ためいきをつく】 sigh [1693]

不承不承に【ふしょうぶしょうに】 grudgingly, halfheartedly [2141] + [0007]

また again

元の【もとの】 former [1226]

経机【きょうづくえ】 sutra-reading desk [0898] + [0549]

観音経【かんのんぎょう】 the sutra of Avalokiteśvara (Kannon) [1212] + [1312] + [0898]

読む【よむ】 read [1038]

帰る【かえる】 return (to doing something) [0098]

　それからまた内供は、絶えず人の鼻を気にしていた。池
の尾の寺は、僧供講説などのしばしば行われる寺である。
寺の内には、僧坊が隙なく建て続いて、湯屋では寺の僧が
日毎に湯を沸かしている。従ってここへ出入する僧俗の類
も甚多い。内供はこういう人々の顔を根気よく物色した。
一人でも自分のような鼻のある人間を見つけて、安心がし
たかったからである。だから内供の眼には、紺の水干も白
の帷子もはいらない。まして柑子色の帽子や、椎鈍の法衣
なぞは、見慣れているだけに、有れども無きが如くである。

6

また moreover
内供【ないぐ】Naigu (person's name) 🐢 [2162] + [0066]
絶えず【たえず】always [0917]
人【ひと】people 🐢 [2111]
鼻【はな】nose 🐢 [1739]
気にする【きにする】worry about, pay attention to [2037]
池の尾【いけのお】Ike-no-O (place name) [0160] + [1942]
寺【てら】temple 🐢 [1367]
僧供【そうぐ】offerings to monks [0119] + [0066]
講説【こうせつ】giving lectures on the sutras [1078] + [1042]
〜など and so on
しばしば frequently
行う【おこなう】hold, conduct, do [0157]
内【うち】inside, within [2162]

僧坊【そうぼう】monks' living quarters [0119] + [0171]
隙【すき】crack, gap, break [-]
建て続く【たてつづく】be built side by side [1965] + [0921]
湯屋【ゆや】bathing room [0446] + [1973]
僧【そう】monk [0119]
日毎に【ひごとに】every day [1915] + [1283]
湯【ゆ】hot water [0446]
沸かす【わかす】boil [0244]
従って【したがって】therefore [0309]
出入する【しゅつにゅうする】go in and out [2180] + [2113]
僧俗【そうぞく】monks and laymen [0119] + [0079]
類【たぐい】type, variety [1176]
甚【はなはだ】extremely, greatly [1689]
多い【おおい】numerous [1372]
こういう such
人々【ひとびと】people [2111]

In addition, Naigu also fretted incessantly about other people's noses. The temple at Ike-no-O was one at which offerings to the monks, sermons on the sutras and other such ceremonies were held frequently. In the temple precincts, the monks' cells were built side by side with no space in between, and the monks heated water at the bathhouse every day. The result was that all sorts of monks and laymen came and went in great numbers. Naigu used to inspect all their faces thoroughly. He wanted to be reassured by the discovery of at least one person with a nose like his. Dark blue overgarments and white hempen kimonos never registered in his eyes; the saffron headgear and priestly black robes (to the sight of which he was so accustomed) might as well not have existed.

....

顔【かお】face [1177]

根気よく【こんきよく】patiently, untiringly [0631] + [2037]

物色する【ぶっしょくする】look, search, select [0587] + [1280]

一人【ひとり】one person [2105] + [2111]

自分【じぶん】himself [2195] + [1247]

〜のような like

人間【にんげん】person [2111] + [2094]

見つける【みつける】find [1615]

安心【あんしん】comfort, ease, peace of mind [1373] + [0004]

眼【め】eye [0796]

紺【こん】dark blue [0899]

水干【すいかん】outer garment worn in Heian and Edo periods [0003] + [2116]

白【しろ】white [2175]

帷子【かたびら】hemp summer kimono [-] + [2125]

はいる enter

まして still more, much less, not to mention, to say nothing of

柑子色【こうじいろ】orange, saffron [-] + [2125] + [1280]

帽子【ぼうし】hat [0416] + [2125]

椎鈍【しいにび】black [0679] + [1108]

法衣【ころも】monk's garment [0248] + [1270]

〜なぞ and so on (colloquial form of 〜など)

見慣れる【みなれる】be accustomed to seeing [1615] + [0487]

〜だけに simply because, to the extent that

有れども無きが如く【あれどもなきがごとく】as though ... does not exist even when it does [1895] + [1351] + [0154]

内供は人を見ずに、唯、鼻を見た。──しかし鍵鼻はあっても、内供のような鼻は一つも見当らない。その見当らない事が度重なるに従って、内供の心は次第にまた不快になった。内供が人と話しながら、思わずぶらりと下っている鼻の先をつまんで見て、年甲斐もなく顔を赤めたのは、全くこの不快に動かされての所為である。

　最後に、内供は、内典外典の中に、自分と同じような鼻のある人物を見出して、せめても幾分の心やりにしようとさえ思った事がある。

内供【ないぐ】Naigu (person's name) ☗ [2162] + [0066]

人【ひと】person, people ☗ [2111]

見ずに【みずに】without looking [1615]

唯【ただ】only, just [0339]

鼻【はな】nose ☗ [1739]

見る【みる】see, look at [1615]

しかし but, however

鍵鼻【かぎばな】hooked nose [-] + [1739]

～のような like

一つも【ひとつも】(+ negative) not one [2105]

見当る【みあたる】find ☗ [1615] + [1378]

事【こと】occasion, experience ☗ [2220]

度重なる【たびかさなる】occur frequently [1974] + [2223]

～に従って【～にしたがって】as, in proportion to [0309]

心【こころ】heart, soul, mind [0004]

次第に【しだいに】gradually [0038] + [1706]

また again

不快【ふかい】unpleasant, uncomfortable ☗ [2141] + [0182]

話す【はなす】talk [1027]

思わず【おもわず】unthinkingly, unconsciously, instinctively [1633]

ぶらりと (+ verb) droop, say

下る【さがる】hang down [2115]

先【さき】tip, end [1552]

つまむ pinch

～て見る【～てみる】try to ～ [1615]

年甲斐もなく【としがいもなく】foolishly, in a way ill-befitting one's age [1284] + [2169] + [-]

顔【かお】face [1177]

赤める【あからめる】redden, blush [1389]

全く【まったく】totally, truly, indeed [1277]

動かす【うごかす】move, affect [1163]

所為【しょい】act, deed [0568] + [2225]

7

最後に【さいごに】finally [1599] + [0267]

内典外典【ないてんげてん】books on Buddhism and other religions [2162] + [1680] + [0135] + [1680]

Naigu was not looking at the people; he was looking only at their noses. Even if there was the odd hooked nose, he never once saw a nose like his own. And as his failures to spot a similar nose mounted, Naigu felt more and more unhappy. When he spoke to people, he would unconsciously squeeze the tip of his dangling nose, before blushing scarlet in a manner unbecoming to his years. This mannerism was wholly attributable to that same unhappiness.

In the end, Naigu thought that it would afford him at least some consolation, if he could find a person with a nose like his somewhere in the scriptures.

· ·

中【なか】among, within [2150]
自分【じぶん】himself [2195] + [1247]
同じ【おなじ】the same [1897]
～ような like
人物【じんぶつ】person [2111] + [0587]
見出す【みいだす】discover, detect [1615] +
　　[2180]
せめて at least
幾分【いくぶん】some degree [2229] + [1247]
心やり【こころやり】consolation [0004]
～さえ even, just
思う【おもう】think, feel [1633]

けれども、目連や、舎利弗の鼻が長かったとは、どの経文にも書いてない。勿論竜樹や馬鳴も、人並の鼻を備えた菩薩である。内供は、震旦の話の序に蜀漢の劉玄徳の耳が長かったという事を聞いた時に、それが鼻だったら、どの位自分は心細くなくなるだろうと思った。

　内供がこういう消極的な苦心をしながらも、一方ではまた、積極的に鼻の短くなる方法を試みた事は、わざわざここにいうまでもない。内供はこの方面でも、殆出来るだけの事をした。

8

But in none of the sutras did it mention anything about Mahāmaud or Śāriputra having had long noses. Nāgārjuna and Aśvaghoṣa may have been holy men, but they were equipped only with standard noses. When Naigu heard the story from China about Liu Xuande of the Kingdom of Shu having long ears, he thought how heartwarming it would have been for him had it been his nose that had been oversized.

While Naigu was a passive victim of anxiety on the one hand, there should not be any need for me to tell you that he was also tireless in trying all sorts of techniques to shorten his nose. In fact, he pretty much did everything that he could in this area.

....

[0004]
～ながら while, as
一方では 【いっぽうでは】 on the one hand
  [2105] + [1243]
また moreover, also
積極的に 【せっきょくてきに】 actively, vigorously [0835] + [0695] + [0767]
短い 【みじかい】 short [0801]
方法 【ほうほう】 method, means [1243] +
  [0248]
試みる 【こころみる】 try, attempt [1025]
わざわざ explicitly, expressly
いうまでもない needless to say, it goes
  without saying
方面 【ほうめん】 aspect, point of view, field
  [1243] + [1324]
殆 【ほとんど】 almost [-]
出来るだけ 【できるだけ】 as much as possible [2180] + [2211]

烏瓜を煎じて飲んで見た事もある、鼠の尿を鼻へなすって見た事もある。しかし何をどうしても、鼻は依然として、五六寸の長さをぶらりと唇の上にぶら下げているではないか。

　ところが或年の秋、内供の用を兼ねて、京へ上った弟子の僧が、知己の医者から長い鼻を短くする法を教わって来た。その医者というのは、もと震旦から渡って来た男で、当時は長楽寺の供僧になっていたのである。

烏瓜【からすうり】snake gourd [-] + [-]
煎じる【せんじる】brew, boil [-]
飲む【のむ】drink [1111]
〜て見る【〜てみる】try to 〜 ☃ [1615]
事【こと】fact, experience ☃ [2220]
鼠【ねずみ】mouse, rat [-]
尿【いばり】urine [1944]
鼻【はな】nose ☃ [1739]
なする rub on
しかし but, however
何【なに】whatever [0045]
依然として【いぜんとして】as before [0061] + [1779]
五六寸【ごろくすん】five or six *sun* (1 *sun* = 3 cm) [2142] + [1244] + [1864]
長さ【ながさ】length [1626]
ぶらりと (+ verb) droop, sag
唇【くちびる】lips [1752]
上【うえ】above [2128]
ぶら下げる【ぶらさげる】dangle [2115]

9

ところが but
或年【あるとし】a certain year [-] + [1284]

秋【あき】autumn [0776]
内供【ないぐ】Naigu (person's name) [2162] + [0066]
用【よう】business, affairs [1889]
兼ねる【かねる】combine, do one thing and another [1469]
京【きょう】the capital (Kyoto) [1297]
上る【のぼる】go up (to the capital) [2128]
弟子【でし】disciple [1291] + [2125]
僧【そう】monk [0119]
知己【しるべ】acquaintance, friend [0768] + [2117]
医者【いしゃ】doctor ☃ [1902] + [2047]
長い【ながい】long [1626]
短い【みじかい】short [0801]
法【ほう】method [0248]
教わる【おそわる】be taught [1002]
〜て来る【〜てくる】indicates continuation of an action up to a point ☃ [2211]
もと originally
震旦【しんたん】China [1794] + [1548]
渡る【わたる】cross over (ocean) [0445] + [2211]

He had drunk boiled snake gourd; he had tried rubbing mouse urine on his nose. But no matter what he did, his nose remained the same five- or six-incher dangling down over his lips.

In the autumn one year, a disciple (who had journeyed up to Kyoto partly for a matter concerning Naigu) was told something while there by a doctor acquaintance of his about ways of making long noses shorter. The doctor, who had originally come over from China, was a priest at the Chōrakuji temple at the time.

....

男【おとこ】man [1613]
当時【とうじ】at that time [1378] + [0625]
長楽寺【ちょうらくじ】Chōrakuji temple
    [1626] + [1808] + [1367]
供僧【ぐそう】priest [0066] + [0119]

内供は、いつものように、鼻などは気にかけないという風をして、わざとその法もすぐにやって見ようとはいわずにいた。そうして一方では、気軽な口調で、食事の度毎に、弟子の手数をかけるのが、心苦しいというような事をいった。内心では勿論弟子の僧が、自分を説伏せて、この法を試みさせるのを待っていたのである。弟子の僧にも、内供のこの策略がわからないはずはない。しかしそれに対する反感よりは、内供のそういう策略をとる心もちの方が、より強くこの弟子の僧の同情を動かしたのであろう。弟子の僧は、内供の予期通り、口を極めて、この法を試みる事を勧め出した。そうして、内供自身もまた、その予期通り、結局この熱心な勧告に聴従する事になった。

10

内供【ないぐ】Naigu (person's name) [2162] + [0066]
いつものように as always
鼻【はな】nose [1739]
〜など and so on
気にかける【きにかける】worry about [2037]
風【ふう】manner, air [1908]
わざと on purpose, deliberately
法【ほう】method (of treatment) [0248]
すぐに immediately
やる do
〜て見る【〜てみる】try to 〜 [1615]
いわずに without saying
一方では【いっぽうでは】on the one hand [2105] + [1243]
気軽な【きがるな】lighthearted [2037] + [1015]
口調【くちょう】tone, manner of expression [2119] + [1051]

食事【しょくじ】meal [1316] + [2220]
度【たび】time, occasion [1974]
〜毎に【〜ごとに】each 〜 [1283]
弟子【でし】disciple [1291] + [2125]
手数をかける【てすうをかける】make trouble for [2155] + [1170]
心苦しい【こころぐるしい】painful, regrettable [0004] + [1433]
〜というような to the effect that
事【こと】thing [2220]
いう say, speak
内心では【ないしんでは】inwardly, in one's heart of hearts [2162] + [0004]
勿論【もちろん】of course [-] + [1058]
僧【そう】monk [0119]
自分【じぶん】himself [2195] + [1247]
説伏せる【ときふせる】persuade, argue down [1042] + [0029]
試みる【こころみる】try, attempt [1025]

Naigu—as usual maintaining the fiction that he did not care about his nose—deliberately refrained from suggesting they try the technique right away. On the other hand, he did casually mention how guilty he felt about inconveniencing the disciple every mealtime. Under this facade, of course, hc was waiting for the disciple to talk him round and get him to give the technique a try. The disciple understood his role in Naigu's little ruse. Far from irritating him, the frame of mind which prompted Naigu to resort to this kind of playacting actually made the disciple feel more sympathetic. Just as Naigu had planned, the disciple was a marvel of eloquence as he recommended giving the method a try. And again just as planned, Naigu finally yielded to his enthusiastic exhortations.

....

待つ【まつ】wait [0269]

策略【さくりゃく】ruse, stratagem 憂 [1720] + [0793]

とる devise

わかる understand

～はずはない there is no expectation that ~

しかし but, however

～に対する【～にたいする】toward [0556]

反感【はんかん】aversion, repulsion [1869] + [1814]

心もち【こころもち】feeling, frame of mind [0004]

～の方が【～のほうが】rather (link for comparisons) [1243]

より rather

強く【つよく】strongly [0349]

同情【どうじょう】sympathy [1897] + [0353]

動かす【うごかす】provoke, move [1163]

予期【よき】expectation 憂 [1253] + [1120]

～通り【～どおり】as, in accordance with 憂 [1982]

口を極める【くちをきわめる】be very persuasive [2119] + [0695]

勧め出す【すすめだす】start to recommend [1202] + [2180]

自身【じしん】himself [2195] + [2213]

また again, also

結局【けっきょく】finally, ultimately [0912] + [1943]

熱心な【ねっしんな】enthusiastic [1834] + [0004]

勧告【かんこく】advice, counsel [1202] + [1560]

聴従する【ちょうじゅうする】listen dutifully, defer to [0956] + [0309]

～事になる【～ことになる】come to be that ~ [2220]

その法というのは、唯、湯で鼻を茹でて、その鼻を人に踏ませるという、極めて簡単なものであった。

湯は寺の湯屋で、毎日沸かしている。そこで弟子の僧は、指も入れられないような熱い湯を、すぐに提に入れて、湯屋から汲んで来た。しかしじかにこの提へ鼻を入れるとなると、湯気に吹かれて顔を火傷する惧がある。そこで折敷へ穴をあけて、それを提の蓋にして、その穴から鼻を湯の中へ入れる事にした。鼻だけはこの熱い湯の中へ浸しても、少しも熱くないのである。しばらくすると弟子の僧がいった。

——もう茹った時分でござろう。

法【ほう】method [0248]
唯【ただ】only, just [0339]
湯【ゆ】hot water 🐾 [0446]
鼻【はな】nose 🐾 [1739]
茹でる【ゆでる】boil [-]
人【ひと】person [2111]
踏む【ふむ】trample on [1066]
極めて【きわめて】exceedingly [0695]
簡単な【かんたんな】simple, rudimentary [1746] + [1444]

寺【てら】temple [1367]
湯屋【ゆや】bathing room 🐾 [0446] + [1973]
毎日【まいにち】every day [1283] + [1915]
沸かす【わかす】boil, heat up [0244]
弟子【でし】disciple 🐾 [1291] + [2125]
僧【そう】monk 🐾 [0119]

指【ゆび】finger [0278]
入れる【いれる】put in, insert 🐾 [2113]
熱い【あつい】hot 🐾 [1834]
すぐに immediately
提【ひさげ】bucket 🐾 [0431]
汲む【くむ】draw, ladle [-]
〜て来る【〜てくる】indicates continuation of an action up to a point [2211]
しかし but, however
じかに directly
湯気【ゆげ】steam [0446] + [2037]
吹く【ふく】blow [0170]
顔【かお】face [1177]
火傷する【やけどする】get burnt [2159] + [0118]
惧【おそれ】danger, worry, risk [-]
折敷【おしき】tray (wooden, usually lacquered) [0189] + [1207]

The technique—which involved no more than boiling the nose and getting someone to trample all over it—was exceedingly simple.

Water was heated every day in the temple bathhouse. The disciple filled a bucket with water so hot that you couldn't even dip your finger in it, and carried it over from the bathhouse. If Naigu had just plunged his nose straight into the bucket, there was the risk that the rising steam would scald his face. To prevent this, they punched a hole in a tray, placed it like a lid on the bucket and got him to put his nose into the hot water through it. Even though his nose was soaking in the scalding water, it did not feel the slightest bit hot. After a while, the disciple spoke:

"I think it should be boiled by now."

......

穴【あな】hole 爰 [1366]
あける make (a hole)
蓋【ふた】lid [-]
中【なか】in, into 爰 [2150]
〜事にする【〜ことにする】arrange to 〜, decide to 〜 [2220]
浸す【ひたす】soak, dunk [0326]
少しも【すこしも】(+ negative) not in the least [2163]
しばらくすると after a while
いう say, speak

13

もう already, just about
茹る【うだる】be boiled [-]
時分【じぶん】moment, time [0625] + [1247]
〜でござろう = 〜でしょう (polite form)

内供は苦笑した。これだけ聞いたのでは、誰も鼻の話とは気がつかないだろうと思ったからである。鼻は熱湯に蒸されて、蚤の食ったようにむず痒い。

弟子の僧は、内供が折敷の穴から鼻をぬくと、そのまだ湯気の立っている鼻を、両足に力を入れながら、踏みはじめた。内供は横になって、鼻を床板の上へのばしながら、弟子の僧の足が上下に動くのを眼の前に見ているのである。弟子の僧は、時々気の毒そうな顔をして、内供の禿げ頭を見下しながら、こんな事をいった。

14

内供【ないぐ】Naigu (person's name) ☻ [2162] + [0066]

苦笑する【くしょうする】smile wryly [1433] + [1692]

聞く【きく】hear [2097]

誰も【だれも】(+ negative) nobody [-]

鼻【はな】nose ☻ [1739]

話【はなし】talk, discussion [1027]

気がつく【きがつく】realize [2037]

思う【おもう】think, feel [1633]

熱湯【ねっとう】boiling water [1834] + [0446]

蒸す【むす】steam [1508]

蚤【のみ】flea [-]

食う【くう】eat, bite [1316]

〜ように like, as if

むず痒い【むずがゆい】itchy [-]

15

弟子【でし】disciple ☻ [1291] + [2125]

僧【そう】monk ☻ [0119]

折敷【おしき】tray [0189] + [1207]

穴【あな】hole [1366]

ぬく take out, remove

湯気【ゆげ】steam [0446] + [2037]

立つ【たつ】rise, float up [1257]

両足【りょうあし】both feet/legs [2191] + [1386]

力を入れる【ちからをいれる】strain, put strength into [2114] + [2113]

〜ながら while, as ☻

踏む【ふむ】trample on [1066]

〜はじめる begin to 〜

横になる【よこになる】lie down [0733]

床板【ゆかいた】floorboards [1947] + [0575]

上【うえ】on, upon [2128]

のばす stretch out

足【あし】legs, feet [1386]

上下【うえした】up and down [2128] + [2115]

動く【うごく】move [1163]

眼【め】eyes [0796]

前【まえ】before, in front of [1453]

見る【みる】watch [1615]

Naigu smiled ruefully, thinking that even if someone had over-heard that remark, they would never guess that the topic in question was a nose. His nose had been steam-cooked in the hot water and itched as if it had been bitten by fleas.

After Naigu had extracted his nose from the hole in the tray, the disciple, projecting all his power into his lower limbs, began to stamp on the nose while steam was still rising from it. Naigu, who was lying down with his nose stretched out before him on the floorboards, gazed at the feet of the disciple as they pounded up and down right in front of his eyes. From time to time, the disciple would make a pitying face, look down at Naigu's bald pate and say:

....

時々【ときどき】from time to time [0625]
気の毒そうな【きのどくそうな】pitying,
    apologetic [2037] + [1571]
顔【かお】face, expression [1177]
禿げ頭【はげあたま】bald head [-] + [1073]
見下す【みおろす】look down on [1615] +
    [2115]
事【こと】thing [2220]
いう say, speak

——痛うはござらぬかな。医師は責めて踏めと申したで。じゃが、痛うはござらぬかな。

内供は、首を振って、痛くないという意味を示そうとした。ところが鼻を踏まれているので思うように首が動かない。そこで、上眼を使って、弟子の僧の足に皸のきれているのを眺めながら、腹を立てたような声で、

——痛うはないて。

と答えた。実際は鼻はむず痒い所を踏まれるので、痛いよりも却て気もちのいい位だったのである。

16

痛うはござらぬ【いとうはござらぬ】not painful (polite form of 痛くない) [2065]

〜かな (after a negative) expresses the speaker's hope

医師【いし】doctor [1902] + [0892]

責める【せめる】torture [1595]

踏む【ふむ】trample on [1066]

申す【もうす】say (polite form of いう) [2186]

じゃが however (colloquial form of だが)

17

内供【ないぐ】Naigu (person's name) [2162] + [0066]

首【くび】head, neck [1452]

振る【ふる】shake [0316]

痛い【いたい】painful [2065]

意味【いみ】meaning [1352] + [0206]

示す【しめす】express, communicate [1229]

ところが but

鼻【はな】nose [1739]

思う【おもう】think, feel [1633]

〜ように as

動く【うごく】move [1163]

上眼を使う【うわめをつかう】glance upward [2128] + [1927] + [0068]

弟子【でし】disciple [1291] + [2125]

僧【そう】monk [0119]

足【あし】foot [1386]

皸のきれる【あかぎれのきれる】be chapped [-]

眺める【ながめる】gaze at [0795]

〜ながら while, as

腹を立てる【はらをたてる】get angry [0710] + [1257]

〜ような like

声【こえ】voice [1393]

18

痛うはないて【いとうはないて】It doesn't hurt! (＝痛くないって)

19

答える【こたえる】answer [1722]

"I hope it does not hurt. The doctor told me to trample mercilessly. I hope it does not hurt …"

Naigu shook his head in an attempt to indicate that it was not painful. But since his nose was being trampled on, his head refused to move as expected. So he looked upward, and staring at the disciple's chapped feet, replied in an angry-sounding voice:

"It doesn't hurt!"

If truth be told, since the itchy bits of his nose were being stamped on, far from being painful, it actually felt quite pleasant.

実際 【じっさい】 in fact, really [1416] + [0503]
むず痒い 【むずかゆい】 itchy [-]
所 【ところ】 place, spot, bit [0568]
却て 【かえって】 on the contrary [0761]
気もちのいい 【きもちのいい】 pleasant (of a feeling) [2037]
〜位 【〜くらい】 extent, degree [0042]

しばらく踏んでいると、やがて、粟粒のようなものが、鼻へ出来はじめた。いわば毛をむしった小鳥をそっくり丸炙にしたような形である。弟子の僧はこれを見ると、足を止めて独り言のようにこういった。

——これを鑷子でぬけと申す事でござった。

内供は、不足らしく頬をふくらせて、黙って弟子の僧のするなりに任せておいた。勿論弟子の僧の親切がわからない訳ではない。それは分っても、自分の鼻をまるで物品のように取扱うのが、不愉快に思われたからである。

しばらく for a while
踏む【ふむ】trample on [1066]
やがて at last
粟粒【あわつぶ】grains of millet [-] + [0894]
〜のような like ☠
もの object
鼻【はな】nose ☠ [1739]
出来る【できる】form [2180] + [2211]
〜はじめる begin to 〜
いわば so to speak
毛【け】hair [2152]
むしる pluck
小鳥【ことり】small bird [0002] + [2083]
そっくり exactly like
丸炙にする【まるやきにする】roast whole [2134] + [-]
形【かたち】form, shape [0565]
弟子【でし】disciple ☠ [1291] + [2125]
僧【そう】monk ☠ [0119]
見る【みる】see [1615]

足【あし】leg, foot [1386]
止める【とめる】stop [1868]
独り言【ひとりごと】talking to oneself [0293] + [1233]
〜のように as if ☠
いう say, speak

鑷子【けぬき】tweezers [-] + [2125]
ぬく pick out, pluck, extract
申す【もうす】say, speak (polite form of いう) [2186]
事【こと】thing, fact [2220]
〜でござる ＝〜です (polite form)

内供【ないぐ】Naigu (person's name) [2162] + [0066]
不足【ふそく】dissatisfied, dissatisfaction [2141] + [1386]
頬【ほお】cheeks [-]
ふくらせる puff up
黙る【だまる】be quiet [1833]

After the disciple had been trampling a while, things like grains of millet began to appear on the nose. It looked exactly like a plucked fowl roasted whole. Seeing this, the disciple stopped his stamping and, as if talking to himself, said:

"Ah yes, he told me to pluck these off with tweezers."

Naigu puffed up his cheeks sulkily and stayed mum, letting his disciple do as he must. It was not that he did not appreciate his disciple's kindness; he appreciated it, but nevertheless found it unpleasant to have his nose treated like some inanimate object.

....

～のするなりに任せる【～のするなりにま
　かせる】leave it to someone to do as they
　will [0037]
～ておく ~ (for a future purpose) [1671]
勿論【もちろん】of course [-] + [1058]
親切【しんせつ】kindness [1172] + [0015]
わかる understand
訳【わけ】case, state of affairs, reason [0989]
分る【わかる】understand [1247]
自分【じぶん】himself [2195] + [1247]
まるで～のように as if, just like
物品【ぶっぴん】thing, object [0587] + [1437]
取扱う【とりあつかう】treat, handle [0847] +
　[0159]
不愉快【ふゆかい】unpleasant [2141] + [0426] +
　[0182]
思う【おもう】think, feel [1633]

内供は、信用しない医者の手術をうける患者のような顔をして、不承不承に弟子の僧が、鼻の毛穴から鑷子で脂をとるのを眺めていた。脂は、鳥の羽の茎のような形をして、四分ばかりの長さにぬけるのである。

　やがてこれが一通りすむと、弟子の僧は、ほっと一息ついたような顔をして、

　——もう一度、これを茹でればようござる。

　といった。

　内供はやはり、八の字をよせたまま不服らしい顔をして、弟子の僧のいうなりになっていた。

　さて二度目に茹でた鼻を出して見ると、なるほど、何時になく短くなっている。これではあたりまえの鍵鼻と大した変りはない。内供はその短くなった鼻を撫でながら、弟子の僧の出してくれる鏡を、極りが悪るそうにおずおず覗いて見た。

Naigu pulled a face like a patient being operated on by a doctor he does not trust, and peevishly looked on as the disciple plucked fat with tweezers from the pores of his nose. The fat was shaped like the shafts of a feather and came out in half-inch-long pieces.

When this had finally been completed, the disciple paused a moment, looked relieved, and said:

"Now we have to boil the thing one more time."

Naigu, his frown still firmly in place, looked thoroughly dissatisfied, but still did exactly as he was told.

Now when he pulled his nose out for the second time, sure enough it was shorter than before: it was barely different from your common or garden hooked nose. Stroking his abbreviated nose, Naigu took a shamefaced and nervous look in the mirror the disciple had provided.

....

すむ be completed
ほっと一息つく【ほっとひといきつく】take a breath of relief [2105] + [1693]
〜ような like

24

もう一度【もういちど】one more time [2105] + [1974]
茹でる【ゆでる】cook, boil 裏 [-]
ようござる good, right (polite form of よい)

25

いう say

26

やはり nonetheless, as was to be expected
八の字【はちのじ】the character eight 八 (formed by frown wrinkles) [1859] + [1374]
よせる draw near, pull together
〜まま still
不服【ふふく】unsatisfied, discontented [2141] + [0591]
〜のいうなりになる follow the orders of

27

二度目【にどめ】second time [1224] + [1974] + [1927]
出す【だす】expose, bring out 裏 [2180]
〜て見る【〜てみる】try to ~ [1615]
なるほど indeed, to be sure
何時になく【いつになく】unusually, more than ever before [0045] + [0625]
短い【みじかい】short 裏 [0801]
あたりまえの run-of-the-mill, common or garden
鍵鼻【かぎばな】hooked nose [-] + [1739]
大した【たいした】significant [2133]
変り【かわり】difference [1311]
撫でる【なでる】stroke, caress [-]
〜ながら while, as
鏡【かがみ】mirror [1157]
極りが悪い【きまりがわるい】awkward, embarrassed [0695] + [1758]
おずおず nervously
覗く【のぞく】look at, peer at [-]

鼻は――あの顋の下まで下がっていた鼻は、殆嘘のように萎縮して、今は僅に上唇の上で意気地なく残喘を保っている。所々まだらに赤くなっているのは、恐らく踏まれた時の痕であろう。こうなれば、もう誰も晒うものはないのにちがいない。――鏡の中にある内供の顔は、鏡の外にある内供の顔を見て、満足そうに眼をしばたたいた。

しかし、その日はまだ一日、鼻がまた長くなりはしないかという不安があった。そこで内供は誦経する時にも、食事をする時にも、暇さえあれば手を出して、そっと鼻の先にさわって見た。が、鼻は行儀よく唇の上に納まっているだけで、格別それより下へぶら下って来る気色もない。

鼻【はな】nose ☠ [1739]
顋【あご】chin [-]
下【した】beneath, below ☠ [2115]
下る【さがる】hang down [2115]
殆【ほとんど】almost [-]
嘘【うそ】lie [-]
～のように like
萎縮する【いしゅくする】shrivel, dwindle [-] + [0955]
今【いま】now [1246]
僅に【わずかに】merely [-]
上唇【うわくちびる】upper lip [2128] + [1752]
上【うえ】above ☠ [2128]
意気地なく【いくじなく】weakly, tamely [1352] + [2037] + [0152]
残喘【ざんぜん】short-remaining life [0640] + [-]

保つ【たもつ】maintain, keep [0072]
所々【ところどころ】here and there [0568]
まだらに in spots/patches
赤い【あかい】red [1389]
恐らく【おそらく】perhaps, probably [1696]
踏む【ふむ】trample on [1066]
時【とき】time, occasion ☠ [0625]
痕【あと】traces, marks [-]
誰も【だれも】(+ negative) nobody [-]
晒う【わらう】laugh at [-]
もの people
～にちがいない certainly, no doubt
鏡【かがみ】mirror ☠ [1157]
中【なか】inside, in [2150]
内供【ないぐ】Naigu (person's name) ☠ [2162] + [0066]
顔【かお】face ☠ [1177]

His nose—that nose which once hung all the way down to his chin—had dwindled to an almost incredible degree, and now modestly maintained a reduced existence, barely even encroaching upon his upper lip. The red blotches that were dotted about on it were probably the result of being trampled on. No doubt about it —no one was going to laugh at a nose like this. As the real Naigu looked at the reflection of his face in the mirror, he fluttered his eyelashes in satisfaction.

Still he was uneasy all day lest the nose grow back. When he was chanting the sutras or eating his meals—if he had even one free moment—he would discreetly reach out his hand and touch the tip of his nose. The nose was politely ensconced above his upper lip, and—marvelous to relate—it showed no sign of dangling down any lower.

....

外 【そと】 outside [0135]
見る 【みる】 look at [1615]
満足 【まんぞく】 satisfaction [0441] + [1386]
眼 【め】 eyes [0796]
しばたたく blink

29

しかし but, however
日 【ひ】 day [1915]
一日 【いちにち】 one day, all day [2105] + [1915]
また once again
長い 【ながい】 long [1626]
不安 【ふあん】 uncertainty, anxiety [2141] + [1373]
誦経する 【ずきょうする】 chant sutras [-] + [0898]
食事 【しょくじ】 meal [1316] + [2220]
暇 【ひま】 free time [0691]
〜さえ (+ conditional) if only

手を出す 【てをだす】 reach out [2155] + [2180]
そっと discreetly
先 【さき】 tip, end [1552]
さわる touch, feel
〜て見る 【〜てみる】 try to 〜 [1615]
行儀よく 【ぎょうぎよく】 in a well-mannered way, properly [0157] + [0124]
唇 【くちびる】 lips [1752]
納まる 【おさまる】 stay, be ensconced [0877]
格別 【かくべつ】 exceptionally, remarkably [0627] + [0760]
ぶら下がる 【ぶらさがる】 hang down, dangle [2115]
〜て来る 【〜てくる】 begin to 〜 [2211]
気色 【けしき】 sign, indication, sense [2037] + [1280]

それから一晩寝て、あくる日早く眼がさめると内供は先、第一に、自分の鼻を撫でて見た。鼻は依然として短い。内供はそこで、幾年にもなく、法華経書写の功を積んだ時のような、のびのびした気分になった。

ところが二三日たつ中に、内供は意外な事実を発見した。それは折から、用事があって、池の尾の寺を訪れた侍が、前よりも一層可笑しそうな顔をして、話も碌々せずに、じろじろ内供の鼻ばかり眺めていた事である。

一晩【ひとばん】one night [2105] + [0668]
寝る【ねる】sleep [1503]
あくる日【あくるひ】the next day [1915]
早い【はやい】early [1549]
眼がさめる【めがさめる】wake up [0796]
内供【ないぐ】Naigu (person's name) [2162] + [0066]
先【まず】first of all, first off [1552]
第一に【だいいちに】first of all [1291] + [2105]
自分【じぶん】himself [2195] + [1247]
鼻【はな】nose [1739]
撫でる【なでる】stroke, caress [-]
～て見る【～てみる】try to ~ [1615]
依然として【いぜんとして】as before, still [0061] + [1779]
短い【みじかい】short [0801]
幾年にもなく【いくねんにもなく】after a gap of many years [2229] + [1284]
法華経書写【ほけきょうしょしゃ】transcription of The Lotus Sutra [0248] + [1465] + [0898] + [1703] + [1260]
功【こう】deed [0138]
積む【つむ】pile up [0835]

時【とき】time, occasion [0625]
～のような like, as
のびのびする feel at ease
気分【きぶん】mood [2037] + [1247]

ところが but
二三日【にさんにち】two or three days [1224] + [1225] + [1915]
たつ pass (of time)
～中【～うち】before, within [2150]
意外な【いがいな】unexpected [1352] + [0135]
事実【じじつ】fact, reality [2220] + [1416]
発見する【はっけんする】discover, find out [1634] + [1615]
折から【おりから】just then, right then [0189]
用事【ようじ】business, things to do [1889] + [2220]
池の尾【いけのお】Ike-no-O (place name) [0160] + [1942]
寺【てら】temple [1367]
訪れる【おとずれる】visit [0985]
侍【さむらい】man of the samurai class [0062]
前【まえ】before [1453]

After sleeping through the night, the very first thing Naigu did when he woke up the next day was to stroke his nose: it was as short as before. After an interval of many years, Naigu felt the same sensations of relief he had enjoyed after copying out the Lotus Sutra.

However, before two or three days had passed, Naigu made a surprising discovery. A samurai who was visiting the temple at Ike-no-O on some business just then, looked more amused than ever before; barely able to talk, he just stared mesmerized at Naigu's nose.

··

一層【いっそう】more, all the more [2105] + [2021]

可笑しい【おかしい】strange, odd, funny [1882] + [1692]

顔【かお】face, expression [1177]

話【はなし】talk, chat [1027]

碌々【ろくろく】(+ negative) hardly, barely [-]

〜せずに ＝〜しないで

じろじろ fixedly

〜ばかり only

眺める【ながめる】gaze at [0795]

それのみならず、嘗、内供の鼻を粥の中へ落した事のある中童子なぞは、講堂の外で内供と行きちがった時に、始めは、下を向いて可笑しさをこらえていたが、とうとうこらえ兼ねたと見えて、一度にふっと吹き出してしまった。用をいいつかった下法師たちが、面と向っている間だけは、慎んで聞いていても、内供が後さえ向けば、すぐにくすくす笑い出したのは、一度や二度の事ではない。

内供は始、これを自分の顔がわりがしたせいだと解釈した。しかしどうもこの解釈だけでは十分に説明がつかないようである。

- 31

～のみならず not just ～
嘗【かつて】formerly, before [-]
内供【ないぐ】Naigu (person's name) 象 [2162] + [0066]
鼻【はな】nose [1739]
粥【かゆ】rice porridge [-]
中【なか】into [2150]
落す【おとす】drop, let fall [1494]
事【こと】experience, act, thing [2220]
中童子【ちゅうどうじ】temple pageboy [2150] + [1348] + [2125]
～なぞ and so on (colloquial form of など)
講堂【こうどう】lecture hall [1078] + [1656]
外【そと】outside [0135]
行きちがう【ゆきちがう】cross paths [0157]
時【とき】when [0625]
始めは【はじめは】at first 象 [0211]
下【した】down, below [2115]
向く【むく】look, face [1934]

可笑しさ【おかしさ】humorousness [1882] + [1692]
こらえる suppress, fight down 象
とうとう finally, in the end
～兼ねる【～かねる】fail to ～ [1469]
見える【みえる】seem, appear [1615]
一度に【いちどに】all at once [2105] + [1974]
ふっと吹き出す【ふきだす】laugh explosively [0170] + [2180]
～てしまう expresses completion of an action with regret
用【よう】business [1889] + [-]
いいつかる be ordered (to do something)
下法師【しもほうし】monk of low rank [2115] + [0248] + [0892]
面と向う【めんとむかう】be face to face [1324] + [1934]
～間【～あいだ】while [2094]
慎んで【つつしんで】humbly, modestly [0463]
聞く【きく】listen [2097]

That was not all. When the pageboy who had dropped Naigu's nose into his rice porridge passed him in front of the lecture hall, he first looked down and stifled his laughter, but—seemingly unable to control himself—finally emitted a mocking hoot. When given instructions by Naigu, the lower-ranking monks listened humbly while face-to-face with him, but the instant he turned his back, they started to snigger. This happened on several occasions.

Naigu at first interpreted all this as the result of the change in his appearance. Somehow, though, it seemed that this interpretation was insufficient to explain things.

後 【うしろ】 behind, the other way [0267]
〜さえ (+ conditional) if only
向く 【むく】 turn [1934]
くすくす snickeringly
笑い出す 【わらいだす】 burst into laughter [1692] + [2180]
一度 【いちど】 once [2105] + [1974]
二度 【にど】 twice [1224] + [1974]
事 【こと】 event, happening [2220]

31

自分 【じぶん】 himself [2195] + [1247]
顔がわり 【かおがわり】 change of appearance [1177]
〜せい because
解釈する 【かいしゃくする】 interpret [1017] + [0997]
しかし but, however
どうも somehow
解釈 【かいしゃく】 interpretation [1017] + [0997]

十分 【じゅうぶん】 enough, sufficient [2110] + [1247]
説明がつく 【せつめいがつく】 explain [1042] + [0572]

——勿論、中童子や下法師が晒う原因は、そこにあるのに
ちがいない。けれども同じ晒うにしても、鼻の長かった昔
とは、晒うのにどことなく容子がちがう。見慣れた長い鼻
より、見慣れない短い鼻の方が滑稽に見えるといえば、そ
れまでである。が、そこにはまだ何かあるらしい。

——前にはあのようにつけつけとは晒わなんだて。

内供は、誦しかけた経文をやめて、禿げ頭を傾けながら、
時々こう呟く事があった。

32

33

Obviously, the change in my looks is the reason that the pages and junior monks laugh at me. They may laugh just as they used to in the days when my nose was long, but there's something—it's hard to define what—different in the way they laugh. If you argue that my short nose, which they're not used to, is more comical than my old long nose, which they were used to, then that would be that. But I feel there's something more to it.

"They didn't used to laugh viciously like that before ..."

Sometimes Naigu would whisper these words, pausing in the middle of reading a sutra and tilting his head to one side.

愛すべき内供は、そういう時になると、必ぼんやり、傍に
かけた普賢の画像を眺めながら、鼻の長かった四五日前の
事を憶い出して、「今はむげにいやしくなりさがれる人の、
さかえたる昔をしのぶがごとく」ふさぎこんでしまうので
ある。——内供には、遺憾ながらこの問に答を与える明が
欠けていた。

　　　——人間の心には互に矛盾した二つの感情がある。勿論、
誰でも他人の不幸に同情しない者はない。ところがその人
がその不幸を、どうにかして切りぬける事が出来ると、今
度はこっちで何となく物足りないような心もちがする。

愛すべき【あいすべき】lovable, amiable [1606]

内供【ないぐ】Naigu (person's name) ☃
[2162] + [0066]

そういう such

時【とき】time, occasion, moment [0625]

必【かならず】invariably, without fail [0006]

ぼんやり vaguely, distractedly

傍【そば】nearby [0110]

かける hang

普賢【ふげん】Samantabhadra (a bodhisattva) [1499] + [1817]

画像【がぞう】portrait, picture [1904] + [0123]

眺める【ながめる】gaze at [0795]

〜ながら while, as

鼻【はな】nose [1739]

長い【ながい】long [1626]

四五日【しごにち】four or five days [1928] +
[2142] + [1915]

〜前【〜まえ】before, earlier [1453]

事【こと】event, experience [2220]

憶い出す【おもいだす】recall, remember
[0530] + [2180]

今【いま】now [1246]

むげに out of hand, downright

いやしい low (of social standing, one's place
in the world)

なりさがる sink (to a level), be reduced,
come down (in the world)

人【ひと】person ☃ [2111]

さかえたる flourish (classical form of さ
かえる)

昔【むかし】the old days, long ago [1574]

しのぶ recall, remember

〜ごとく just like

ふさぎこむ get depressed

〜てしまう expresses completion of an
action with regret

遺憾ながら【いかんながら】regrettably,
unfortunately [2023] + [0529]

問【とい】question [2091]

At these moments, the amiable Naigu would always gaze dreamily at the portrait of Samantabhadra which hung nearby. Then remembering how things were four or five days earlier when his nose was long, he would sink into gloom: "As the man who hath sunk to be the lowest of the low recalls his days of glory." Regrettably, though, he lacked the wisdom to understand why.

In the heart of man, there are two emotions which run counter to each other. Everyone, of course, feels sympathy for the misfortunes of another person. If, however, that other person somehow manages to overcome his misfortunes, then they feel slightly cheated.

答【こたえ】answer [1722]
与える【あたえる】furnish, provide [2138]
明【めい】wisdom [0572]
欠ける【かける】lack, be without [1255]

34

人間【にんげん】human [2111] + [2094]
心【こころ】hcart, soul, mind [0004]
互に【たがいに】mutually, reciprocally [2143]
矛盾する【むじゅんする】conflict, be opposed [1266] + [1907]
二つ【ふたつ】two [1224]
感情【かんじょう】emotion [1814] + [0353]
勿論【もちろん】of course [-] + [1058]
誰でも【だれでも】anybody [-]
他人【たにん】another person, other people [0022] + [2111]
不幸【ふこう】unhappiness 爱 [2141] + [1408]
同情する【どうじょうする】sympathize [1897] + [0353]

者【もの】person [2047]
ところが but
どうにかして by doing one's best
切りぬける【きりぬける】overcome, get over [0015]
〜事が出来る【〜ことができる】be able to 〜 [2220] + [2180] + [2211]
今度【こんど】the next time around [1246] + [1974]
何となく【なんとなく】for some reason [0045]
物足りない【ものたりない】dissatisfied, disappointed [0587] + [1386]
心もち【こころもち】feeling, frame of mind [0004]

少し誇張していえば、もう一度その人を、同じ不幸に陥れて見たいような気にさえなる。そうして何時の間にか、消極的ではあるが、或敵意をその人に対して抱くような事になる。——内供が、理由を知らないながらも、何となく不快に思ったのは、池の尾の僧俗の態度に、この傍観者の利己主義をそれとなく感づいたからに外ならない。

　そこで内供は日毎に機嫌が悪くなった。二言目には、誰でも意地悪く叱りつける。しまいには鼻の療治をしたあの弟子の僧でさえ、「内供は法慳貪の罪を受けられるぞ」と陰口をきくほどになった。殊に内供を忿らせたのは、例の悪戯な中童子である。

35
🔊 MP3
5.
Back to
Nature
03:40

少し【すこし】slightly, a bit [2163]

誇張する【こちょうする】exaggerate [1022] + [0348]

いう say, speak

もう一度【もういちど】again [2105] + [1974]

人【ひと】person ⚥ [2111]

同じ【おなじ】the same [1897]

不幸【ふこう】unhappiness [2141] + [1408]

陥れる【おとしいれる】throw into, entrap [0334]

〜て見る【〜てみる】try to 〜 [1615]

〜ような like

気【き】feeling [2037]

〜さえ even ⚥

何時の間にか【いつのまにか】at some point [0045] + [0625] + [2094]

消極的【しょうきょくてき】passive, not active [0327] + [0695] + [0767]

或【ある】a certain [-]

敵意【てきい】enmity, hostility [1204] + [1352]

〜に対して【〜にたいして】toward [0556]

抱く【いだく】have, hold, harbor [0227]

事【こと】state of affairs, circumstance [2220]

内供【ないぐ】Naigu (person's name) ⚥ [2162] + [0066]

理由【りゆう】reason [0659] + [2181]

知る【しる】know, understand [0768]

〜ながら in spite of

何となく【なんとなく】somehow [0045]

不快【ふかい】unpleasant [2141] + [0182]

思う【おもう】think, feel [1633]

池の尾【いけのお】Ike-no-O (place name) [0160] + [1942]

僧俗【そうぞく】clergy and laity, monks and laymen [0119] + [0079]

態度【たいど】attitude [1822] + [1974]

傍観者【ぼうかんしゃ】observer [0110] + [1212] + [2047]

It would only be a slight exaggeration to say that they want to cast that person right back into his original misfortune, and that at some point, they develop a feeling of hostility—albeit passive hostility—toward that person. Naigu felt uncomfortable, but he did not know exactly why. Without a doubt it was because he somehow sensed this third-party coldness in the attitudes of both the laity and clergy of Ike-no-O.

Naigu became more ill-tempered by the day. He only opened his mouth to administer sharp rebukes. In the end, it got to the point that even the disciple who had treated Naigu's nose began to mutter against him, saying, "That Naigu's set up for a fall." It was, however, the mischievous pageboys who most infuriated Naigu.

....

利己主義【りこしゅぎ】 selfishness, egotism [0757] + [2117] + [1231] + [1514]
それとなく indirectly
感づく【かんづく】 sense, realize [1814]
〜に外ならない【〜にほかならない】 without a doubt [0135]

35

日毎に【ひごとに】 day by day [1915] + [1283]
機嫌【きげん】 mood, temper [0736] + [0459]
悪い【わるい】 bad [1758]
二言目には【ふたことめには】 whenever one talks [1224] + [1233] + [1927]
誰でも【だれでも】 anybody and everybody [-]
意地悪い【いじわるい】 cantankerous, peevish [1352] + [0152] + [1758]
叱りつける【しかりつける】 tell off, scold [-]
しまいには finally
鼻【はな】 nose [1739]

療治【りょうじ】 treatment [0250] + [2067]
弟子【でし】 disciple [1291] + [2125]
僧【そう】 monk [0119]
法慳貪【ほうけんどん】 metaphor for perverseness [0248] + [-] + [-]
罪【つみ】 sin [1673]
受ける【うける】 get, receive [1569]
陰口をきく【かげぐちをきく】 mutter darkly, backbite [0397] + [2119]
〜ほど extent, degree [0806]
殊に【ことに】 especially [0639]
忿る【おこる】 get angry [-]
例の【れいの】 that/those (previously referred to ~) [0067]
悪戯な【いたずらな】 mischievous [1758] + [1208]
中童子【ちゅうどうじ】 temple pageboy [2150] + [1348] + [2125]

或日、けたたましく犬の吠える声がするので、内供が何気なく外へ出て見ると、中童子は、二尺ばかりの木の片をふりまわして、毛の長い、痩せた尨犬を逐いまわしている。それも唯、逐いまわしているのではない。「鼻を打たれまい。それ、鼻を打たれまい」と囃しながら逐いまわしているのである。内供は、中童子の手からその木の片をひったくって、したたかその顔を打った。木の片は以前の鼻持上げの木だったのである。

内供はなまじいに、鼻の短くなったのが、反て恨めしくなった。

或日【あるひ】a certain day [-] + [1915]
けたたましい loud, noisy
犬【いぬ】dog [2160]
吠える【ほえる】bark [-]
声【こえ】sound [1393]
内供【ないぐ】Naigu (person's name) ☠ [2162] + [0066]
何気なく【なにげなく】casually, unthinkingly [0045] + [2037]
外【そと】outside [0135]
出る【でる】go out [2180]
見る【みる】have a look [1615]
中童子【ちゅうどうじ】temple pageboy ☠ [2150] + [1348] + [2125]
二尺【にしゃく】two *shaku* (1 *shaku* = 30 cm) [1224] + [2146]
〜ばかり about 〜
木【き】wood ☠ [2149]
片【きれ】piece ☠ [2158]

ふりまわす brandish, wave about
毛の長い【けのながい】long-haired [2152] + [1626]
痩せる【やせる】be thin, be scrawny [-]
尨犬【むくいぬ】shaggy dog [-] + [2160]
逐いまわす【おいまわす】chase about ☠ [1975]
唯【ただ】only, just [0339]
鼻【はな】nose ☠ [1739]
打つ【うつ】hit, strike ☠ [0142]
囃す【はやす】jeer at, taunt [-]
〜ながら while, as
手【て】hand [2155]
ひったくる snatch away
したたか hard, heavily
顔【かお】face [1177]
以前【いぜん】before [0025] + [1453]
鼻持上げ【はなもたげ】nose-supporter [1739] + [0275] + [2128]

One day, drawn by the loud barking of a dog, Naigu had wandered nonchalantly outside. A page waving a two-foot piece of wood was chasing a long-haired, underfed dog around. In fact, he was not just chasing it around, he was chasing it and yelling, "Watch out for your nose! I'm going to whack your nose!" Tearing the bit of wood from the pageboy's hand, Naigu smacked him hard in the face with it. The piece of wood was the very one that had previously been used to hold up his nose.

Naigu now began to regret that he had had his nose shortened without thinking things through properly.

36

なまじいに recklessly
短い 【みじかい】 short [0801]
反て 【かえって】 on the contrary [1869]
恨めしい 【うらめしい】 regrettable [0272]

するとか或夜の事である。日が暮れてから急に風が出たと
見えて、塔の風鐸の鳴る音が、うるさいほど枕に通って来
た。その上、寒さもめっきり加わったので、老年の内供は
寝つこうとしても寝つかれない。そこで床の中でまじまじ
していると、ふと鼻が何時になく、むず痒いのに気がつい
た。手をあてて見ると少し水気が来たようにむくんでいる。
どうやらそこだけ、熱さえもあるらしい。

――無理に短うしたで、病が起ったのかも知れぬ。

或夜【あるよる】a certain night [-] + [1301]

事【こと】event, occurrence [2220]

日【ひ】day [1915]

暮れる【くれる】get dark [1522]

急に【きゅうに】suddenly [1328]

風【かぜ】wind [1908]

出る【でる】come out [2180]

見える【みえる】seem [1615]

塔【とう】tower, pagoda [0411]

風鐸【ふうたく】wind-bell [1908] + [-]

鳴る【なる】sound, ring [0481]

音【おと】sound [1312]

うるさい bothersomely noisy

～ほど extent, degree [0806]

枕【まくら】pillow [-]

通う【かよう】travel, be conveyed [1982]

～て来る【～てくる】indicates progression in the direction of Naigu [2211]

その上【そのうえ】moreover, in addition [2128]

寒さ【さむさ】coldness, chill [1490]

めっきり remarkably

加わる【くわわる】be added to [0023]

老年【ろうねん】old age [2040] + [1284]

内供【ないぐ】Naigu (person's name) [2162] + [0066]

寝つく【ねつく】get to sleep 😴 [1503]

床【とこ】futon, bed [1947]

中【なか】in, inside [2150]

まじまじする move around restlessly

ふと suddenly

鼻【はな】nose [1739]

何時になく【いつになく】unusually [0045] + [0625]

むず痒い【むずかゆい】itchy [-]

気がつく【きがつく】notice, realize [2037]

手【て】hand [2155]

あてる place, touch, put

～て見る【～てみる】try to ~ [1615]

少し【すこし】slightly, a bit [2163]

水気【すいき】dropsy, moisture [0003] + [2037]

One night the sun was seen to set and the wind to rise suddenly, bearing the chime of the pagoda's wind-bells all the way to Naigu's pillow. It was also remarkably cold, so that try as he might, Naigu (who was an old man) found himself unable to sleep. Turning this way and that in his bed, he suddenly became aware of an unusual itchy sensation in his nose. When he touched it, it was swollen as if with a touch of the dropsy. It (and it alone) seemed to be burning hot, too.

"Shortening it in that unnatural way, it's probably gone and got ill."

⋯⋯

来る【くる】come [2211]
〜ように as if, like
むくむ swell up
どうやら likely
熱【ねつ】fever, heat [1834]
〜さえ even, also, too

38

無理に【むりに】forcefully, unnaturally [1351] [0659]
短うする【みじこうする】shorten (colloquial form of 短くする) [0801]
病【やまい】sickness [2059]
起る【おこる】happen [2079]
〜かも知れぬ【〜かもしれぬ】perhaps [0768]

内供は、仏前に香花を供えるような恭しい手つきで、鼻を抑えながら、こう呟いた。

翌朝、内供が何時ものように早く眼をさまして見ると、寺内の銀杏や橡が、一晩の中に葉を落したので、庭は黄金を敷いたように明い。塔の屋根には霜が下りているせいであろう。まだうすい朝日に、九輪がまばゆく光っている。禅智内供は、蔀を上げた橡に立って、深く息をすいこんだ。

殆、忘れようとしていた或感覚が、再内供に帰って来たのはこの時である。

....

内供【ないぐ】Naigu (person's name) ⚲ [2162] + [0066]

仏前【ぶつぜん】Buddhist altar (*lit.*, "before the Buddha") [0010] + [1453]

香花を供える【こうげをそなえる】offer incense and flowers [1637] + [1405] + [0066]

〜ような like, akin to

恭しい【うやうやしい】respectful, reverential [1591]

手つき【てつき】gesture [2155]

鼻【はな】nose [1739]

抑える【おさえる】press [0193]

〜ながら while, as

呟く【つぶやく】mutter [-]

翌朝【よくあさ】the next morning [1712] + [1114]

何時もの【いつもの】usual [0045] + [0625]

〜ように like

早い【はやい】early [1549]

眼をさます【めをさます】wake up [0796]

〜て見ると【〜てみると】when [1615]

寺内【じない】within the temple grounds [1367] + [2162]

銀杏【いちょう】gingko tree [1133] + [1554]

橡【とち】horse chestnut [-]

一晩【ひとばん】one evening [2105] + [0668]

中【うち】within, during [2150]

葉【は】leaves [1497]

落す【おとす】drop, let fall [1494]

庭【にわ】garden [1987]

黄金【きん】bright yellow gold [1596] + [1302]

敷く【しく】spread out [1207]

〜ように like, as if

明い【あかるい】bright [0572]

塔【とう】tower, pagoda [0411]

屋根【やね】roof [1973] + [0631]

霜【しも】frost [1801]

So whispered Naigu, cupping his nose reverently between his hands as if proffering incense and flowers at the altar.

The next morning when Naigu woke up early (as he usually did), the gingkos and horse chestnuts in the temple precincts had shed all their leaves overnight, so the garden looked as bright as if it were paved with gold. Perhaps because frost had settled on the roof of the pagoda, the crown of copper rings shone brilliantly in the pale morning sun. Zenchi Naigu pushed up the shutter, stood on the veranda and breathed in deeply.

It was then that a certain almost forgotten sensation came back to him.

下りる【おりる】 descend, fall [0335]
〜せいである is due to, is because
うすい weak, thin
朝日【あさひ】 morning sun [1114] + [1915]
九輪【くりん】 nine-ring decoration on top of a pagoda [2112] + [1067]
まばゆい bright
光る【ひかる】 shine [1550]
禅智内供【ぜんちないぐ】 Zenchi Naigu (person's name) [0708] + [1781] + [2162] + [0066]
蔀【しとみ】 latticed shutters [-]
上げる【あげる】 lift up [2128]
椽【えん】 open corridor, veranda [-]
立つ【たつ】 stand [1257]
深い【ふかい】 deep [0385]
息【いき】 breath [1693]
すいこむ inhale, breathe in

殆【ほとんど】 almost [-]

忘れる【わすれる】 forget [1285]
或【ある】 a certain [-]
感覚【かんかく】 feeling, sensation [1814] + [1668]
再【ふたたび】 once again [2192]
帰る【かえる】 come back [0098]
〜て来る【〜てくる】 indicates progression in the direction of Naigu [2211]
時【とき】 time, occasion, moment [0625]

内供は慌てて鼻へ手をやった。手にさわるものは、昨夜
の短い鼻ではない。上唇の上から頤の下まで、五六寸あま
りもぶら下っている、昔の長い鼻である。内供は鼻が一夜
の中に、また元の通り長くなったのを知った。そうしてそ
れと同時に、鼻が短くなった時と同じような、はればれし
た心もちが、どこからともなく帰って来るのを感じた。

　――こうなれば、もう誰も晒うものはないにちがいない。
　内供は心の中でこう自分に囁いた。長い鼻をあけ方の秋
風にぶらつかせながら。

....

内供【ないぐ】Naigu (person's name) 要
　[2162] + [0066]

慌てる【あわてる】panic [0425]

鼻【はな】nose 要 [1739]

手をやる【てをやる】put one's hand to
　[2155]

手【て】hand 要 [2155]

さわる touch

昨夜【ゆうべ】the night before [0601] + [1301]

短い【みじかい】short [0801]

上唇【うわくちびる】upper lip [2128] + [1752]

上【うえ】above [2128]

頤【あご】chin [-]

下【した】beneath, below [2115]

五六寸【ごろくすん】five or six sun (1 sun
　= 3 cm) [2142] + [1244] + [1864]

〜あまり a little more than 〜

ぶら下がる【ぶらさがる】hang down [2115]

昔【むかし】the old days, long ago [1574]

長い【ながい】long 要 [1626]

一夜【いちや】one night [2105] + [1301]

中【うち】within [2150]

また once again [2108]

元の通り【もとのとおり】the way it used to
　be [1226] + [1982]

知る【しる】understand [0768]

〜と同時に【〜とどうじに】at the same time
　[1897] + [0625]

短い【みじかい】short [0801]

時【とき】time [0625]

同じ【おなじ】the same [1987]

〜ような like

はればれする be cheerful, be refreshed,
　be delighted

心もち【こころもち】feeling, frame of mind
　[0004]

どこからともなく from nowhere

帰る【かえる】return [0098]

〜て来る【〜てくる】indicates progres-
　sion in the direction of Naigu [2211]

感じる【かんじる】feel [1814]

Panic-stricken, Naigu brought his hand to his nose. What he touched was not the short nose of the previous night. It hung over his upper lip and right down to his chin and was more than five or six inches long: it was his old nose. Naigu realized that his nose had returned to its original length in the course of that one night. At the same instant, he also felt again an inexplicable delight—exactly what he had felt when his nose had been made shorter.

"No doubt about it—no one is going to laugh at a nose like this" were the words that Naigu whispered to himself, as he dangled forth his nose in the autumnal breezes of the dawn.

....

43

誰も【だれも】(+ negative) nobody [-]
哂う【わらう】laugh [-]
もの person
〜にちがいない certainly, no doubt

44

心【こころ】heart, soul, mind 象 [0004]
中【なか】inside [2150]
自分【じぶん】himself [2195] + [1247]
囁く【ささやく】whisper [-]
あけ方【あけがた】dawn [1243]
秋風【あきかぜ】autumn breeze [0776] +
  [1908]
ぶらつく swing, dangle
〜ながら while, as

Rashōmon 羅生門

Two thieves debate before an audience of corpses

Akira Kurosawa's film *Rashōmon* won the Grand Prix at the Venice Film Festival in 1951 and ushered in the golden age of Japanese cinema. Despite its name, the film is actually based on "In a Grove," and the Rashomon gate was used as no more than a framing device suggesting a world of physical and moral decay. While "In a Grove" is a highly cinematic *Usual Suspects*-style thriller, "Rashōmon" is a static tale dominated by descriptions of the ruined gate and the bodies that litter its dimly lit upper story. With its whiff of necrophilia, *Rashōmon* is a classic of the *ero-guro* (erotic grotesque), a uniquely Japanese genre which adds a dash of perverse eroticism to compelling Poe-like hallucinations. Budding *ero-guro* fans might also enjoy the stories of Tanizaki Jun'ichirō and the bondage photographs of Nobuyoshi Araki.

This story is available as an MP3 sound file at **www.speaking-japanese.com**. To reduce download times, the audio version has been divided into five chapters. These are (1) An Idle Servant, (2) Into the Gate, (3) A Shocking Sight, (4) Honor of Thieves and (5) Decision Time. The chapters are numbered and marked with an ◀)) ᴹᴾ³ icon in the left margin of the page containing the Japanese text.

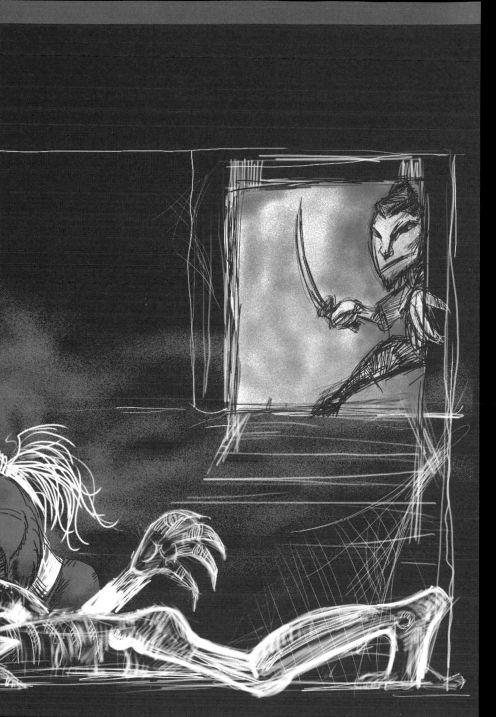

或日の暮方の事である。一人の下人が、羅生門の下で雨やみを待っていた。

広い門の下には、この男の外に誰もいない。唯、所々丹塗の剝げた、大きな円柱に、蟋蟀が一匹とまっている。羅生門が、朱雀大路にある以上は、この男の外にも、雨やみをする市女笠や揉烏帽子が、もう二三人はありそうなものである。それが、この男の外には誰もいない。

何故かというと、この二三年、京都には、地震とか辻風とか火事とか饑饉とかいう災がつづいて起った。そこで洛中のさびれ方は一通りではない。旧記によると、仏像や仏具を打砕いて、その丹がついたり、金銀の箔がついたりした木を、路ばたにつみ重ねて、薪の料に売っていたという事である。

1

或日【あるひ】on a certain day [-] + [1915]

暮方【くれがた】nightfall [1522] + [1243]

事【こと】thing, event, state of affairs 🐟 [2220]

一人【ひとり】one person [2105] + [2111]

下人【げにん】servant [2115] + [2111]

羅生門【らしょうもん】Rashōmon gate 🐟 [1679] + [2179] + [0597]

下【した】beneath 🐟 [2115]

雨やみ【あめやみ】the letup of the rain 🐟 [2218]

待つ【まつ】wait for [0269]

2

広い【ひろい】big, wide [1921]

門【もん】gate [0597]

男【おとこ】man 🐟 [1613]

〜の外に【〜のほかに】except for, other than 🐟 [0135]

誰も【だれも】(+ negative) nobody 🐟 [-]

唯【ただ】just, only [0339]

所々【ところどころ】here and there [0568]

丹塗の【にぬりの】red-painted, vermilion-lacquered [2147] + [1818]

剝げる【はげる】peel off [-]

大きな【おおきな】big [2133]

円柱【まるばしら】round pillar [1875] + [0603]

蟋蟀【きりぎりす】cricket [-] + [-]

一匹【いっぴき】one (of animals) [2105] + [1878]

とまる sit on, settle on

朱雀大路【すざくおおじ】Suzaku Avenue [2200] + [-] + [2133] + [1031]

以上は【いじょうは】since, as, seeing that [0025] + [2128]

市女笠【いちめがさ】broad-brimmed hat worn by women (here used to represent women) [1258] + [2135] + [-]

揉烏帽子【もみえぼし】lightly crumpled hat worn by men (here used to represent men) [-] + [-] + [0416] + [2125]

二三人【にさんにん】two or three people

One day, in the evening, a servant was waiting beneath the Rashō-mon gate for the rain to stop.

There was no one but this one man beneath the broad gate. A single cricket sat on a thick, round pillar from which the red lacquer was peeling in places. Since the gate stands on Suzaku Avenue, one would have expected to see the distinctive headgear of two or three other men or women waiting out the rain; but there was no one but this one man.

The reason was that over the last two or three years, a succession of disasters—earthquakes, whirlwinds, fires and famine—had occurred in Kyoto. The city's decline was multifaceted. According to old chronicles, it even happened that people broke up wooden effigies of the Buddha and sacred objects, heaped the pieces—still covered with red lacquer, or gold and silver leaf—on the roadside, and sold them to use as firewood.

....

[1224] + [1225] + [2111]

3

何故【なぜ】 why [0045] + [0778]

いう say, explain 🦮

二三年【にさんねん】 two or three years [1224] + [1225] + [1284]

京都【きょうと】 Kyoto [1297] + [1106]

地震【じしん】 earthquake [0152] + [1794]

～とか～とか such things as ~ and ~ 🦮

辻風【つじかぜ】 whirlwind [-] + [1908]

火事【かじ】 fire [2159] + [2220]

饑饉【ききん】 famine [-] + [-]

災【わざわい】 calamity, disaster [1400]

つづく happen one after another, occur continuously

起る【おこる】 take place, occur [2079]

洛中【らくちゅう】 in Kyoto [-] + [2150]

さびれ方【さびれかた】 manner of decline [1243]

一通り【ひととおり】 simple, of one type,

uncompounded [2105] + [1982]

旧記【きゅうき】 old chronicles/histories [0005] + [0974]

～によると according to

仏像【ぶつぞう】 images/statues of Buddha [0010] + [0123]

仏具【ぶつぐ】 religious artifacts [0010] + [1622]

打砕く【うちくだく】 smash, break [0142] + [0773]

丹【に】 red paint, vermilion lacquer [2147]

つく stick to 🦮

金銀【きんぎん】 silver and gold [1302] + [1133]

箔【はく】 foil, leaf, gilt [-]

木【き】 wood [2149]

路ばた【みちばた】 roadside [1031]

つみ重ねる【つみかさねる】 pile up [2223]

薪【たきぎ】 firewood [1538]

料【しろ】 material [0870]

売る【うる】 sell [1391]

洛中がその始末であるから、羅生門の修理などは、元より誰も捨てて顧る者がなかった。するとその荒れ果てたのをよい事にして、狐狸が棲む。盗人が棲む。とうとうしまいには、引取り手のない死人を、この門へ持って来て、棄てて行くという習慣さえ出来た。そこで、日の目が見えなくなると、誰でも気味を悪るがって、この門の近所へは足ぶみをしない事になってしまったのである。

　その代りまた鴉が何処からか、たくさん集って来た。昼間見ると、その鴉が、何羽となく輪を描いて、高い鴟尾のまわりを啼きながら、飛びまわっている。殊に門の上の空が、夕焼けであかくなる時には、それが胡麻をまいたように、はっきり見えた。

洛中【らくちゅう】in Kyoto [-] + [2150]

始末【しまつ】circumstances, situation [0211] + [2184]

羅生門【らしょうもん】Rashōmon gate [1679] + [2179] + [0597]

修理【しゅり】repair (usually read しゅうり) [0092] + [0659]

元より【もとより】of course, from the very start [1226]

誰も【だれも】(+ negative) nobody [-]

捨てる【すてる】ignore, leave as is, get rid of, throw away [0369]

顧る【かえりみる】have regard for, care about [1220]

者【もの】person [2047]

荒れ果てる【あれはてる】go to ruin, become dilapidated [1447] + [2217]

よい good, positive

事【こと】thing, state of affairs 🐛 [2220]

狐狸【こり】foxes and badgers [-] + [-]

棲む【すむ】live 🐛 [-]

盗人【ぬすびと】robbers, thieves [1714] + [2111]

とうとう finally

しまいには in the end

引取り手【ひきとりて】person who receives [0133] + [0847] + [2155]

死人【しにん／しびと】dead person, corpse [2194] + [2111]

門【もん】gate 🐛 [0597]

持つ【もつ】have, carry [0275] + [2211]

〜て来る【〜てくる】indicates continuation of an action up to a point 🐛 [2211]

棄てる【すてる】throw away, get rid of [1353]

〜て行く【〜てゆく】~ and go away [0157]

習慣【しゅうかん】custom, practice [1711] + [0487]

〜さえ even

出来る【できる】be established, come into being [2180] + [2211]

日の目【ひのめ】sunlight [1915] + [1927]

With Kyoto in this state, no one even thought about the Rashomon gate, let alone worried about its repair. Foxes and badgers took advantage of its decay to nest in it; robbers, too, lodged there. And in time the custom was even established of bringing dead people with no one to receive their remains to the gate, and abandoning them there. The sinister atmosphere made sure people gave the place a wide berth after sunset.

In place of people, crows had flocked to the gate in great numbers. By day you could see countless numbers of the birds flying around in circles and cawing at the high ornamental ridgepiece tiles. When the sky above the gate turned red as the sun set, they were especially noticeable and looked like a handful of sesame flung into the air. They came, of course, to peck at the flesh of the dead in the gate's upper story.

. . . .

見える【みえる】 be visible 悪 [1615]
誰でも【だれでも】 everybody
気味を悪るがる【きみをわるがる】 get a bad feeling from, find spooky [2037] + [0206] + [1758]
近所【きんじょ】 neighborhood, vicinity [1941] + [0568]
足ぶみをする【あしぶみをする】 set foot in [1386]
〜てしまう expresses completion with regret

4

その代り【そのかわり】 instead, in their place [0018]
鴉【からす】 crows 悪 [-]
何処からか【どこからか】 from somewhere or other [0045] + [1918]
集る【あつまる】 gather, assemble [1772]
昼間【ひるま】 daytime [1972] + [2094]
見る【みる】 look [1615]
何羽となく【なんわとなく】 in countless numbers (of birds) [0045] + [0167]

輪【わ】 circle [1067]
描く【えがく】 draw [0358]
高い【たかい】 high, tall [1330]
鴟尾【しび】 ornamental corner rooftile [-] + [1942]
まわり around
啼く【なく】 caw [-]
〜ながら while, as
飛びまわる【とびまわる】 fly around [2222]
殊に【ことに】 particularly, especially [0639]
上【うえ】 above, on top [2128]
空【そら】 the sky [1418]
夕焼け【ゆうやけ】 sunset [2123] + [0681]
あかい red
時【とき】 when [0625]
胡麻【ごま】 sesame [0623] + [1995]
まく scatter
はっきりと clearly

鴉は、勿論、門の上にある死人の肉を、啄みに来るのである。──尤も今日は、刻限が遅いせいか、一羽も見えない。唯、所々、崩れかかった、そうしてその崩れ目に長い草のはえた石段の上に、鴉の糞が、点々と白くこびりついているのが見える。下人は七段ある石段の一番上の段に、洗いざらした紺の襖の尻を据えて、右の頬に出来た、大きな面皰を気にしながら、ぼんやり、雨のふるのを眺めていた。

作者はさっき、「下人が雨やみを待っていた」と書いた。しかし、下人は雨がやんでも、格別どうしようという当てはない。ふだんなら、勿論、主人の家へ帰るべきはずである。ところがその主人からは、四五日前に暇を出された。

鴉【からす】crows 쪲 [-]
勿論【もちろん】of course [-] + [1058]
門【もん】gate [0597]
上【うえ】above, on top, upon 쪲 [2128]
死人【しにん／しびと】corpse [2194] + [2111]
肉【にく】flesh, meat [2042]
啄む【ついばむ】peck at [0299]
来る【くる】come (to do something) [2211]
尤も【もっとも】indeed, if truth be told [-]
今日【きょう】today [1246] + [1915]
刻限【こくげん】time [0851] + [0296]
遅い【おそい】late [1999]
〜せい because
一羽【いちわ】one bird [2105] + [0167]
見える【みえる】be visible, be seen 쪲 [1615]
唯【ただ】only, just [0339]
所々【ところどころ】here and there [0568]
崩れかかる【くずれかかる】begin to moulder and break up [1478]
崩れ目【くずれめ】crack [1478] + [1927]
長い【ながい】long [1626]

草【くさ】grass [1450]
はえる grow (of vegetation)
石段【いしだん】stone steps 쪲 [1884] + [0780]
糞【くそ】droppings [-]
点々と【てんてんと】here and there, in patches [1322]
白い【しろい】white [2175]
こびりつく stick to
下人【げにん】servant 쪲 [2115] + [2111]
七段【ななだん／しちだん】seven steps [2109] + [0780]
一番【いちばん】the most, the first, the top [2105] + [1761]
段【だん】step [0780]
洗いざらす【あらいざらす】wear out from washing [0288]
紺【こん】dark blue [0899]
襖【あお】everyday garment worn by men [-]
尻を据える【しりをすえる】sit oneself down [-] + [0365]
右【みぎ】right [1888]

But today—perhaps because it was late—there was not a single bird to be seen. Their sticky white droppings were spattered about on the crumbling stone steps, from the cracks of which long weeds sprouted. The servant, after lowering his faded blue kimono-clad bottom onto the seventh and top step of the stone staircase, blankly watched the rain fall while picking at a large pimple on his right cheek.

I wrote earlier that "A servant was waiting for the rain to stop." But in fact the servant had nothing in particular to do even after the rain stopped. Normally, of course, he would have returned to his master's house. However, he had been discharged from the service of that master some four or five days before.

頬【ほお】cheek [-]
出来る【できる】come out (of a growth, pimple) [2180] + [2211]
大きな【おおきな】big [2133]
面皰【にきび】pimple, spot [1324] + [-]
気にする【きにする】fuss about, worry about [2037]
〜ながら while, as
ぼんやり vacantly, absentmindedly
雨【あめ】rain [2218]
ふる fall
眺める【ながめる】look at [0795]

5

作者【さくしゃ】author [0049] + [2047]
さっき previously, before
雨やみ【あめやみ】the letup of the rain [2218]
待つ【まつ】wait for [0269]
書く【かく】write [1703]
しかし but, however
雨【あめ】rain [2218]

やむ stop, abate
格別【かくべつ】specially, particularly [0627] + [0760]
当て【あて】aim, purpose [1378]
ふだんなら normally, in normal conditions
勿論【もちろん】of course [-] + [1058]
主人【しゅじん】master 🗨 [1231] + [2111]
家【いえ】house [1458]
帰る【かえる】return, go back to [0098]
〜べき should 〜, ought to 〜
〜はず one would expect that 〜
ところが but
四五日【しごにち】four or five days [1928] + [2142] + [1915]
〜前【〜まえ】before, earlier [1453]
暇を出す【ひまをだす】send away, fire [0691] + [2180]

前にも書いたように、当時京都の町は一通りならず衰微していた。今この下人が、永年、使われていた主人から、暇を出されたのも、実はこの衰微の小さな余波に外ならない。だから「下人が雨やみを待っていた」というよりも「雨にふりこめられた下人が、行き所がなくて、途方にくれていた」という方が、適当である。その上、今日の空模様も少からず、この平安朝の下人の Sentimentalisme に影響した。申の刻下りからふり出した雨は、未に上るけしきがない。そこで、下人は、何を措いても差当り明日の暮しをどうにかしようとして——いわばどうにもならない事を、どうにかしようとして、とりとめもない考えをたどりながら、さっきから朱雀大路にふる雨の音を、聞くともなく聞いていたのである。

前【まえ】before [1453]
書く【かく】write [1703]
〜ように like, as
当時【とうじ】at that time [1378] + [0625]
京都【きょうと】Kyoto [1297] + [1106]
町【まち】city, town [0756]
一通りならず【ひととおりならず】not simple, not of one type, extreme [2105] + [1982]
衰微する【すいびする】decline, decay 夏 [1333] + [0461]
今【いま】now [1246]
下人【げにん】servant 夏 [2115] + [2111]
永年【ながねん】for a long time [1230] + [1284]
使う【つかう】employ [0068]
主人【しゅじん】master [1231] + [2111]
暇を出す【ひまをだす】send away, fire [0691] + [2180]
実は【じつは】truly, in fact [1416]

小さな【ちいさな】small [0002]
余波【よは】secondary effect, consequence [1289] + [0245]
〜に外ならない【〜にほかならない】be no more than [0135]
雨やみ【あめやみ】the letup of the rain [2218]
待つ【まつ】wait for [0269]
雨【あめ】rain 夏 [2218]
ふりこめる rain in, keep indoors with rain
行き所【ゆきどころ】place to go [0157] + [0568]
途方にくれる【とほうにくれる】be at a loss [1980] + [1243]
方【ほう】way (of saying something) [1243]
適当【てきとう】fit, proper [2020] + [1378]
その上【そのうえ】in addition [2128]
今日【きょう】today [1246] + [1915]
空模様【そらもよう】weather (*lit.,* "sky appearance") [1418] + [0720] + [0723]

As I said earlier, the city of Kyoto was experiencing a multifaceted decline. The fact that the servant had been discharged by the master who had employed him for so many years was no more than one insignificant, secondary effect of this overall decline. So, perhaps rather than saying, "A servant was waiting for the rain to stop," it would be more appropriate to say, "The rain-trapped servant had nowhere to go and was at the end of his tether." The dull weather further darkened the mood of our Heian-period servant. The rain, which had started falling at around five in the afternoon, showed no sign of stopping. The servant was thinking incoherent thoughts about what he could do to scrape through at least tomorrow—about how to make something of his hopeless situation. From a while back he had been listening—without really hearing anything—to the rain falling on Suzaku Avenue.

....

少からず 【すくなからず】 not a little [2163]

平安朝 【へいあんちょう】 Heian period (794 –1185) [2167] + [1373] + [1114]

影響する 【えいきょうする】 influence [1216] + [1840]

申の刻 【さるのこく】 the hour of the Monkey (3:00–5:00 P.M.) [-] + [0851] + [2115]

～下がり 【～さがり】 just past ～

ふり出す 【ふりだす】 start to fall [2180]

未に 【いまだに】 (+ negative) not yet [2185]

上る 【あがる】 let up (of rain) [2128]

けしき appearance, look

そこで at which point, so

何を措いても 【なにをおいても】 first of all [0045] + [-]

差当り 【さしあたり】 for the time being [2082] + [1378]

明日 【あす】 the next day [0572] + [1915]

暮し 【くらし】 living, livelihood [1522]

どうにかする manage, get through

いわば so to speak

どうにもならない hopeless

事 【こと】 situation, state of affairs [2220]

とりとめもない rambling

考え 【かんがえ】 thoughts [2039]

たどる trace, follow

さっき before

朱雀大路 【すざくおおじ】 Suzaku Avenue [2200] + [-] + [2133] + [1031]

ふる fall

音 【おと】 sound [1312]

聞く 【きく】 listen [2097]

～ともなく not really ～

雨は、羅生門をつつんで、遠くから、ざあっという音をあつめて来る。夕闇は次第に空を低くして、見上げると、門の屋根が、斜につき出した甍の先に、重たくうす暗い雲を支えている。

どうにもならない事を、どうにかするためには、手段を選んでいる遑はない。選んでいれば、築土の下か、道ばたの土の上で、饑死をするばかりである。そうして、この門の上へ持って来て、犬のように棄てられてしまうばかりである。選ばないとすれば——下人の考えは、何度も同じ道を低徊したあげくに、やっとこの局所へ逢着した。

6

雨【あめ】rain [2218]
羅生門【らしょうもん】Rashōmon gate [1679]+[2179]+[0597]
つつむ wrap up, cover
遠い【とおい】far, distant [2013]
ざあっ onomatopoeic expression that describes the sound of heavy rain falling
音【おと】sound [1312]
あつめる accumulate
～て来る【～てくる】come and ~ [2211]
夕闇【ゆうやみ】evening darkness, dusk [2123]+[-]
次第に【しだいに】gradually [0038]+[1706]
空【そら】the sky [1418]
低い【ひくい】low [0054]
見上げる【みあげる】look up [1615]+[2128]
門【もん】gate 🔊 [0597]
屋根【やね】roof [1973]+[0631]

斜に【ななめに】diagonally [0999]
つき出す【つきだす】stick out [2180]
甍【いらか】rooftile [-]
先【さき】tip [1552]
重たい【おもたい】heavy [2223]
うす暗い【うすぐらい】dim, dark [0689]
雲【くも】cloud [1774]
支える【ささえる】support, hold up [1251]

7

どうにもならない hopeless
事【こと】situation, state of affairs [2220]
どうにかする manage, get through
～ために in order to ~, so as to ~
手段【しゅだん】means, method [2155]+[0780]
選ぶ【えらぶ】choose, select 🔊 [2026]
遑【いとま】spare time, leisure [-]
築土【ついじ】roofed mudwall [1743]+[2127]
下【した】beneath, below [2115]

The rain, enveloping the gate, beat down in violent torrents that swept in from far away. Dusk pushed the sky down low, and if you looked up, you got the impression that the tile-ends that protruded at a slant from the roof of the gate were holding up the heavy, dark clouds.

The servant did not have the luxury of being fastidious as to how he was going to "make something of his hopeless situation." Were he fussy, it would only mean starving to death beneath a mud wall or by the side of the road, before being brought to the upper part of the gate and abandoned like a dog. "If I can do whatever it takes …"—his thoughts had traveled the same path over and over again before he had finally reached this conclusion.

....

道ばた 【みちばた】 roadside [2000]
土 【つち】 earth [2127]
上 【うえ】 on, upon 炙 [2128]
餓死 【うえじに】 death by hunger [-] + [2194]
〜ばかり only, just 炙
持つ 【もつ】 have, carry [0275] [2211]
〜て来る 【〜てくる】 indicates progression up to a point [2211]
犬 【いぬ】 dog [2160]
〜のように like, the same as
棄てる 【すてる】 throw away, abandon [1353]
〜てしまう expresses completion of an action with regret
下人 【げにん】 servant [2115] + [2111]
考え 【かんがえ】 thought, idea [2039]
何度も 【なんども】 many times [0045] + [1974]
同じ 【おなじ】 the same [1897]
道 【みち】 track, road, path [2000]
低徊する 【ていかいする】 linger, hover

[0054] + [-]
〜あげく (after a verb in the past tense) after, in the end
やっと finally
局所 【きょくしょ】 point [1943] + [0568]
逢着する 【ほうちゃくする】 encounter [-] + [2086]

しかしこの「すれば」は、何時_{いつ}までたっても、結局「すれば」であった。下人は、手段を選ばないという事を肯定しながらも、この「すれば」のかたをつけるために、当然、その後_{のち}に来_{きた}るべき「盗人になるより外_{ほか}に仕方がない」という事を、積極的に肯定するだけの、勇気が出ずにいたのである。

下人は、大きな嚔_{くさめ}をして、それから、大儀_{たいぎ}そうに立上った。夕冷えのする京都は、もう火桶_{ひおけ}が欲しいほどの寒さである。風は門の柱と柱との間を、夕闇と共に遠慮なく、吹きぬける。丹塗の柱にとまっていた蟋蟀_{きりぎりす}も、もうどこかへ行ってしまった。

しかし but, however

何時までたっても【いつまでたっても】no matter how much time passes [0045] + [0625]

結局【けっきょく】finally, in the final analysis [0912] + [1943]

下人【げにん】servant 桑 [2115] + [2111]

手段【しゅだん】means, method [2155] + [0780]

選ぶ【えらぶ】choose, select [2026]

事【こと】position, point of view 桑 [2220]

肯定する【こうていする】endorse, affirm 桑 [1567] + [1420]

〜ながらも even though

かたをつける bring to a conclusion

〜ために in order to 〜, so as to 〜

当然【とうぜん】of course, naturally [1378] + [1779]

後【のち】after [0267]

来るべき【きたるべき】coming, eventual [2211]

盗人【ぬすびと】robber [1714] + [2111]

〜より外に【〜よりほかに】other than [0135]

仕方がない【しかたがない】have no alternative [0021] + [1243]

積極的に【せっきょくてきに】vigorously, enthusiastically [0835] + [0695] + [0767]

勇気【ゆうき】courage [1326] + [2037]

出ず【でず】not muster [2180]

8

大きな【おおきな】big [2133]

嚔【くさめ】sneeze [-]

大儀【たいぎ】tired, exhausted, worn out [2133] + [0124]

立上る【たちあがる】stand up [1257] + [2128]

夕冷え【ゆうびえ】evening chill [2123] + [0057]

京都【きょうと】Kyoto [1297] + [1106]

火桶【ひおけ】bucket of coals, brazier [2159] + [-]

欲しい【ほしい】want, desire [0990]

However, this "if I can" remained no more than an abstract idea. Even though the servant had decided that he had to do what he had to do, he did not have the courage to admit wholeheartedly to himself that the logical next step was for him to become a robber, pure and simple.

The servant sneezed loudly and raised himself wearily to his feet. The evening chill of Kyoto was so biting that he longed for a brazier. Together with the dusk, the pitiless wind blew through the pillars of the gate. The cricket which had been sitting on the red-lacquered pillar was long gone.

〜ほど to the extent that 〜
寒さ【さむさ】coldness [1190]
風【かぜ】wind [1908]
門【もん】gate [0597]
柱【はしら】pillar, column ⚱ [0603]
間【あいだ】between [2094]
夕闇【ゆうやみ】evening darkness [2123] + [-]
〜と共に【〜とともに】together with [1551]
遠慮【えんりょ】hesitation, reserve [2013] +
　　[2057]
吹きぬける【ふきぬける】blow through [0170]
丹塗の【にぬりの】red-painted, vermil-
　　ion-lacquered [2147] + [1818]
とまる sit on, settle on
蟋蟀【きりぎりす】cricket [-] + [-]
どこか somewhere
行く【いく】go [0157]
〜てしまう expresses completion of an
　　action with regret

　下人は、頸をちぢめながら、山吹の汗衫に重ねた、紺の襖の肩を高くして、門のまわりを見まわした。雨風の患のない、人目にかかる惧のない、一晩楽にねられそうな所があれば、そこでともかくも、夜を明かそうと思ったからである。すると、幸門の上の楼へ上る、幅の広い、これも丹を塗った梯子が眼についた。上なら、人がいたにしても、どうせ死人ばかりである。下人はそこで、腰にさげた聖柄の太刀が鞘走らないように気をつけながら、藁草履をはいた足を、その梯子の一番下の段へふみかけた。

The servant tucked his head into his chest, pulled the blue kimono he wore over his yellow undergarment up around his shoulders and inspected the gate. If there were a spot that was out of reach of rain and wind, he thought, a spot where he wouldn't be seen and where he could sleep comfortably the night through, then he would spend the night there. By a stroke of good luck, the broad lacquered ladder, which led to the tower above the gate, caught his eye precisely at that instant. If anyone were up there, they would all be dead anyway, so no matter! Making sure that the sword hanging at his side, with its unadorned wooden hilt, did not slip from its scabbard, the servant placed his sandal-clad foot on the bottom rung of the ladder.

塗る【ぬる】paint [1818]

梯子【はしご】ladder 🔥 [-] + [2125]

眼につく【めにつく】come into view [0796]

人【ひと】person, people [2111]

どうせ in any event, in any case, only

死人【しにん／しびと】corpse [2194] + [2111]

〜ばかり only, just, merely

腰【こし】waist [0711]

さげる hang

聖柄【ひじりづか】plain wooden sword hilt (NOTE: normally sword hilts were covered in sharkskin) [1812] + [0604]

太刀【たち】sword [1360] + [1857]

鞘走る【さやばしる】slip out of the scabbard [-] + [1390]

〜ように so that

気をつける【きをつける】be careful [2037]

藁草履【わらぞうり】straw sandals [-] + [1450] + [2028]

はく wear (on the feet)

足【あし】feet [1386]

一番【いちばん】the most [2105] + [1761]

下【した】bottom [2115]

段【だん】step [0780]

ふみかける place one's foot on, step on

それから、何分かの後である。羅生門の楼の上へ出る、幅の広い梯子の中段に、一人の男が、猫のように身をちぢめて、息を殺しながら、上の容子を窺っていた。楼の上からさす火の光が、かすかに、その男の右の頬をぬらしている。短い鬚の中に、赤く膿を持った面皰のある頬である。下人は、始めから、この上にいる者は、死人ばかりだと高を括っていた。それが、梯子を二三段上って見ると、上では誰か火をとぼして、しかもその火を其処此処と、動かしているらしい。これは、その濁った、黄いろい光が、隅々に蜘蛛の巣をかけた天井裏に、揺れながら映ったので、すぐにそれと知れたのである。この雨の夜に、この羅生門の上で、火をともしているからは、どうせ唯の者ではない。

何分か【なんぷんか／なんふんか】a few minutes [0045] + [1247]

後【のち】after, later [0267]

羅生門【らしょうもん】Rashōmon gate ☠ [1679] + [2179] + [0597]

楼【ろう】tower, lookout place, story ☠ [0697]

上【うえ】above, on top ☠ [2128]

出る【でる】emerge [2180]

幅【はば】breadth, width [0417]

広い【ひろい】broad [1921]

梯子【はしご】ladder ☠ [-] + [2125]

中段【ちゅうだん】halfway up, middle stair [2150] + [0780]

一人【ひとり】a single person [2105] + [2111]

男【おとこ】man ☠ [1613]

猫【ねこ】cat [0391]

～のように like

身【み】body [2213]

ちぢめる scrunch up, make smaller

息を殺す【いきをころす】hold one's breath [1693] + [0889]

～ながら while, as ☠

容子【ようす】appearance, state of things [1462] + [2125]

窺う【うかがう】look, peep [-]

さす emit (light)

火【ひ】fire ☠ [2159]

光【ひかり】light, glow [1550]

かすかに faintly, weakly, dimly

右【みぎ】right [1888]

頬【ほお】cheek ☠ [-]

ぬらす soak, pour on, illuminate

短い【みじかい】short [0801]

鬚【ひげ】beard (around the chin), chin whiskers [-]

中【なか】inside, among [2150]

赤い【あかい】red [1389]

膿【うみ】puss, foul secretion [-]

持つ【もつ】have, hold, contain [0275]

It was some minutes later. The man—now halfway up the ladder that led to the tower room of the Rashōmon gate—held his breath, scrunched up his body like a cat and looked up. The light of a flame from the tower illuminated his right cheek faintly. It was the cheek with the angry, puss-gorged pimple amongst the stubble. The servant had optimistically assumed that everyone up there would be dead. Climbing a further two or three rungs up the ladder, however, he saw that someone not only had a light, but that they were moving it to and fro. He realized that immediately because the glow of the muddy yellow light was wobbling on the cobweb-covered ceiling. Whoever was burning a light in the upper floor of the Rashomon gate that rainy evening was no normal being.

....

面皰【にきび】pimple [1324] + [-]
下人【げにん】servant [2115] + [2111]
始めから【はじめから】from the start [0211]
者【もの】person, people [2047]
死人【しにん／しびと】dead people [2194] + [2111]
〜ばかり just
高を括る【たかをくくる】underrate, not take seriously [1330] + [0276]
二三段【にさんだん】two or three steps [1224] + [1225] + [0780]
上る【あがる】go up [2128]
見る【みる】see [1615]
誰か【だれか】someone [-]
火をとぼす【ひをとぼす】light (a candle, torch) [2159]
しかも furthermore
其処此処【そздесь】here and there [-] + [1918] + [-] + [1918]
動かす【うごかす】move around [1163]

濁る【にごる】be muddy, be unclear [0533]
黄いろい【きいろい】yellow [1596]
隅々【すみずみ】every corner [0450]
蜘蛛の巣【くものす】spider's web [-] + [-] + [1477]
かける hang
天井裏【てんじょううら】ceiling [2148] + [2153] + [1354]
揺れる【ゆれる】wobble, shake, tremble [0434]
映る【うつる】be reflected, be visible [0600]
すぐに immediately
知れる【しれる】be known, be evident [0768]
雨【あめ】rain [2218]
夜【よる】night [1301]
火をともす【ひをともす】light (a candle, torch) (variant of 火をとぼす) [2159]
どうせ in any event, in any case, anyway
唯の者【ただのもの】normal/ordinary person [0339] + [2047]

下人は、守宮のように足音をぬすんで、やっと急な梯子を、一番上の段まで這うようにして上りつめた。そうして体を出来るだけ、平にしながら、頸を出来るだけ、前へ出して、恐る恐る、楼の内を覗いて見た。

見ると、楼の内には、噂に聞いた通り、幾つかの屍骸が、無造作に棄ててあるが、火の光の及ぶ範囲が、思ったより狭いので、数は幾つともわからない。唯、おぼろげながら、知れるのは、その中に裸の屍骸と、着物を着た屍骸とがあるという事である。勿論、中には女も男もまじっているらしい。そうして、その屍骸は皆、それが、嘗、生きていた人間だという事実さえ疑われるほど、土を捏ねて造った人形のように、口を開いたり手を延ばしたりして、ごろごろ床の上にころがっていた。

11

下人【げにん】 servant [2115] + [2111]

守宮【やもり】 lizard [1375] + [1459]

〜のように like ☠

足音をぬすむ【あしおとをぬすむ】 be stealthy, go on silent feet (*lit.,* "steal foot-noise") [1386] + [1312]

やっと finally, with great effort

急な【きゅうな】 steep [1328]

梯子【はしご】 ladder [-] + [2125]

一番【いちばん】 the most [2105] + [1761]

上【うえ】 top ☠ [2128]

段【だん】 step [0780]

這う【はう】 crawl [-]

〜ようにする make as if to 〜

上りつめる【のぼりつめる】 climb the whole way, climb to the top [2128]

体【からだ】 body [0052]

出来るだけ【できるだけ】 as much as possible ☠ [2180] + [2211]

平にする【たいらにする】 make flat [2167]

〜ながら while, as

頸【くび】 neck, head [-]

前【まえ】 forward, in front [1453]

出す【だす】 stick out [2180]

恐る恐る【おそるおそる】 fearfully, in trepidation [1696]

楼【ろう】 tower, lookout place, story ☠ [0697]

内【うち】 inside ☠ [2162]

覗く【のぞく】 have a look [-]

〜て見る【〜てみる】 try to 〜 [1615]

12

見る【みる】 look [1615]

噂【うわさ】 rumor [-]

聞く【きく】 hear [2097]

〜通り【〜とおり】 just as, in accordance with [1982]

幾つか【いくつか】 some, a certain number [2229]

The servant, crawling as quietly as a lizard, reached the steep ladder's topmost rung. Flattening his body as much as possible, he stuck his head as far forward as it would go and peeped fearfully into the tower.

Looking in, he saw—as the rumors had said—several corpses strewn carelessly about. Since the light of the flame did not reach as far as he had thought, he could not tell how many there were. What he could vaguely make out was that some of the bodies were naked and some were clothed. As was to be expected, there was a mixture of men and women. The corpses were lying higgledy-piggledy on the floor, their mouths gaping, their arms thrown wide. They looked so like dolls of clay, you could scarcely believe they had once been living beings.

· ·

屍骸【しがい】corpses 🦎 [-] + [-]
無造作に【むぞうさに】carelessly, casually [1351] + [1983] + [0049]
棄てる【すてる】abandon, throw out [-]
火【ひ】fire [2159]
光【ひかり】light, glow [1550]
及ぶ【およぶ】extend, reach [2122]
範囲【はんい】scope, range [1740] + [1949]
思う【おもう】think, expect [1633]
〜より more than
狭い【せまい】small, narrow [0294]
数【かず】number [1170]
幾つ【いくつ】how many [2229]
わかる understand
唯【ただ】but, just [0339]
おぼろげ vague, misty, unclear
〜ながら while
知れる【しれる】be known, be evident [0768]
中【なか】among 🦎 [2150]
裸の【はだかの】naked [0819]
着物【きもの】clothes [2086] + [0587]
着る【きる】wear [2086]
事【こと】state of affairs, situation [2220]

勿論【もちろん】of course [-] + [1058]
女【おんな】women [2135]
男【おとこ】men [1613]
まじる be mixed together
皆【みな】all [1581]
嘗て【かつて】previously, before [-]
生きる【いきる】be alive [2179]
人間【にんげん】human beings [2111] + [2094]
事実【じじつ】fact, reality [2220] + [1416]
〜さえ even, indeed
疑う【うたがう】doubt, disbelieve [1050]
〜ほど to the extent that 〜
土【つち】earth, mud, clay [2127]
捏ねる【こねる】knead [-]
造る【つくる】make [1983]
人形【にんぎょう】dolls [2111] + [0565]
口【くち】mouths [2119]
開く【あく】open [2092]
手【て】arms, hands [2155]
延ばす【のばす】stretch out, extend [1952]
ごろごろ higgledy-piggledy
床【ゆか】floor [1947]
ころがる lie around

しかも、肩とか胸とかの高くなっている部分に、ぼんやり
した火の光をうけて、低くなっている部分の影を一層暗く
しながら、永久に啞の如く黙っていた。

下人は、それらの屍骸の腐爛した臭気に思わず、鼻を掩
った。しかし、その手は、次の瞬間には、もう鼻を掩う事
を忘れていた。或る強い感情が、殆 悉 この男の嗅覚を奪
ってしまったからである。

下人の眼は、その時、はじめて、その屍骸の中に蹲って
いる人間を見た。檜皮色の着物を着た、背の低い、痩せた、
白髪頭の、猿のような老婆である。その老婆は、右の手に
火をともした松の木片を持って、その屍骸の一つの顔を覗
きこむように眺めていた。髪の毛の長い所を見ると、多分
女の屍骸であろう。

しかも furthermore, moreover
肩【かた】shoulder [1238]
胸【むね】chest [0647]
高い【たかい】high, uppermost [1330]
部分【ぶぶん】part 🔥 [1099] + [1247]
ぼんやりした vague, indistinct
火【ひ】fire [2159]
光【ひかり】light, glow [1550]
うける get, receive
低い【ひくい】low [0054]
影【かげ】shadow [1216]
一層【いっそう】one degree, all the more
　[2105] + [2021]
暗い【くらい】dark [0689]
永久に【えいきゅう】forever [1230] + [2121]
啞【おし】deaf-mute (NOTE: now pejora-
　tive; do not use) [-]
如く【ごとく】like [0154]
黙る【だまる】be silent, not talk [1833]

13

下人【げにん】servant 🔥 [2115] + [2111]
屍骸【しがい】corpse 🔥 [-] + [-]
腐爛する【ふらんする】decompose, rot
　[2022] + [-]
臭気【しゅうき】foul odor, stench [1682] + [2037]
思わず【おもわず】without thinking, invol-
　untarily [1633]
鼻【はな】nose 🔥 [1739]
掩う【おおう】cover 🔥 [-]
しかし but, however
手【て】hand 🔥 [2155]
次【つぎ】next [0038]
瞬間【しゅんかん】moment [0841] + [2094]
事【こと】act [2220]
忘れる【わすれる】forget [1285]
或る【ある】a certain [-]
強い【つよい】strong [0349]
感情【かんじょう】emotion [1814] + [0353]

The bits of them that jutted up, like their shoulders and chests, caught the light's dim glow, but this only emphasized the darkness of the shadows on the lower-lying parts of their bodies. Like mutes they kept an eternal silence.

The servant instinctively covered his nose at the foul odor of decomposition. The next moment he forgot even to complete the gesture. A powerful emotion had robbed him completely of his sense of smell.

His eyes caught sight of someone squatting amongst the corpses. Clad in a brown kimono, short, emaciated, and with gray hair, it was an old, monkey-like woman. She had a pine torch in her right hand and was gazing intently at the face of one of the corpses. Judging from the long hair, it was probably the body of a woman.

....

殆【ほとんど】almost [-]
悉【ことごとく】fully, altogether, completely [-]
男【おとこ】man [1613]
嗅覚【きゅうかく】sense of smell [-] + [1668]
奪う【うばう】rob, take away [1517]
〜てしまう thoroughly ~

14
眼【め】eyes [0796]
時【とき】time, moment [0625]
はじめて first
中【なか】among [2150]
蹲る【うずくまる】crouch, squat [-]
人間【にんげん】human being [2111] + [2094]
見る【みる】see ⚥ [1615]
檜皮色【ひわだいろ】color of cypress bark, dark brown [-] + [1923] + [1280]
着物【きもの】clothes [2086] + [0587]
着る【きる】wear [2086]
背の低い【せのひくい】short [1641] + [0054]
痩せる【やせる】be thin [-]
白髪頭【しらがあたま】white-haired head

[2175] + [1821] + [1073]
猿【さる】monkey [0479]
〜のような like ⚥
老婆【ろうば】old woman ⚥ [2040] + [1768]
右【みぎ】right [1888]
手【て】hand, arm [2155]
火をともす【ひをともす】light (a candle, torch) [2159]
松【まつ】pine [0580]
木片【きぎれ】branch [2149] + [2158]
持つ【もつ】carry, hold [0275]
一つ【ひとつ】one [2105]
顔【かお】face [1177]
覗きこむ【のぞきこむ】peer closely at, scrutinize [-]
〜ように like, as if
眺める【ながめる】gaze at [0795]
髪の毛【かみのけ】hair [1821] + [2152]
長い【ながい】long [1626]
所【ところ】fact, circumstance [0568]
多分【たぶん】probably [1372] + [1247]
女【おんな】woman [2135]

　下人は、六分の恐怖と四分の好奇心とに動かされて、暫時（ざんじ）は呼吸（いき）をするのさえ忘れていた。旧記の記者の語を借りれば、「頭身の毛も太（ふと）る」ように感じたのである。すると、老婆は、松の木片を、床板の間に挿（さ）して、それから、今まで眺めていた屍骸の首に両手をかけると、丁度（ちょうど）、猿の親が猿の子の虱（しらみ）をとるように、その長い髪の毛を一本ずつ抜きはじめた。髪は手に従って抜けるらしい。

　その髪の毛が、一本ずつ抜けるのに従って、下人の心からは、恐怖が少しずつ消えて行った。そうして、それと同時に、この老婆に対するはげしい憎悪が、少しずつ動いて来た。——いや、この老婆に対するといっては、語弊（ごへい）があるかも知れない。

下人【げにん】servant 🅰 [2115] + [2111]

六分【ろくぶ】six parts (out of ten) [1244] + [1247]

恐怖【きょうふ】fear 🅰 [1696] + [1247]

四分【しぶ】four parts (out of ten) [1928] + [1247]

好奇心【こうきしん】curiosity [0155] + [1409] + [0004]

動かす【うごかす】move, stir, touch [1163]

暫時【ざんじ】for a short while, for a moment [1832] + [0625]

呼吸【いき】breath, breathing [0205] + [0150]

〜さえ even

忘れる【わすれる】forget [1285]

旧記【きゅうき】old chronicles/histories [0005] + [0974]

記者【きしゃ】writers, chroniclers [0974] + [2047]

語【ご】phrase, expression [1040]

借りる【借りる】borrow [0091]

頭身【とうしん】head and body [1073] + [2213]

毛【け】hair 🅰 [2152]

太る【ふとる】thicken, stand thick [1360]

〜ように like

感じる【かんじる】feel [1814]

老婆【ろうば】old woman 🅰 [2040] + [1768]

松【まつ】pine [0580]

木片【きぎれ】branch [2149] + [2158]

床板【ゆかいた】floorboards [1947] + [0575]

間【あいだ】between [2094]

挿す【さす】push in [0317]

今まで【いままで】until now [1246]

眺める【ながめる】gaze at [0795]

屍骸【しがい】corpse [-] + [-]

首【くび】head [1452]

両手【りょうて】both hands [2191] + [2155]

かける place, put

丁度【ちょうど】exactly [2106] + [1974]

For a short while the servant, moved six parts by fear and four parts by curiosity, forgot even to breathe. To borrow a phrase from one of the old chroniclers, he felt "the hairs of his head and body stand thick." Then the old woman stuck the pine torch into a gap in the floorboards. She placed both hands on the head of the corpse she had been looking at and, like a monkey picking lice off its young, started plucking out the long hair, strand by strand. The hair seemed to come out with very little effort.

As the strands of hair were plucked out one by one, so the fear in the servant's heart slowly began to melt away. At the same time, an intense hatred of the old woman began to move inside him. —No, to say "of the old woman" is, I think, inaccurate.

猿【さる】monkey 🐒 [0479]
親【おや】parent, mother [1172]
子【こ】baby, child, young [2125]
虱【しらみ】lice [-]
とる pick off, remove
長い【ながい】long [1626]
髪の毛【かみのけ】hair 🐒 [1821] + [2152]
一本【いっぽん】one strand 🐒 [2105] + [2183]
〜ずつ at a time, individually 🐒
抜く【ぬく】pull out [0183]
〜はじめる begin to 〜
髪【かみ】hair [1821]
手【て】hand [2155]
従う【したがう】follow, be obedient to [0309]
抜ける【ぬける】come out 🐒 [0183]

16

心【こころ】heart, mind [0004]
少し【すこし】a little 🐒 [2163]
消える【きえる】disappear, vanish [0327]

〜て行く【〜ていく】indicates progression away from the servant [0157]
〜と同時に【〜とどうじに】at the same time as [1897] + [0625]
〜に対する【〜にたいする】toward 🐒 [0556]
はげしい intense, passionate
憎悪【ぞうお】hatred [0489] ١ [1758]
動く【うごく】move, stir [1163]
〜て来る【〜てくる】begin to 〜 [2211]
〜といっては to say 〜
語弊【ごへい】inaccurate/misleading expression [1040] + [1843]
〜かも知れない【〜かもしれない】maybe, perhaps [0768]

寧(むしろ)、あらゆる悪に対する反感が、一分毎(ごと)に強さを増して来たのである。この時、誰(だれ)かがこの下人に、さっき門の下でこの男が考えていた、饑死をするか盗人になるかという問題を、改めて持出したら、恐らく下人は、何の未練もなく、饑死を選んだ事であろう。それほど、この男の悪を憎む心は、老婆の床に挿した松の木片のように、勢よく燃え上り出していたのである。

17 下人には、勿論(もちろん)、何故(なぜ)老婆が死人の髪の毛を抜くかわからなかった。従って、合理的には、それを善悪の何れ(いずれ)に片づけてよいか知らなかった。しかし下人にとっては、この雨の夜に、この羅生門の上で、死人の髪の毛を抜くという事が、それだけで既(すで)に許すべからざる悪であった。勿論(もちろん)、下人は、さっきまで、自分が、盗人になる気でいた事なぞは、とうに忘れているのである。

寧【むしろ】on the contrary [1519]
あらゆる each and every, all
悪【あく】wickedness, evil ☠ [1758]
〜に対する【〜にたいする】toward [0556]
反感【はんかん】feeling of revulsion [1869] + [1814]
一分【いっぷん】one minute [2105] + [1247]
〜毎に【〜ごとに】each, every [1283]
強さ【つよさ】strength [0349]
増す【ます】increase, make more [0483]
〜て来る【〜てくる】begin to ~ [2211]
時【とき】time, moment [0625]
誰か【だれか】someone [-]
下人【げにん】servant ☠ [2115] + [2111]
さっき before, just now ☠
門【もん】gate [0597]
下【した】beneath, under [2115]
男【おとこ】man ☠ [1613]
考える【かんがえる】think [2039]
饑死【うえじに】death by starvation ☠ [-] + [2194]
盗人【ぬすびと】robber, thief ☠ [1714] + [2111]
問題【もんだい】question, problem [2091] + [2103]
改めて【あらためて】once again [0180]
持出す【もちだす】bring up, broach (a topic) [0275] + [2180]
恐らく【おそらく】perhaps, probably [1696]
何の【なんの】(+ negative) with no trace of [0045]
未練【みれん】regret [2185] + [0931]
選ぶ【えらぶ】choose, select [2026]
事【こと】situation, act, deed, fact ☠ [2220]
それほど to such an extent
憎む【にくむ】hate [0489]
心【こころ】heart, mind, feelings [0004]
老婆【ろうば】old woman ☠ [2040] + [1768]
床【ゆか】floor [1947]

It was rather that his antipathy to all forms of evil was growing stronger by the minute. At that moment, if someone had again raised the question that he had been thinking about under the gate—namely, whether to starve to death or become a robber—he would probably have chosen starvation without a trace of regret. That was how much the servant's loathing for evil had flared up: as vigorously as the pine torch that the old woman had wedged in between the floorboards.

Of course, the servant had no idea why the old woman was plucking the dead woman's hair. So, in rational terms, he could not really know whether to define what she was doing as either good or bad. But as far as the servant was concerned, plucking the hair of the dead on that rain-swept night in the Rashōmon gate was self-evidently an unpardonable evil. Of course, he had already forgotten that it was only a little while ago that he had made up his mind to become a thief himself.

挿す【さす】push in [0317]
松【まつ】pine [0580]
木片【きぎれ】branch [2149] + [2158]
〜のように like
勢よく【いきおいよく】energetically, vigorously [1829]
燃え上り出す【もえあがりだす】begin to burst into flames [0739] + [2128] + [2180]

17

勿論【もちろん】of course 🐾 [-] + [1058]
何故【なぜ】why [0045] + [0778]
死人【しにん／しびと】corpse 🐾 [2194] + [2111]
髪の毛【かみのけ】hair 🐾 [1821] + [2152]
抜く【ぬく】take out, pluck 🐾 [0183]
わかる understand
従って【したがって】therefore, so [0309]
合理的に【ごうりてきに】rationally [1274] + [0659] + [0767]
善悪【ぜんあく】good and evil, right and wrong [1501] + [1758]

何れ【いずれ】one or the other, one of two [0045]
片づける【かたづける】deal with, sort out, define [2158]
よい appropriate, good
知る【しる】know [0768]
しかし but, however
〜にとって for
雨【あめ】rain [2218]
夜【よる】night [1301]
羅生門【らしょうもん】Rashōmon gate [1679] + [2179] + [0597]
上【うえ】above, on top [2128]
既に【すでに】already [0791]
許すべからざる【ゆるすべからざる】unforgivable [0986]
自分【じぶん】oneself, himself [2195] + [1247]
気【き】feeling, desire, spirit [2037]
とうに already, long ago
忘れる【わすれる】forget [1285]

そこで、下人は、両足に力を入れて、いきなり、梯子から上へ飛び上った。そうして聖柄の太刀に手をかけながら、大股に老婆の前へ歩みよった。老婆が驚いたのはいうまでもない。

老婆は、一目下人を見ると、まるで弩にでも弾かれたように、飛び上った。

「おのれ、どこへ行く。」

下人は、老婆が屍骸につまずきながら、慌てふためいて逃げようとする行手を塞いで、こう罵った。老婆は、それでも下人をつきのけて行こうとする。下人はまた、それを行かすまいとして押しもどす。二人は屍骸の中で、暫、無言のまま、つかみ合った。しかし勝敗は、はじめから、わかっている。下人はとうとう、老婆の腕をつかんで、無理にそこへ扭じ倒した。丁度、鶏の脚のような、骨と皮ばかりの腕である。

18

そこで and so, then
下人【げにん】servant 🏃 [2115] + [2111]
両足【りょうあし】both legs [2191] + [1386]
力【ちから】strength, force [2114]
入れる【いれる】put in [2113]
いきなり suddenly
梯子【はしご】ladder [-] + [2125]
上【うえ】up, above [2128]
飛び上る【とびあがる】fly upward 🏃 [2222] + [2128]
聖柄【ひじりづか】plain wooden sword handle [1812] + [0604]
太刀【たち】sword [1360] + [1857]
手【て】hand [2155]
かける put, place
大股に【おおまたに】with long strides [2133] + [-]

老婆【ろうば】old woman 🏃 [2040] + [1768]
前【まえ】in front of [1453]
歩みよる【あゆみよる】walk up to [1566]
驚く【おどろく】be surprised [1848]
いうまでもない it goes without saying, needless to say

19

一目【ひとめ】glimpse, single glance [2105] + [1927]
見る【みる】see [1615]
まるで〜ように as if
弩【いしゆみ】sling [-]
弾く【はじく】shoot, propel [0418]
〜ように as if

20

おのれ you (pejorative)
行く【いく／ゆく】go 🏃 [0157]

Tensing both his legs, the servant suddenly sprang up off the ladder. His hand upon the wooden hilt of his sword, he strode over to the old woman. No need for me to tell you that the old woman was flabbergasted.

When the old woman caught sight of the servant, she leapt up as if she had been shot out of a sling.

"You wretch! Where do you think you're going?"

The servant cursed the old woman and barred her way as she stumbled over the corpses in her panicky eagerness to escape. Undeterred, she tried to push him to one side and slip by. But he had no intention of letting her go, and pushed her right back. For a while the two of them grappled wordlessly among the corpses. The outcome, however, was a foregone conclusion. In the end, the servant grabbed the arms of the old woman and twisted her down to the floor, despite her resistance. Her arms were just skin and bone—like chicken feet.

21

屍骸【しがい】corpse 愛 [-] + [-]
つまずく trip over
〜ながら while, as
慌てふためく【あわてふためく】be in a panic [0425]
逃げる【にげる】escape, flee, run off [1970]
行手【ゆくて】route, way [0157] + [2155]
塞ぐ【ふさぐ】block, obstruct [-]
罵る【ののしる】revile, curse [-]
つきのける thrust aside
また once again, moreover
行かす【ゆかす】allow to go [0157]
〜まい would not 〜
押しもどす【おしもどす】push back [0234]
二人【ふたり】two people [1224] + [2111]
中【なか】among [2150]
暫【しばらく】for a while [1832]
無言【むごん】without a word, speechless [1351] + [1233]
〜のまま still

つかみ合う【つかみあう】hold/clasp each other [1274]
しかし but, however
勝敗【しょうはい】outcome, result [0686] + [0991]
はじめから from the start
わかる know, understand
とうとう finally
腕【うで】arm 愛 [0687]
つかむ grab
無理に【むりに】against one's will, by force [1351] + [0659]
扭じ倒す【ねじたおす】twist down, wrestle to the floor [-] + [0093]
丁度【ちょうど】exactly, precisely [2106] + [1974]
鶏【とり】chicken [1158]
脚【あし】legs, limbs [0664]
〜のような like
骨【ほね】bone [1699]
皮【かわ】skin [1923]
〜ばかり only, nothing but

「何をしていた。いえ。いわぬと、これだぞよ。」

　下人は、老婆をつき放すと、いきなり、太刀の鞘を払って、白い鋼の色を、その眼の前へつきつけた。けれども、老婆は黙っている。両手をわなわなふるわせて、肩で息を切りながら、眼を眼球が瞼の外へ出そうになるほど、見開いて、唖のように執拗く黙っている。これを見ると、下人は始めて明白に、この老婆の生死が、全然、自分の意志に支配されているという事を意識した。そうしてこの意識は、今までけわしく燃えていた憎悪の心を、何時の間にか冷ましてしまった。後に残ったのは、唯、或仕事をして、それが円満に成就した時の、安らかな得意と満足とがあるばかりである。そこで、下人は、老婆を見下しながら、少し声を柔げてこういった。

"What were you doing? Tell me! Or it's this for you!"

The servant pushed her away, whipped his sword from the scabbard and thrust the pale steel up before her eyes. But the old woman said nothing. Her hands shook uncontrollably; her shoulders jerked as she gasped for breath. She opened her eyes so wide that it seemed her eyeballs would pop out of their sockets. But like a deaf-mute, she remained stubbornly silent. Seeing this, the servant became conscious that the fate of the old woman was completely his to decide. This awareness quickly cooled the loathing that had burned so intensely in his heart. What remained were the calm feelings of egotism and satisfaction that you experience after doing a job and bringing it to a smooth and successful conclusion. The servant looked down at the old woman and said in a slightly softened tone of voice:

....

明白に【めいはくに】clearly, obviously [0572] + [2175]

生死【せいし】life or death, survival [2179] + [2194]

全然【ぜんぜん】completely, utterly [1277] + [1779]

自分【じぶん】himself [2195] + [1247]

意志【いし】will, wish [1352] + [1394]

支配する【しはいする】dominate, control [1251] + [0981]

事【こと】fact, state of affairs [2220]

意識する【いしきする】become aware/conscious of 変 [1352] + [1086]

今まで【いままで】until now [1246]

けわしい angry, fierce

燃える【もえる】burn [0739]

憎悪【ぞうお】hate [0489] + [1758]

心【こころ】heart, mind, emotions [0004]

何時の間にか【いつのまにか】at some point [0045] + [0625] + [2094]

冷ます【さます】cool down [0057]

～てしまう expresses completion of an action with regret

後に【あとに】afterward [0267]

残る【のこる】remain, be left over [0640]

唯【ただ】just, only [0339]

或【ある】a certain [-]

仕事【しごと】work, job [0021] + [2220]

円満に【えんまんに】smoothly [1875] + [0441]

成就する【じょうじゅする】fulfill, complete [2202] + [1113]

時【とき】time, occasion [0625]

安らかな【やすらかな】tranquil, calm [1373]

得意【とくい】elation, conceit [0351] + [1352]

満足【まんぞく】satisfaction [0441] + [1386]

～ばかり just, nothing but

見下す【みおろす】look down on [1615] + [2115]

少し【すこし】a little [2163]

声【こえ】voice [1393]

柔げる【やわらげる】soften [1325]

いう say, speak

「己は検非違使の庁の役人などではない。今し方この門の下を通りかかった旅の者だ。だからお前に縄をかけて、どうしようというような事はない。唯、今時分、この門の上で、何をしていたのだか、それを己に話しさえすればいいのだ。」

　すると、老婆は、見開いていた眼を、一層大きくして、じっとその下人の顔を見守った。眶の赤くなった、肉食鳥のような、鋭い眼で見たのである。それから、皺で、殆、鼻と一つになった唇を、何か物でも嚙んでいるように、動かした。細い喉で、尖った喉仏の動いているのが見える。その時、その喉から、鴉の啼くような声が、喘ぎ喘ぎ、下人の耳へ伝わって来た。

己【おれ】I (masculine) 숮 [2117]
検非違使【けびいし】police chief with judicial powers [0674] + [0598] + [2014] + [0068]
庁【ちょう】office, department [1920]
役人【やくにん】government official [0181] + [2111]
今し方【いましがた】just now [1246] + [1243]
門【もん】gate 숮 [0597]
下【した】under, below 숮 [2115]
通りかかる【とおりかかる】come along, pass by [1982]
旅の者【たびのもの】traveler, wanderer [0624] + [2047]
お前【おまえ】you [1453]
縄をかける【なわをかける】arrest (lit., "put rope on") [0942]
〜ような like, as if 숮

事【こと】intention, scenario [2220]
唯【ただ】just, only [0339]
今時分【いまじぶん】about now [1246] + [0625] + [1247]
上【うえ】above, upon [2128]
何【なに】what [0045]
話し【はなし】talk, explanation [1027]
〜さえ (+ conditional) if only

老婆【ろうば】old woman [2040] + [1768]
見開く【みひらく】open wide [1615] + [2092]
眼【め】eyes 숮 [0796]
一層【いっそう】one degree, all the more [2105] + [2021]
大きい【おおきい】big [2133]
じっと fixedly
下人【げにん】servant 숮 [2115] + [2111]
顔【かお】face [1177]

"I'm no official from the police chief's department. I'm just a traveler who happened to pass by this gate. I'm not planning to arrest you or anything like that. All I want you to do is to tell me what you were doing up here in this gate just now."

The old woman opened her wide-stretched eyes even wider and stared unblinkingly at the servant's face. She looked at him with the piercing red eyes of a bird of prey. She moved her lips (so wrinkled was she, that they seemed to be of a piece with her nose) as if she were chewing something. The point of her Adam's apple could be seen moving in her scrawny throat. Then from that throat emerged a pant-broken voice like the cawing of a crow, and she said to the servant:

見守る【みまもる】stare at [1615] + [1375]
眶【まぶた】eyelids [-]
赤い【あかい】red [1389]
肉食鳥【にくしょくちょう】carnivorous bird [2042] + [1316] + [2083]
〜のような like
鋭い【するどい】sharp, shrewd [1140]
見る【みる】look at, watch [1615]
皺【しわ】wrinkles [-]
殆ど【ほとんど】almost [-]
鼻【はな】nose [1739]
一つ【ひとつ】one [2105]
唇【くちびる】lips [1752]
何か【なにか】something or other [0045]
物【もの】thing, object [0587]
噛む【かむ】chew [-]
〜ように like, as if
動かす【うごかす】move [1163]

細い【ほそい】thin, slight [0900]
喉【のど】throat 🦌 [-]
尖る【とがる】be pointed [-]
喉仏【のどぼとけ】Adam's apple [-] + [0010]
動く【うごく】move [1163]
見える【みえる】be visible [1615]
時【とき】time, moment [0625]
鴉【からす】crow [-]
啼く【なく】caw [-]
声【こえ】voice, sound [1393]
喘ぎ喘ぎ【あえぎあえぎ】pantingly [-]
耳【みみ】ear [2190]
伝わる【つたわる】be transmitted, be communicated [0028]
〜て来る【〜てくる】indicates progression in the direction of the servant [2211]

「この髪を抜いてな、この髪を抜いてな、鬘にしょうと思うたのじゃ。」

　下人は、老婆の答が存外、平凡なのに失望した。そうして失望すると同時に、また前の憎悪が、冷な侮蔑と一しょに、心の中へはいって来た。すると、その気色が、先方へも通じたのであろう。老婆は、片手に、まだ屍骸の頭から奪った長い抜け毛を持ったなり、蟇のつぶやくような声で、口ごもりながら、こんな事をいった。

「なるほどな、死人の髪の毛を抜くという事は、何ぼう悪い事かも知れぬ。じゃが、ここにいる死人どもは、皆、その位な事を、されてもいい人間ばかりだぞよ。

髪【かみ】hair ♨ [1821]
抜く【ぬく】pull out, pluck ♨ [0183]
〜な you see, you know ♨
鬘【かずら】wig [-]
〜しょうと思う【〜しようとおもう】plan to do [1633]

下人【げにん】servant [2115] + [2111]
老婆【ろうば】old woman ♨ [2040] + [1768]
答【こたえ】answer [1722]
存外【ぞんがい】contrary to expectation [1894] + [0135]
平凡な【へいぼんな】commonplace, ordinary [2167] + [1866]
失望する【しつぼうする】be disappointed ♨ [2189] + [1756]
〜と同時に【〜とどうじに】at the same time as [1897] + [0625]
また once again
前【まえ】before [1453]
憎悪【ぞうお】hatred [0489] + [1758]
冷な【ひややかな】cold [0057]
侮蔑【ぶべつ】contempt [0059] + [-]
〜と一しょに【〜といっしょに】together with [2105]
心【こころ】heart, mind [0004]
中【なか】inside [2150]
はいる enter
〜て来る【〜てくる】indicates progression in the direction of the servant [2211]
気色【けしき】feeling, emotion [2037] + [1280]
先方【せんぽう】the other party, counterpart [1552] + [1243]
通じる【つうじる】be communicated [1982]

"I'm taking this hair, you know … I'm taking this hair to make a wig."

The servant was disappointed by the unexpected banality of the old woman's answer. With this sense of disappointment, his former loathing—now mingled with a cold contempt—re-entered his heart. These feelings must have been transmitted to the other party, for the old woman, still clutching in one hand the long hair she had torn from the head of the corpse, and mumbling in a voice like the croak of a toad, said:

"I know what you're thinking—so perhaps pulling out the hair of the dead is a very wicked thing to do. But all the dead people up here are the kind of people that deserve no better.

- -

片手【かたて】one hand [2158] + [2155]
屍骸【しがい】corpse [-] + [-]
頭【あたま】head [1073]
奪る【とる】seize, steal [1517]
長い【ながい】long [1626]
抜け毛【ぬけげ】plucked hair [0183] + [2152]
持つ【もつ】hold [0275]
〜なり (after a verb in the past tense) still
蟇【ひき】toad [-]
つぶやく croak, mutter
〜のような like
声【こえ】voice [1393]
口ごもる【くちごもる】mumble, speak unclearly [2119]
〜ながら while, as
事【こと】thing, act, deed 𡧃 [2220]
いう say, speak

28

なるほど to be sure, as you say [2202] + [0806]
〜な sentence-ending particle expressing emotion
死人【しびと】dead person 𡧃 [2194] + [2111]
髪の毛【かみのけ】hair [1821] + [2152]
何ぼう【なんぼう】how much, very [0045]
悪い【わるい】evil, wicked [1758]
〜かも知れぬ【〜かもしれぬ】maybe, perhaps [0768]
じゃが but (colloquial form of だが)
〜ども them, these (suffix that makes the preceding word plural)
皆【みな】all, everyone [1581]
位【くらい】degree, extent [0042]
人間【にんげん】person [2111] + [2094]
〜ばかり only, all, just (and nothing more)

現在、わしが今、髪を抜いた女などはな、蛇を四寸ばかり
ずつに切って干したのを、干魚だというて、太刀帯の陣へ
売りに往んだわ。疫病にかかって死ななんだら、今でも売
りに往んでいた事であろ。それもよ、この女の売る干魚は、
味がよいというて、太刀帯どもが、欠かさず菜料に買って
いたそうな。わしは、この女のした事が悪いとは思うてい
ぬ。せねば、饑死をするのじゃて、仕方がなくした事であ
ろ。されば、今また、わしのしていた事も悪い事とは思わ
ぬよ。これとてもやはりせねば、饑死をするじゃて、仕方
がなくする事じゃわいの。じゃて、その仕方がない事を、
よく知っていたこの女は、大方わしのする事も大目に見て
くれるであろ。」

現在【げんざい】now, at present [0657] +
　[1896]

わし I (form of わたし that in premodern
　times was used especially by women) 愛

今【いま】now 愛 [1246]

髪【かみ】hair [1821]

抜く【ぬく】pluck, pull out [0183]

女【おんな】woman 愛 [2135]

～な you see, you know 愛

蛇【へび】snake [0907]

四寸【しすん】four *sun* (1 *sun* = 3 cm) [1928] +
　[1864]

～ばかり about ～

～ずつ individually, each

切る【きる】cut [0015]

干す【ほす】dry [2116]

干魚【ほしうお】dried fish 愛 [2116] + [1345]

いう say 愛

太刀帯【たてわき】palace guards, court
　guards 愛 [1360] + [1857] + [1648]

陣【じん】camp, barrack [0332]

売る【うる】sell [1391]

往ぬ【いぬ】go (to do something) 愛 [0217]

疫病【えやみ】plague [2058] + [2059]

かかる be infected with

死ななんだら【しななんだら】if … had
　not died (colloquial form of 死ななかっ
　たら) [2194]

今でも【いまでも】even now 愛 [1246]

事【こと】thing, act, state of affairs 愛 [2220]

～であろ ＝～であろう 愛

それも more than that

味【あじ】taste, flavor [0206]

よい good

The woman whose hair I was plucking just now, she used to cut and dry snakes in five-inch pieces, say it was dried fish, and go and sell it to the court guards at the barracks. If she hadn't caught the plague and died, she'd probably still be going off to sell it right now. Seems that the guards thought that the dried fish she sold was very tasty, and used to buy it all the time for food. Now for myself, I don't think that what this woman did was wicked. If she hadn't done it, she'd have starved to death—so she just did what she had to do. Likewise, I don't think what I'm doing here is bad. After all, if I didn't do this, I'd starve to death—so I'm just doing what I have to do, aren't I? So I'm sure that this lady here—who knew all about doing the things you've got to do—I'm sure she's looking on with forgiving eyes at what I'm doing here."

．．．

～ども them, those (suffix that makes the preceding word plural)

欠かさず【かかさず】always [1255]

菜料【さいりょう】food, meal [1486] + [0870]

買う【かう】buy [1662]

悪い【わるい】evil, wicked 🜨 [1758]

思う【おもう】think 🜨 [1633]

～ていぬ =～ていない

せねば =しなければ 🜨

餓死【うえじに】death from starvation 🜨 [1141] + [2194]

じゃて therefore (colloquial form of だから) 🜨

仕方がない【しかたがない】have no alternative 🜨 [0021] + [1243]

されば as such, therefore, thus (= そうであれば)

また once more [2108]

思わぬ【おもわぬ】 = 思わない

やはり after all, all the same, just the same

～じゃわいの = ～なのだ

知る【しる】know, understand [0768]

大方【おおかた】probably [2133] + [1243]

大目に見る【おおめにみる】look on with indulgence, tolerate [2133] + [1927] + [1615]

老婆は、大体こんな意味の事をいった。

　下人は、太刀を鞘におさめて、その太刀の柄を左の手でおさえながら、冷然として、この話を聞いていた。勿論、右の手では、赤く頬に膿を持った大きな面皰を気にしながら、聞いているのである。しかし、これを聞いている中に、下人の心には、或勇気が生まれて来た。それは、さっき門の下で、この男には欠けていた勇気である。そうして、またさっきこの門の上へ上って、この老婆を捕えた時の勇気とは、全然、反対な方向に動こうとする勇気である。下人は、饑死をするか盗人になるかに、迷わなかったばかりではない。その時の、この男の心もちからいえば、饑死などという事は、殆、考える事さえ出来ないほど、意識の外に追い出されていた。

29

老婆【ろうば】old woman 😊 [2040] + [1768]
大体【だいたい】more or less, roughly [2133]+[0052]
意味【いみ】meaning, gist [1352] + [0206]
事【こと】thing 😊 [2220]
いう say 😊

30

下人【げにん】servant 😊 [2115] + [2111]
太刀【たち】sword 😊 [1360] + [1857]
鞘【さや】scabbard, sheath [-]
おさめる put into, put away
柄【つか】hilt, pommel [0604]
左【ひだり】left [1887]
手【て】hand 😊 [2155]
おさえる press, push down
〜ながら while, as
冷然と【れいぜんと】coldly [0057] + [1779]

話【はなし】speech, utterance [1027]
聞く【きく】listen 😊 [2097]
勿論【もちろん】of course [-] + [1058]
右【みぎ】right [1888]
赤い【あかい】red [1389]
頬【ほお】cheek [-]
膿【うみ】puss [-]
持つ【もつ】hold, bear [0275]
大きな【おおきな】big [2133]
面皰【にきび】pimple [1324] + [-]
気にする【きにする】worry about [2037]
しかし but, however
〜中に【〜うちに】while [2150]
心【こころ】heart [0004]
或【ある】a certain [-]
勇気【ゆうき】courage 😊 [1326] + [2037]
生まれる【うまれる】be born, come into being [2179]

This is more or less the gist of what the old woman said.
The servant had returned his sword to its sheath. He clasped
the hilt of his sword with his left hand while listening coldly to the
above outpourings. As he listened, he fingered the big red puss-
gorged pimple on his cheek with his right hand. As he listened, a
kind of courage was born in his heart. It was exactly the courage
he had lacked before, under the gate. But it was courage of quite the
opposite tendency to the courage that had made him climb up the
gate and seize the old woman. It was not just that he no longer felt
any doubt about whether to starve or become a robber. The way he
felt right then was that a fate like starving to death had been driven
so far out of his mind that it was beyond even thinking about.

～て来る【～てくる】begin to ~ [2211]

さっき before, previously 衆

門【もん】gate 衆 [0597]

下【した】beneath [2115]

男【おとこ】man 衆 [1613]

欠ける【かける】lack [1255]

また moreover [2108]

上【うえ】above, top [2128]

上る【あがる】climb up [2128]

捕まえる【つかまえる】grab [0315]

時【とき】time, moment 衆 [0625]

全然【ぜんぜん】completely, utterly [1277] + [1779]

反対な【はんたいな】opposite [1869] + [0556]

方向【ほうこう】direction [1243] + [1934]

動く【うごく】move [1163]

饑死【うえじに】death by starvation 衆 [-] + [2194]

盗人【ぬすびと】robber, thief [1714] + [2111]

迷う【まよう】be at a loss, be unsure [1967]

～ばかり just, only

心もち【こころもち】feelings, emotional state [0004]

～など and so on

殆【ほとんど】almost

考える【考える】think, consider [2039]

～さえ even

出来る【できる】be capable of [2180] + [2211]

～ほど to the extent that ~

意識【いしき】consciousness, awareness [1352] + [1086]

外【そに】outside [0135]

追い出す【おいだす】drive out, expel [1971] + [2180]

「きっと、そうか。」

老婆の話が完ると、下人は嘲るような声で念を押した。そうして、一足前へ出ると、不意に右の手を面皰から離して、老婆の襟上をつかみながら、噛みつくようにこういった。

33

「では、己が引剝をしようと恨むまいな。己もそうしなければ、餓死をする体なのだ。」

下人は、すばやく、老婆の着物を剝ぎとった。それから、足にしがみつこうとする老婆を、手荒く屍骸の上へ蹴倒した。梯子の口までは、僅に五歩を数えるばかりである。下人は、剝ぎとった檜皮色の着物をわきにかかえて、またたく間に急な梯子を夜の底へかけ下りた。

31

きっと indeed, certainly

32

老婆【ろうば】old woman 👤 [2040] + [1768]

話【はなし】speech, utterance [1027]

完る【おわる】come to an end [1396]

下人【げにん】servant 👤 [2115] + [2111]

嘲る【あざける】mock, jeer [-]

〜ような like, as if

声【こえ】voice [1393]

念を押す【ねんをおす】say emphatically, make sure [1304] + [0234]

一足前【ひとあしまえ】one step forward [2105] + [1386] + [1453]

出る【でる】come out, advance [2180]

不意に【ふいに】suddenly [2141] + [1352]

右【みぎ】right [1888]

手【て】hand [2155]

面皰【にきび】pimple [1324] + [-]

離す【はなす】withdraw, take away [1195]

襟上【えりがみ】collar [0845] + [2128]

つかむ grab

〜ながら while, as

噛みつく【かみつく】bite [-]

いう say

33

己【おれ】I (masculine) 👤 [2117]

引剝【ひはぎ】tearing off clothes [0133] + [-]

恨む【うらむ】hate [0272]

〜まい will not 〜

〜な =ね

餓死【うえじに】death by starvation [-] + [2194]

"No doubt you're right," the servant said with emphatic sarcasm when the old woman finished speaking. He advanced a step, withdrew his right hand from the pimple and suddenly seized the old woman's collar. In biting tones, he said:

"Well then, don't hold it against me when I rip off your clothes. You see, if I didn't do this, this poor body of mine would starve."

The servant hastily tore off the old woman's kimono. As the old woman tried to grab hold of his legs, he kicked her brutally back onto the corpses. To the trapdoor with the ladder was a mere five paces. With the brown kimono he had torn off tucked under his arm, the servant slipped down the steep ladder and off into the bowels of the night in the blink of an eye.

....

体 【からだ】 position, circumstance [0052]

34

すばやく very quickly
着物 【きもの】 clothes 🐾 [2086] + [0587]
剝ぎとる 【はぎとる】 tear off, strip off 🐾 [-]
それから then, after that
足 【あし】 legs [1386]
しがみつく cling to
手荒く 【てあらく】 roughly [2155] + [1447]
屍骸 【しがい】 corpse [-] + [-]
上 【うえ】 on top [2128]
蹴倒す 【けたおす】 kick down [-] + [0093]
梯子 【はしご】 ladder 🐾 [-] + [2125]
口 【くち】 mouth, exit, trapdoor [2119]
僅に 【わずかに】 merely [-]
五歩 【ごほ】 five paces [2142] + [1566]

数える 【かぞえる】 count [1170]
〜ばかり just, only
檜皮色 【ひわだいろ】 color of cedar bark, dark brown [-] + [1923] + [1280]
わき underarm
かかえる hold, carry
またたく間に 【またたくまに】 in no time, in a flash [2094]
急な 【きゅうな】 steep [1328]
夜 【よる】 night [1301]
底 【そこ】 depths, bottom [1961]
かけ下りる 【かけおりる】 climb down [2115]

　暫、死んだように倒れていた老婆が、屍骸の中から、その裸の体を起こしたのは、それから間もなくの事である。老婆は、つぶやくような、うめくような声を立てながら、まだ燃えている火の光をたよりに、梯子の口まで、這って行った。そうして、そこから、短い白髪を倒にして、門の下を覗きこんだ。外には、唯、黒洞々たる夜があるばかりである。

　下人の行方は、誰も知らない。

暫【しばらく】for a while [1832]
死ぬ【しぬ】die [2194]
〜ように like, as if
倒れる【たおれる】fall down, collapse [0093]
老婆【ろうば】old woman 🐍 [2040] + [1768]
屍骸【しがい】dead bodies [-] + [-]
中【なか】among [2150]
裸の【はだかの】naked [0819]
体【からだ】body [0052]
起こす【おこす】lift, raise up [2079]
間もなく【まもなく】in no time, quickly [2094]
事【こと】act, state of affairs [2220]
つぶやく moan, mutter
〜ような like 🐍
うめく groan
声【こえ】voice [1393]
立てる【たてる】make (a sound) [1257]
〜ながら while, as
燃える【もえる】burn [0739]
火【ひ】fire, flame [2159]
光【ひかり】light [1550]

〜をたよりに relying on 〜
梯子【はしご】ladder [-] + [2125]
口【くち】exit, trapdoor [2119]
這う【はう】crawl [-]
〜て行く【〜ていく】~ and go away [0157]
短い【みじかい】short [0801]
白髪【しらが】white hair, gray hair [2175] + [1821]
倒に【さかさまに】upside down [0093]
門【もん】gate [0597]
下【した】beneath, below [2115]
覗きこむ【のぞきこむ】gaze intently [-]
外【そと】outside [0135]
唯【ただ】only [0339]
黒洞々たる【こくとうとうたる】as dark as a cave [1754] + [0280]
夜【よる】night [1301]
〜ばかり only, just, all

下人【げにん】servant [2115] + [2111]
行方【ゆくえ】whereabouts [0157] + [1243]
誰も【だれも】(+ negative) no one [-]
知る【しる】know [0768]

The old woman lay as if dead for a while, but it was not long before she lifted her naked body upright from among the bodies. Emitting a sound somewhere between a whisper and a groan, she crawled over to the ladder by the light of the burning torch. Her short gray hair hanging upside down (as she poked her head over the edge of the ladder door), she peered down at the lower part of the gate. Outside there was nothing but pitch-black night.

Where the servant went to, no one knows.

SELECTED BIBLIOGRAPHY

This short list provides a rough overview of the various works of reference used in the making of this book. It omits the electronic version of the *Kōjien* (the classic Japanese-Japanese dictionary published by Iwanami Shoten) which I highly recommend for speed of use, for definitions of even archaic words and for providing greater brain exercise than a Japanese-English dictionary!

If you wish to read more of Sôseki's *Dreams* or Akutagawa's short stories, the Japanese editions in Section 3 below are strongly recommended, as their contemporary *kana* usage and *furigana* superscript make them the most accessible of all the editions currently available.

A search on amazon.com is probably the best way to find translations of further works by the two authors, so no list is provided here.

1. Dictionaries & Encyclopedias

The Compact Nelson Japanese-English Character Dictionary Based on the Revised Version of the Classic Edition by Andrew N. Nelson. Abridged by John H. Haig and the Department of East Asian Languages and Literatures, University of Hawaii at Manoa. Tokyo: C. E. Tuttle, 1999.

Japan: An Illustrated Encyclopedia. Tokyo: Kodansha, 1993.

Kenkyusha's New Japanese-English Dictionary, Fourth Edition, Revised and Enlarged. Edited by Masuda Koh. Tokyo: Kenkyusha, 1974.

The Kodansha Kanji Learner's Dictionary. Edited by Jack Halpern. Tokyo: Kodansha International, 2001.

Makino, Seiichi, and Michio Tsutsui. *A Dictionary of Basic Japanese Grammar.* Tokyo: The Japan Times, 1996.

———. *A Dictionary of Intermediate Japanese Grammar.* Tokyo: The Japan Times, 1996.

2. Biographical Information

Gessel, Van C. *Three Modern Novelists: Soseki, Tanizaki, Kawabata.* Tokyo: Kodansha International, 1993.

Healey, G. H. Introduction to *Kappa*, by Akutagawa Ryûnosuke. Translated by Geoffrey Bownas. Tokyo: C. E. Tuttle, 2000.

Hibbett, Howard. "Akutagawa Ryûnosuke." In *Modern Japanese Writers,* edited by Jay Rubin, 19–30. New York: Charles Scribner's Sons, 2001.

Japan: An Illustrated Encyclopedia. Tokyo: Kodansha, 1993.

Rubin, Jay. "Sôseki (Natsume Sôseki)." In *Modern Japanese Writers,* edited by Jay Rubin, 349–84. New York: Charles Scribner's Sons, 2001.

3. Japanese Originals

Akutagawa Ryûnosuke. "Hana." 1917. Reprint in *Rashōmon, Hana,* Shincho bunko. Tokyo: Shincho-Sha, 1995.

———. "Rashōmon." 1915. Reprint in *Rashōmon, Hana,* Shincho bunko. Tokyo: Shincho-Sha, 1995.

———. "Yabu no naka." 1922. Reprint in *Jigokuben, Jajūmon, Kōshoku, Yabu no naka: Hoka nana hen,* Iwanami bunko. Tokyo: Iwanami Shoten, 2001.

Natsume Sôseki. *Yume jūya.* 1908. Reprint in *Yume jūya: Hoka ni hen,* Iwanami bunko. Tokyo: Iwanami Shoten, 2002.

4. Translations

Akutagawa Ryûnosuke. *Rashomon and Other Stories.* Translated by Takashi Kojima. New York: Liveright, 1999.

———. *Ryunosuke Akutagawa Japanese Short Stories.* Translated by Takashi Kojima. Tokyo: C. E. Tuttle, 2000.

Natsume Sôseki. *Ten nights of dream, Hearing things, The heredity of taste.* Translated by Aiko Itô and Graeme Wilson. Tokyo: C. E. Tuttle, 1974.

———. *Ten Nights' Dreams.* Translated by Takumi Kashima and Loretta R. Lorenz. New Bern, NC: Trafford, 2000.

にほんご よ なな ものがたり
日本語を読むための七つの物語
Breaking into Japanese Literature

2003 年 1 月　第 1 刷発行
2008 年 6 月　第 7 刷発行

著　者　ジャイルズ・マリー
発行者　富田　充
発行所　講談社インターナショナル株式会社
　　　　〒 112-8652　東京都文京区音羽 1-17-14
　　　　電話　03-3944-6493（編集部）
　　　　　　　03-3944-6492（営業部・業務部）
　　　　ホームページ www.kodansha-intl.com

印刷・製本所　　大日本印刷株式会社

落丁本、乱丁本は購入書店名を明記のうえ、講談社インターナショナル業務部宛にお送りください。送料小社負担にてお取替えいたします。なお、この本についてのお問い合わせは、編集部宛にお願いいたします。本書の無断複写（コピー）は著作権法上での例外を除き、禁じられています。

定価はカバーに表示してあります。

© ジャイルズ・マリー 2003
Printed in Japan

ISBN 978-4-7700-2899-0